calling the shots

MY FIVE DECADES IN THE NBA

EARL STROM

with BLAINE JOHNSON

SIMON AND SCHUSTER

New York   London   Toronto   Sydney   Tokyo   Singapore

Simon and Schuster
Simon & Schuster Building
Rockefeller Center
1230 Avenue of the Americas
New York, New York 10020

SIMON AND SCHUSTER and colophon are registered trademarks
of Simon & Schuster Inc.

Designed by Irving Perkins Associates
Manufactured in the United States of America

1 3 5 7 9 10 8 6 4 2

Library of Congress Cataloging in Publication Data
Strom, Earl, date.
Calling the shots: my five decades in the NBA/Earl Strom with Blaine
Johnson.
p.   cm.
1. Strom, Earl, date.   2. Basketball—United States—Referees—
Biography.   3. National Basketball Association.   I. Johnson,
Blaine, date.   II. Title.
GV884.S77A3   1990
796.323′092—dc20
[B]   90–42984
CIP

ISBN 0-671-66108-6

Photo on page 251 courtesy of
Glenn Freudenberger.

This book is dedicated with love and affection to:

Yvonne, my wife of thirty-eight years, without whom my career and this book would never have been possible;

My five wonderful children, Margie, Susan, Stephen, Eric, and Jonathan, who lived this book from beginning to end;

Max and Bessie Strom, my late parents, who would have been very proud to have seen this all happen;

My mother-in-law, Dorothy Trolling, who gave me much needed moral support;

My sisters, Esther and Kathryn, and my brother Mort, as well as my three late brothers, Izzie, Len and Ben, who always took such great pride in their youngest brother;

And my seven terrific grandchildren, Brooke, Katelynn, Jason, Kyle, Kari, Michael, and Andrew, who give me tremendous joy.

acknowledgments

I would like to thank the following people for their time and efforts: Blaine Johnson, Jacques de Spoelberch, and Jeff Neuman, who kept the faith during a long process and waited until we could do this book right; Marie Kehs and Jamie and Russell Diesinger, who suggested the title; Mendy Rudolph, Norm Drucker, Arnold Heft, Jim Duffy, Sid Borgia, and Willie Smith—all great pro referees who taught me; and Jocko Collins, Pete Lewis, and Walt Foley, who had the insight to start and mold my officiating career.

—Earl Strom

This book came to be after a long and circuitous journey spanning twelve years from first interview to publication. Long journeys are best shared with special people, and I had the company of four of them on this one: Catherine, for her encouragement and patience as vacations and weekends went toward the quest; Jacques de Spoelberch, for having the faith to keep scouting until we found the very best home for this story; Jeff Neuman, for seeing the potential, then masterfully challenging and guiding the story through the

ACKNOWLEDGMENTS

editing process; and especially Earl, for his willingness to be so self-revealing in relating his story. One of the keys to his success as a referee was that internal toughness that all great competitors possess. What was enjoyable for me as we shared this journey was to learn how that internal toughness melded with his humor and compassion, making him a truly unique person. My thanks to all for helping bring this story to print.

—Blaine Johnson

contents

foreword
by Julius Erving

I had just finished playing in my last game as a pro. As I was walking off the court in Milwaukee, Earl Strom made sure I got the game ball. He came over and stuck it in my chest and said, "This is yours." As he walked beside me, he told me, "I really wanted to work your last game." I asked him why, and he said, "Because I did your first one." I hadn't remembered that until then and it made the occasion a special one for both of us.

By then I had come to know Earl not only as an outstanding official, but also as a person who seemed to genuinely enjoy the players and coaches he governed. He could be tough, but he cared. Earl had been refereeing professional basketball for thirteen years when I came in, and after my sixteen years as a professional player he worked three more. That first game was back in the ABA, where the officials wore those red and white striped shirts. It was an exhibition game in Petersburg, Virginia, the Virginia Squires versus the Kentucky Colonels. Artis Gilmore was a rookie for Kentucky and I was a rookie for Virginia. I somehow managed to kind of steal the show that evening, and Earl made a comment to

7

some Philadelphia writers that I was something special. He ended up getting fined for that.

As I went along in my career, I learned about all the officials and their styles. It wasn't just how they called the game, but their mannerisms as well. Earl had that unique "tweet-pause-tweet-tweet" way of whistling a foul. He also had a special way of flipping you the ball at the foul line, almost like he was bowling. He held it in this sort of contorted way, like he was cuddling it with his left hand. He'd stand there making sure everybody was in their positions. I mean, this was his show, there was no doubt about who was in charge. Then he'd flip it to you with a little pace on it, and if you weren't paying attention you'd catch it right in your chest.

The difference between the officials who are just starting out or those who are below grade and those who are masters of what they do is judgment. The real good official knows what's important to call. Professional basketball is part of the entertainment business, but the first order of business is allowing the play to be at its highest level. An official can encourage that or he can destroy it. Earl knew as well as any official I've ever been around how to encourage a good game. He understood the fan's expectations and the players' needs.

An inexperienced official will often jump the gun on a play. They'll think they know what's going to happen and they'll blow the whistle in anticipation. I was hit with a lot of offensive fouls in my career for driving to the basket and going up and around a guy. The official would guess that I was going to hit the defender, when often I'd graze him at most. They didn't realize that a good professional basketball player can maneuver around a guy standing in front of him trying to draw the charge. An inexperienced official might see me make a move and say, Well, there's no way he could do that without traveling, and blow his whistle. But the film would show that I had made it cleanly. Earl knew what he was seeing and knew how to wait out a play until he could determine just what had happened.

Officials are supposed to call an infraction when someone unfairly takes advantage. The problem is some officials get confused when the advantage has been taken fairly. Veterans are *supposed* to take advantage of rookies. The veteran is supposed to use his savvy and experience to gain an edge over a rookie who might be his equal physically. The veteran should know how to get a guy off balance, out of position, into a situation where he almost has to foul you to keep you from breaking loose for a basket. Taking a guy to school is an acceptable way of taking advantage. Physically manhandling him is not acceptable. A good official knows the difference. In fact, a good official will appreciate it.

Earl earned his stature not by being around professional basketball for thirty-two years, but by making the right calls for all those years. He knew his craft. He knew how to reassure you that he knew what he was doing. There are officials who cause you to have an anxiety attack the minute you walk out onto the court about what you're going to face that night. Suddenly your pregame preparation has had an unwelcome dimension added to it. A poor official can throw you off-balance. He can make you start worrying about what he might take away from you. It isn't even a conscious thing, like, this guy always calls steps. It's more instinctive, where you start thinking about how consistent he'll be or how itchy he'll be about calling the little things. It might be the official's limited competence or whether he'll be intimidated by the home crowd, or you might feel he has a grudge against you. Earl didn't carry over hard feelings from the last time you saw him. He never let the crowd affect him. Earl knew what he was doing on the court because he understood what everybody else was doing.

He had a great way of communicating what he expected. He kept it simple and he could get his point across without shouting. Even when he had a confrontation, I never saw him do anything that was embarrassing to a player or a coach. He could put them in their place without blatantly embarrassing them. It was as though he respected each person's role out there, and all he asked was that you respected his efforts to conduct a fair game. You knew he was tough, but he wasn't arrogant.

The game has changed dramatically since Earl began refereeing in the NBA in 1957. Back then, big guys moved more slowly, more methodically. They stayed in one position on the court. There wasn't as much mobility in the game and there wasn't as much banging all over the floor. Most teams play deeper into their benches now, so it's more of an up-tempo game. It's a more exciting brand of basketball and it certainly has to be a tougher game to call as an official. That's what makes Earl's career all the more impressive. He came in and was immediately successful in an era that is totally different than the game of today, and he was the best in the business when he retired. It's amazing when you think about it. He's a dinosaur.

introduction

I was born on December 15, 1927. A part of me died sixty-two years later when I finally retired as a pro basketball referee; it had become that much a part of my life. Some people figured if I stayed any longer, I'd expire right on the court. But that would give too much satisfaction to all those loudmouths who have been yelling, "Kill that SOB referee!" I knew it was time to step aside when I realized I was old enough to be a grandfather to some of the kids coming into the league. So, in virtually one motion, I went from being regarded as the best official in the National Basketball Association to social security. It wasn't something I set out to do. There were many occasions along the way that could have seen my career come to an abrupt end. There certainly were people trying to orchestrate that at times. I'm competitive enough to feel some satisfaction that I outlasted 'em all.

Maybe that reflects how much I had molded myself to the job. How I had learned to stand up to everyone. How I had run the gauntlet of challenges: the politics, the miles across this country and across the floor, the wear and tear on the body, the strain on family life, the test of courage and judg-

11

ment. I had proven how tough I was, how good I was, how fair I was. I had found a sense of myself that allowed me to stand in there and take command in an arena full of big men and big egos night after night.

Does that mean I have the biggest ego of them all? A guy must have some sort of an inflated ego to want to write a book in which he can explore himself and everything he's rubbed up against. I guess a guy writes a book about his life—or in this case, about the world of pro basketball that dominated virtually his whole adult life—to crow, to set the record straight, to teach, to reflect, and to have some fun. Maybe Dave Cowens had it right several years ago when I mentioned to him that I was thinking of writing a book. He laughed and said, "Earl, a referee writing a book makes about as much sense as players' wives signing autographs." One thing I know, I'll speak my mind without fear of recrimination—and I haven't been able to do that for a good many years.

There are few places in life where you're in charge, yet you're supposed to be anonymous. The whole show rests on your judgment, yet the better the job you do, the less anyone notices. Being a pro basketball referee was how I was known and how I knew myself. It tested me against some notion of perfection every time out. I was measured by my ability to take charge of this group of high-powered, intensely competitive, celebrated men in a center-stage showdown. In thirty-two years of involvement with pro basketball, I saw careers, dynasties, eras come and go. I like to see myself as a guy who was in the middle of all that's happened in the pro game going all the way back into the fifties with the perspective of an impartial witness. But then, I guess I made too many waves and created too much turmoil to get off as merely a witness. I was a *judge*. I made two hundred decisions a night. I fought the system and met a lot of misery as a consequence. But as I finally stepped away, I realized how much I loved all of it. I guess that's why I stayed so long.

chapter 1

VOICES IN A GAME

They had me wired with a hidden microphone for a playoff game, Lakers vs. Celtics in Boston Garden. It was just another one of those inconsistencies that makes the NBA the wonderful world of contradictions that it is. In the thirty years since I had broken in with the NBA, there had been a pretty steady process of trying to erase the referee's personality from the game. It had gotten to the point where there were to be no interviews with the media, no chatter with fans, no conversations with players and coaches off the floor, and nothing but business on it. The NBA *Official's Manual* didn't leave any doubt about what was expected: "Refrain from talking to players, coaches or trainers during the game, unless it is absolutely necessary. At no time should officials speak to fans seated about the court. Do not initiate conversation with fans, coaches, players or other club personnel. Remember, legitimate questions may require a brief response, but statements need not be answered."

When I broke in, the league was rowdy and ribald and if you wanted to survive, you had to show 'em who you were. I had succeeded, in part, because I knew how to deal with all these folks we were now supposed to just avoid. I felt it had come to where the league wanted to clamp any expression of human emotion.

So, while it struck me as a little odd that they wanted to put a microphone on me for this game, I figured, what the hell, I've got nothing to hide. The idea was to pick up some of the flavor of the game from the perspective of the referee for a possible video feature by NBA Entertainment. They got more than they bargained for, especially when a reporter intercepted the signal and wrote it up in a big article that hit *USA Today* and dozens of other papers across the country. Even though the article was censored, what was recorded through my microphone that evening of game four of the 1987 NBA finals conveyed a sense of what it's like out there.

I was working the game with Hugh Evans, who had been in the league about ten years and was a pretty competent official, but tended to get a little nervous. The alternate was Jake O'Donnell, another capable official, but at that time I wouldn't have asked him for help if both my eyes fell out and rolled across the parquet floor. Boston Garden was packed solid. The place is a throwback to the old-time arenas: dark, worn, and kind of ripe on this hot, sticky night. The Lakers had been based in Minneapolis when I broke in, but they moved to Los Angeles for the 1960–61 season, the year I ended up working every game of the finals with Mendy Rudolph. The Celtics, who were down 2–1 in the best-of-seven series, were trying to repeat as NBA champs. No team had won back-to-back titles since 1969 when Bill Russell wrapped up a career of eleven titles in thirteen years. K.C. Jones had played with Russell in college and all those seasons with the Celtics; now he was coaching the Celtics. This evening would turn out to be the closest he would get to another ring. At midcourt, several rows up in the stands, perfectly positioned to communicate with the world around him— especially the referees—was Red Auerbach. He was the club's president, but seemed to have as much of a presence in the building as he did all those years as coach.

Things were rolling along pretty well through the first

half. The microphone was picking up my usual chatter with the guys, telling them to keep their hands off each other, trying to keep the game moving and off the foul line. Just before the half, James Worthy of the Lakers broke loose on a fast break, but Dennis Johnson caught him high on the head and flipped him over. Worthy came up swinging and got into it with Greg Kite. I jumped in between them. "Hey, hey, hey, that's enough!" There were players everywhere. I pushed them back toward their benches. "Get off the court. Get the hell off the court!" I felt like a sheepherder, rounding 'em up and sitting 'em down. The crowd erupted into a chant of "Beat L.A., Beat L.A." while I called Worthy and Kite together. Each was trying to plead his case. "I know, I know. James, you've got a foul shot coming. We're all right. Now we've got a double technical foul on you guys. If you get another unsportsmanlike call, you're gone. We're all right. Let's go." Always keep the game moving.

Usually, when a couple players squared up, all I had to say was, "Go ahead. I'm gonna throw ya out and the commissioner will hit the crap out of you with a fine. If that's the way you want to spend your money, be a fool." It usually helped. Most fights now are more shoving and grabbing than real fisticuffs. When I came into the league in 1957, pro basketball was played in arenas operated by men who founded the NBA to fill in dates around their hockey teams. Their hockey background made them think fans favored the rough stuff and a good fight made the night. If a Jim Loscutoff and an Andy Johnson squared up to fight, there was no way you could tell 'em to go ahead and fight because they'd try to kill each other. There were some damn good fights, the heavyweight haymakers coming in from left and right. A lot of times you didn't get it stopped until one guy went down. Jumping in between those guys was a helluva lot different.

The league has really cracked down on teammates getting into it, especially off the bench. It's a way to cool off the peer pressure. Ask Don Nelson about that. Nellie was with the Lakers before going on to become a great role player for years with the Celtics and then coach at Milwaukee and

Golden State. He got into it one night with Tom Hoover, a big, tough guy with the Knicks, and Hoover kicked the hell out of him. As Nelson was lying on the training table getting some stitches, the game ended and the Lakers started filing in. Nellie started getting on some of them for not helping him during the fight. "Hey, Dick, why didn't you help me out?" he called out to Dick Barnett, who shot back, "Hey, baby, when I looked over, you was winnin'."

Anyway, back to the game. The Celtics were cruising in the third period, the crowd was hungry for more, and one heavyset guy on the baseline was getting pretty rambunctious. I told a security guard, "Make sure that fat guy stays put." In the old days we would have preferred he step onto the court so we could deck him, but we're beyond that now. Changes, changes.

Midway through the third quarter with the Celtics up by 16, there was a play where Kareem Abdul-Jabbar, at 7'2", was going up with a forward virtually seven feet tall in Kevin McHale. And here you had a 6'9" guard in Magic Johnson who might come in and get the ball away from both of them. You want to look for ways the game has changed in the thirty-two years I worked the pro game, think about how dominant Russell was as a 6'9" center, and now you have Magic as the league's premier *point guard* at 6'9". Magic can rebound with the best of them, but he's a guard, an outside player who can handle the ball and shoot as well as the flashiest guards that were around in the old days. Bigger, faster, stronger, more developed skills . . . making it an ever tougher game to call.

On this particular play, we blew it. I was the lead official underneath the basket. I glanced up at the shot taken by Larry Bird. I saw Kareem hit the ball on the way down. I didn't hear Hugh's whistle and I blew mine. Ordinarily this call is made by the trail official, or Hugh in this case, but I was scoring the goal. The Los Angeles players started pointing to Hugh and yelling their objections. I went out to Hugh. "I have goaltending against Kareem. What do you have?"

He said, "I have Kevin McHale hitting the ball off the rim."

I said, "McHale! My God, I didn't even see him being part of it. Okay. Jeez, Hugh, are you sure?"

"Yeah."

I then waved off the goal and called offensive-basket interference. Needless to say, the place went nuts. Kevin just kept shaking his head. He couldn't believe it. He's a good guy and usually doesn't say much to me, so when he does, I tend to listen. He kept saying he never touched the ball. I had to be inclined to believe him, but I also had to support Hugh at this point. Naturally the Boston bench was really on me for changing the call. "That's what he saw, that's what he called! That's it!" I yelled at them.

I was over at the scorer's table later during a time-out and Hugh came over. "Earl, I want to apologize."

"For what?"

"That call with Kevin."

"You're kidding. Whatdidya have?"

"I shouldn't have called basket interference. I should have called a loose-ball foul against Kevin."

I thought, oh, my God. The goaltending would have superseded the loose-ball foul and it would have been two for Boston. Here everyone's thinking I kicked the hell out of the call, and the instant replay that was shown to all the millions of viewers out there watching the finals clearly showed that Kareem had hit the ball. The only person in the place who had it wrong was my partner, who had the responsibility to make that call. I took a deep breath and said, "Okay, let's just move ahead and not let it bother you." Had he come up to me immediately and we'd discussed it, we would have been able to straighten it out.

That's one of the problems with "The System." As supervisor of officials, Darell Garretson wants the trail official to have the primary responsibility for goaltending because he feels he has a better look at it. But that's the most ridiculous thing I've ever heard. It's the guy underneath who is going to be able to pick up the swipes off the board and those little flicks. He's right there looking up at it. Instead of just saying, go out and referee the damn game, it's all broken up into precise positions each guy is supposed to have on the floor and who has what primary responsibility to make some particular call. I worked for eight different supervisors, and they had eight different ways of wanting it done. But if you have guys who have poor judgment or poor play-calling selection, then it doesn't matter where you put the officials on the floor. If you want to run the pro game, you've gotta learn to make the pro call.

We hadn't made it this time, and K.C. Jones started riding me. McHale started sticking in his needle. I recognized Red's as one of those loud voices coming at me from the crowd and caught a few of his customary gestures. I had learned long ago to expect nothing less from Red. From the first time we met, it was probably evident we had the same kind of personalities—neither of us was going to back off from anybody or anything. I think we're also the kind of guys who know that when the shouting is over, it's over. You don't hold grudges, you don't go looking to start it up again the next time you're together, you leave it behind and start fresh. Red understands that because he came from that era. He was always tough on officials, jawing and picking at them. He always seemed to know what he was doing, how much to get away with and when to pull up if he didn't want to get tossed out. But if his team was going bad and he figured he'd better get ejected to get them going, he'd start screaming and calling us gutless bastards and really digging into our character. I can't tell you how many times he pulled that with me, and it always seemed to spark his players. Why they couldn't see through it, I don't know. It was just like taking an upper for them. It would work on the road, it would work at home. He'd get a couple T's and get bounced, and they'd start playing tough defense, ram through about a dozen points on the break, and that would be the game. It was always at the expense of the ref's nerves, but nobody worried much about that.

About two minutes after the goaltending call, Bird lost control of the ball in a crowd and fumbled it out of bounds. He claimed he was fouled. He gestured with his arms, bringing the crowd out. He started riding me as we went up and down the court. "You better get off my ass," I told him. He gave me another shot. I warned him again, "Get off my ass. You heard me."

Bird is very smart at picking his spots, and I'm sure he gets away with things with some officials by playing those games. The thing I like about him is that he has his say and then it's over. Generally, he doesn't harp and harp and harp. He's a throwback to the old players; they had their say and got away from you. (Oscar Robertson and Rick Barry were a couple notable exceptions.) Bird was caught up in a notable exception himself this night. I was along the baseline, eyes on the action, and he was on offense, staying close to me, talking out of the side of his mouth. "You're full of shit and can go fuck yourself," he said.

"Well, fuck you then," my microphone says I said.

"You blew it, Earl."

"Aw, you're full of crap."

He circled under the basket and came back in front of me. "I'm tellin' ya, I was fouled."

"You make a goddamn lousy play and want to lay it on me, that's bullshit."

The play headed back downcourt. Robert Parish was struggling behind. "Let's go, Robert. Let's go." Byron Scott went flying in for a lay-in, but it was blocked by Bird. As Hugh blew his whistle for the foul on Bird, McHale pushed A.C. Green, Scott pushed McHale, and I held back for a couple seconds to study the melee. "Okay, okay, knock it off," I said, wading in. "We've got a double technical foul here and here," I said, pointing at McHale and Green. As Scott went to the line, Bird was crabbing to Dennis Johnson. I looked at him, but I intended it for all of them. "I told you we're gonna stop this fucking bullshit and we're gonna stop it."

Obviously I was not eager to run anybody out of such a big

game, but I'd just about had enough. I had learned from Mendy, if you can head off more serious problems with a warning, do it. But never give a warning that you aren't willing to back up. If you don't follow through, they know they've got your number. Young referees say, "You can do this because of your stature." Hey, when I saw Mendy do it and I tried it, I was a young ref and it still worked. They'll come to respect you as soon as they believe you're consistent, fair, and follow through with your verbal intentions. Nobody hands out instant respect, but you can be around twenty years and never earn it.

At the break before the fourth quarter I went to the L.A. huddle. According to the tape, I said: "Before ya start, let me say something. The next guy that gets into somebody's face, I'm gonna throw their ass out of here. I'm tellin' them the same thing." I got out of there before they could start in telling me their woes, and I headed for the Boston bench. I poked my head into their huddle. "Excuse me, K.C., I just want to say one thing. I just told those guys and I'm tellin' you guys, we're gonna stop the fucking bullshit and we're gonna play ball. The next . . . wait a minute, I'm doing the talking here. Hey, you're talking on my dime! The next guy that gets in somebody's face I'm gonna throw his fuckin' ass out. Okay, now you can talk," I said over my shoulder as I got out of there.

Boston's lead was down to five with ten minutes to go. Magic hurt his knee. I asked him if he was okay. "Nothing serious, this is the finals." With seven minutes to go, McHale fouled Mychal Thompson. "What was that foul for? He pushed me," McHale said. "Yeah, he said you pushed him," I said. "Who should I believe this time?" Thompson went to the line and tied the game. The microphone heard me say, "I should have been a priest."

Boston banged it back out to 8, then L.A. clawed back and took the lead by 1 with fifty-eight seconds to go. Boston was back up by 2 with eight seconds left when Kareem went to the line. He made the first. He missed the second, but the rebound kicked out of bounds. The Celtics screamed that

McHale had been fouled. Hugh made the call and it looked right to me: "It's off white, Lakers' ball." Magic came down the lane and nailed a skyhook with two seconds left. The Lakers were up 1. Boston time-out. I checked the clock and the foul situation. I told Hugh, "The Lakers have a foul to waste. As soon as they throw it in, I would foul. I'd let a second go and then hack someone." I never tried to predict scenarios, because that's where you get into trouble anticipating a call you think you're going to make rather than just reacting to what actually happens in front of you. I never worried how many personal fouls a guy had or how many points he had or even paid that much attention to what the score was. But I was always alert to the time on the game and shooting clocks, the time-out situation, things that were my responsibility to coordinate.

While the time-out was winding down, I noticed that jerk down on the endline was going berserk, screaming and swearing at me. I told a courtside security guard, "Do me a favor. Bring that guy to my locker room after the game. I want to beat the crap out of him." I probably just said that for the benefit of the video. I wouldn't do anything like that—anymore.

The time-out was over, Boston couldn't get off a decent shot, and L.A. was up 3–1 and on its way to what would become the first of their back-to-back titles. It seemed as if people were yelling at me from everywhere. The police pushed us through the crowd. "Great game, great game," I said to no one in particular. I felt good. We got to the locker room and here came Red, screaming like a madman. He had chased us through the crowd, cussing all the way. I hadn't heard him till now. He was saying that if I had any balls, the Lakers would never have gotten back in the game. He was furious that I hadn't called a foul when Kareem missed his free throw, so that McHale would have been on the line, instead of L.A.'s having the ball to set up Magic's winning shot. He was calling me every dirty-rotten-lowlife name he had called me over the previous thirty years, kicking the same old door. Usually when someone started in challenging my character, calling me gutless and the like, I would be all over him. But I had vowed to take a more controlled approach by this point in my career, and I just said, "Arnold, you're showing all the class I always knew you had."

When you go back as far as Red and I do, you don't worry about a guy's screaming in your face. You don't even worry about screaming back. It just reminds you where you came from.

Given that, and even though I was within months of being sixty years old and he was within months of seventy, there's no telling what we might have gotten into if I hadn't been operating with a new attitude at the time of that particular game. I had a very dear and longtime friend who was an official in the NFL for eighteen years, Walt Peters. He had died that previous summer and I had made up my mind that all this garbage that was going on with me and the NBA front office and other officials really was pretty unimportant in the big scheme of things. I worked hard to keep myself from getting involved in any verbal tirades or shouting matches with any of the players, coaches, general managers, owners, people in the league office, fans, media, anybody. I saw that there was more than one way to deal with this type of situation. A little humor and the ability to shrug and walk away works pretty well. But I also don't particularly regret that it took me sixty years to consider that option. Things wouldn't have been nearly as interesting otherwise.

chapter 2

THE PRO CALL

Larry Bird and Bill Laimbeer were charging after a loose ball on Detroit's end of the court. They jostled each other and fumbled for the ball before Bird dove and Laimbeer pulled up, thinking Bird would get called for traveling as he scrambled for the ball. Flat on the floor, Bird finally controlled the ball and flipped it downcourt. As Boston scored the fast-break basket, Laimbeer shouted at me, "That's traveling!" I told him, "No, that's sliding, and we don't have a rule on that." By the letter of the rules, he was right, but to me, that was a good "pro call," or in this case a good pro *non* call. When a guy risks life and limb with extra hustle, the fan is getting the best kind of pro basketball action. And I firmly believe the referee has to look for opportunities to encourage that kind of action, not cripple it with technicalities. Enter judgment—the pro call.

No one officiating the pro game would disagree with the assertion that players have become increasingly bigger, stronger, faster, and armed with greater skills. As a result, they've taken the level of play to a height Naismith wouldn't recognize as the game he invented one hundred years ago.

Back then you had 4'11" guys walking the ball up the court, and now you've got 6'11" super athletes who don't seem to touch the court at all. If you called a game strictly by the rules, you'd be blowing the whistle every two seconds, you couldn't finish it in a week, and nobody would care who won anyway. The game is an athletic contest, granted, but it's also a product. Call it entertainment. Call it a presentation. However you want to characterize it, the pro game can only succeed as a forum for all this talent. You have to let the energy and the skills of these athletes come through. The referee, or the set of three officials now being used, has the responsibility to let that happen.

It takes a feeling for the game to maintain control while still letting the action flow. An official has to sense when someone has actually gained an unfair advantage through a violation of the rules, yet try at all times to keep the game moving. As an official, you can't play the game for them, but you do have an enormous influence on how they're going to play. By not calling the jostling or the traveling in the Bird play, I was sending a message that encouraged all-out effort.

Unlike the built-in parameters of play you get in football (the down) and baseball (the batter), there is no natural break in basketball. Theoretically, it's possible to have nonstop action for twelve minutes each quarter. Other than someone's calling a time-out, the referee is the only one who interrupts play. With that kind of influence on the game's character, an official becomes in effect a kind of gatekeeper for the flow of the game. This leaves a lot of room for being second-guessed, challenged, and intimidated.

That intimidation is especially intense because of the physical environment of a pro basketball game. Unlike the other major sports, there are no fences, walls, or moats between the official and the fans; they're right on top of him. So are the coaches and the players on the bench. The players on the floor don't have a defined position; they can maneuver around and take all kinds of verbal shots at him. Everyone involved, from players to fans, is going to work the official. They aren't objective, and they aren't concerned with whether the official is doing a solid, fair, balanced job out there; they just want to win. The official has nothing to fall back on but his own judgment. That's why it's so important that he know the rules, know how he wants to apply them, and have the confidence to put his views across.

When I talk about the pro call, I mean a philosophy of officiating that recognizes that pro basketball is bigger than the rule book, and that officials need latitude to interpret the game. The league can present its idea of what each call should be, written into the *Official's Manual* according to the opinions of the supervisor of officials, but ultimately it must rely on our judgment about what's a violation and what isn't.

A man makes a steal, and as he lets go with a pass to a teammate downcourt, the man whose pocket he picked tries to grab him to stop the pass. He doesn't get enough of him to prevent it, but he makes contact. Do you call the foul and deny the team a layup? The pro call is to let the play go; that rewards the team for the steal and rewards the fans with continued action.

Over the years, each supervisor has placed his own signature on the style of play he wants for the NBA. When I broke in, and for most of the years I officiated, we were given the leeway to develop our own judgment. But in the later years of my career, the league placed increasing emphasis on exact conformity. I feel that this approach takes away the personal judgment that makes the game work. Sure, the league has a "let 'em play" attitude compared to college and high school ball, but they don't let 'em play quite as openly as I'd advocate. The league would expect me to call traveling on that sliding Larry Bird. I think that puts the ref and the players into the wrong frame of mind.

An official in any sport has to be extremely alert, but you have to concentrate on the action without getting pumped up and coming out there with whistle blazing, as if you're getting paid by the call. When I first came into the league, I'd zero in on some play, call a foul, and think, boy, I'm sharp—they can't get anything by me. Then I'd go into the locker room and Mendy or Sid Borgia or Norm Drucker would jump my ass. "Boy, you sure kicked the shit out of that call. That's not a pro call. Think about what a call like that does to the game." I got the point. You have to use your head, not just your eyes. Despite what it says in the rules, you have to make instantaneous decisions based on how you interpret what you see. *He touched the shooter. The rules say you can't do that. But did he really cause the shooter to miss?* It all comes down to determining the effect the "infraction" had on the play.

Al Bianchi, who is now general manager of the Knicks, made this comment when he was an assistant coach with Phoenix: "When we were playing in the fifties, the league was full of veterans, and officials were able to work a different game. Earl comes out nowadays and tries to treat it like his game. He calls it common sense. I say there are rules and they are supposed to be called a certain way. He's one of these guys who just runs his own show, and that doesn't work with the athlete of today."

I say it does if you're consistent and you use good judgment. Remember, the point of a pro call is to make sure nobody abuses the rules to gain an unfair advantage while keeping the game moving. The unprecedented popularity the game enjoys today tells me that fans are becoming more sophisticated and can follow the whole game. There are so many subtle things going on if you watch for them: the maneuvering away from the ball, the continual adjustments between the offense and defense. Teams are just a collection of individuals; they get hot, they cool off, they get a little tired, they lose concentration, they make adjustments to take away what the other guy was doing, and they find ways to get things rolling themselves. It doesn't take much to shift the balance of a game. Sometimes a guy is burying shots like crazy, so the defense forces him out a couple feet and he's getting tired and now he's missing and setting up fast breaks off the rebounds. The game is played in a constant state of adjustment. How well those adjustments flow is keyed by the officials and their ability to let it happen.

Someone once described refereeing as eye-brain-whistle coordination. We work with the whistle always in the mouth, ready. That's why you have inadvertent whistles on occasion. But for every call that's instantaneous, there is one where you have to suck on the whistle, wait it out, see what's really happening. In college and high school, if you see an infraction, boom, you're supposed to nail it right there. The beauty of refereeing professional basketball is that we can delay half a second to determine the outcome of a particular incident. Five people go up in air for a rebound. Do they bump? Sure. But did the guy with position who jumped the highest get the ball? If so, why call anything? Fans see lots of things and say we missed them. But the challenge is to determine what is really affecting the game, and the let-goes are part of it.

Some people call this frontier justice; I think it's like being a cop on the street. You ignore the jaywalkers and watch for the muggers. You earn respect with your voice, your body language, knowledge of the facts, instincts, and judgment. I reward aggressive play, but I never condone the hatchet-men, the bullies who inhibit the play of the biggest talents. That's the primary role of an official—to ensure that talent has a fair chance to display itself in the spirit of the game.

That's why I tell guys to keep their hands off. I give 'em a warning, tell 'em what I want, set the guidelines. I'd much rather talk to a player first than just blow my whistle all night. If he's gained an unfair advantage, I'll call it, but if there's no edge yet, then get him shaped up and keep the game moving. Some guys think you have to call everything you see to control the game. That's ridiculous. They'll play to whatever guidelines you set. Too many of today's officials lack that feeling for where to draw the line. That throws off the whole game. Ticky-tacky fouls keep guys from getting into a rhythm; they spend too much time standing around, and they start reaching, grabbing, poking, holding, playing defense with their hands instead of their feet. You've got to encourage the game to take off.

There's a purpose for every rule and it's important to keep

in mind what that purpose is. Take the three-second rule. It was brought in to keep the big, dominant centers from planting themselves in the key. If some guy wanders into a corner of the key and the play isn't even around him, you don't say, "Ha, I got ya!" and nail the guy unless he got some unfair advantage. I prefer to say, "Get in and out of there, so and so." If they move, the game keeps moving; if they don't, I nail 'em. I think that's one of the worst calls in basketball, not just in the pros but at all levels. I see times when a guy's not even in the play, has nothing to do with what's going on at that minute, and he gets called. Sure, if he's gaining an advantage, then you take action. But I don't worry so much about where he's planted his feet. What I do watch for is if he's grabbing guys cutting through the key or stepping into the path of someone rolling across. If I see a player get loose from the guy who's guarding him and someone else steps out and blocks his path, I'm quick to call that unless he was clearly there in time. That's a lot more important than looking for someone's feet on the three-second line.

Traveling. I don't think we let that much of it go. Sure, there's a little stutter-stepping. Guys stumble or slip a little on a wet spot. Did he get an advantage by slipping? If you have a Michael Jordan break loose for a big slam dunk and it's a 30-point game with a minute left and he takes a little skip or a hop, why not let him bring the house down? But if it's a 2-point game, you don't let him get that advantage regardless of how spectacular the play is. If a player palms the ball to get around a man, that should be called as traveling. But some of these guys are so good at getting the ball up high and guiding it with their hand on the side, and that's okay. Palming has to be really blatant to be worth a whistle.

Most of the time on a shot you have the offensive and defensive players coming at each other. Neither of them usually goes straight up, so there's bound to be some contact. That's just a part of the pro game; it shouldn't be an automatic call. A guy slams one home and he's got his arm in the basket up to his elbow. The ball's through and someone goes up and makes contact with his arm. Some referees will call that on the defense. Why? It didn't affect the shot. A guy goes up to shoot, the ball is already released, and the defender taps the shooter's arm. Let it go. If a man dribbling toward the basket gets bumped or slapped, hold the whistle until you see the outcome of the play. Instead of calling the foul immediately, let him go through and try to score, unless he loses the ball because of the foul. Try to avoid the cheap three-point plays, where incidental contact doesn't really affect the shot. I figure if the defender doesn't actually nail the shooter on his arm, let it go. Sure, if some guy creams the body, then it's a foul. But so often when a guy gets bumped while hitting a shot, you'll hear the bench yell out, "And one!" signifying he made the basket, now give him the foul shot, too. I figure, he got the hoop, let's move the show down to the other end. A guy goes in for a lay-up and the defender bumps him after the shot. Why call it, unless it's flagrant? A guy goes up to shoot, the defender comes down on the ball, and they bump bodies. Guys call the foul: "Ya got the body." Body my ass, he got the ball cleanly. Who's to say who caused the contact, anyway? Again, I'm not talking about plays where the defensive guy really nails him and takes him down with the body. If a guy hammers someone, nail him with a flagrant foul. I threw Rory Sparrow out of a playoff game a few years ago. He was playing for the Knicks against the Celtics. I had just warned these guys that we were going to stop the head-hunting when Larry Bird went sailing in for a shot and Rory unloaded on him and knocked him down. I threw Rory out of the game. He said I was just protecting Larry. I told him I'd have thrown him out if he'd done that to my mother-in-law.

In the pivot we allow the defensive player to put his forearm on the offensive player's back, as long as it's up against his body and not extended to where he's denying the offensive player the opportunity to maneuver to the side or is just pushing him out from the basket. They can brace against a player, but if they stick their knee up into the guy, it's a foul. If they start bumping and I'm the underneath official, I'm going to watch this closely because if you let yourself watch the action on the ball, invariably these two guys will get into a fight. Nothing is touchier than the hand-check, which is holding, impeding the progress of the offensive man. But there's a difference between holding and touching. If a guy has his hand out there and it's not actually holding a guy up, we allow that. But if there's force on it, where the guy is trying to maneuver the offensive player, then it's a foul. I watch for defensive guys who are trying to goad the offensive player by sticking a hand into him. It always follows: the offensive guy slaps it away. Defender sticks it back. Slaps it away. Sticks it back. Now the offensive guy is totally distracted from his game. He's just thinking of a way to break this guy's hand. The defender has taken the guy out of his game, which is what he wants. He's taken advantage of the rules. The official needs to get that stopped right now. I'll give 'em a verbal: "Get your hands off, knock off the bumping. Play the game." It usually works, and you can do it without bringing play to a halt.

Just as the official tries to keep a player from distracting others by banging, grabbing, and challenging, he also has to be sure extracurricular activities don't distract his own concentration. If a coach or player is raising a ruckus, that's when you have to cool them off, first with a warning that you've had enough, and then with technicals if they persist.

I'm not eager to call jump balls. I probably let players tug at the ball a little longer than most referees. Let one guy come up with it and keep the game moving; that's what the fans came for—movement, action. If there is a likely jump-ball situation and the ball is rolling around, guys are grabbing at it, I just let it go. Yeah, it looks bad with everybody scrambling and scratching, but many times out of just that kind of a situation you'll see a beautiful breakaway basket. Hold the whistle and you let it happen.

The pro call isn't all let-goes. It's also looking for the clever maneuvers that give a guy an advantage, like a guy's grabbing a hand or arm as a defender tries to get around a screen. I look for the defensive guy who puts his foot into the path of an offensive player, trying to trip him or force him to step around. I look for the defender who tries to block the shot with his top hand and jabs the shooter with his lower hand to throw his shot off. Offensively, I look for the guy in the pivot hooking his elbow on the defender and spinning around him. I look for shooters driving to the basket and warding off the defender with the nonball arm. These are all judgment calls, trying to determine if a guy took enough advantage of the rules that it's necessary to stop the game with a foul.

I probably didn't call illegal defenses as much as most officials. The rules covering illegal defenses are quite intricate, with all sorts of details concerning 2.9-second counts, imaginary lines, and double-team dos and don'ts. I didn't worry so much that a defensive player might technically be in violation of these elaborate rules. I just called illegal defense when a player or players gained an unfair advantage by abusing the requirements. Sometimes it was all I could do to keep from laughing when I'd look at a guy sagging in the lane and then he'd see me and start looking around frantically for his man. He wouldn't be moving his feet, but he'd be making all kinds of motion with his head. When you're camped in there, not double-teaming the ball or playing your own man, it's a zone. Acting doesn't work. Still, many times calling it just stops play when it isn't necessary.

It keeps coming back to judgment, having a feeling for the pro game and reacting with confidence. Certainly experience helps, getting so you can watch the routine things like the game and shot clocks, the scorer's table, substitutions, team fouls, coach and bench behavior, and commercial timeouts almost by instinct. But the test is still how you judge the game. I've seen young referees come in with plenty of enthusiasm and determination, only to wilt under the pressure. I've known guys who started out strong and were courageous enough to make tough calls against the home team late in a game if they had to be made, but you could see them change as the players and the coaches and the fans got to them. "Why bring the house down on my head? Why get

killed for something nobody really appreciates anyway?"
I've had guys say that to me. If you ever stop to say, "What's
going to happen to me if I make this call?" you might as well
take your whistle and shove it because that's all the respect
you're giving it. I was taught from the beginning, and it has
stuck with me through all these years, that it's much easier
to fight your way out of a place than to have to go look in the
mirror and admit you backed down from a tough call.

It's been said that in any game two-thirds of the plays are
pretty black-and-white and the remaining third are in the
grays, calls that could go either way, and that the referee
should make sure those even out between the two teams. I
can't subscribe to that. How can you referee a game and
keep track of who got the last "break"? Each play has to be
judged on its own merits. That's like saying referees should
use makeup calls. Is a makeup call supposed to be made up?
I was taught early on that if you feel you've kicked the hell
out of a call and you have a team upset with you as a result,
a makeup call will only get the other team upset, too. You
make a pretty long night for yourself going about your business that way. If you kick a play, you just have to swallow it,
or change it if you discover it right away. You can't do that
very often or they're going to start wondering where your
head is, but you'll get a lot more respect by admitting you
blew one than by trying to even things out by making up a
call the other way. If there's a loose-ball situation and I call
some guy for a foul, then realize it really isn't the best call
because of other things I sense have simultaneously happened, I might just wave off the foul and call a jump ball.
Other refs say, "Well, yeah, you can get away with that
because you're Earl Strom. I can't get away with it." I tell
them any official can get away with it if you do it in a way
that sells it, that shows you're in control. You'll hear from the
league office, but so what if you know you got the call right?

You can get into trouble anticipating a foul. These guys are
so fast and such incredible athletes, they can fool you. If you
blow your whistle anticipating a foul and it doesn't occur,
own up to it. I've had situations where the defensive player

comes flying up and looks as if he's going to hammer the offensive player on his shot, I blow the whistle, and whoa, the guy gets the ball cleanly. Rather than trying to sell the call with some bullshit like "With the body!" admit you guessed and guessed wrong. As long as the team that was shooting knows they're going to get the same call on the other end, they'll buy it. You're trying to get the call right, and that's what this game is all about.

Consistency is the key. That's true for the calls you make at both ends of the court and throughout the course of the game. Guys just want to know where the line is being drawn. They'll adjust to it. But you can't keep moving that line around on them. If you haven't been calling three seconds in the key all night, don't do it in the final thirty seconds with the game on the line.

Just as I try to avoid anticipating a call, I try hard not to prejudge a game. Naturally, we spend a lot of time in the dressing room before a game going over player matchups and what to look for in certain situations. If Larry Bird is playing, we might discuss how he likes to sag into the passing lanes, so we have to keep him honest, don't let him play a zone. Don Nelson is probably the best among all coaches in disguising illegal defenses. We might talk about what to watch for from his players. If we know there is a particular grudge between players, we discuss that matchup. Sleepy Floyd and Jeff Hornacek have a real thing going; we'll remind ourselves to be particularly alert to these guys if they start banging. Akeem Olajuwon likes to back into guys when he's on offense, bumping them back under the basket. Kevin McHale is the same way. These guys use their legs and butts to gain position. We might remind ourselves to let the defensive guy have an extra bump back, let him have just a little bit more license to fight his way around as a defender. Buck Williams and Karl Malone are two very physical guys. We might talk about how they're going to bang on each other and how we should let 'em play, unless someone is taking advantage of the other. We'll talk about guys who like to kick a leg out when they're shooting, trying to draw contact with the defender and get the foul shot to go with the basket. Dennis Johnson is good at that. Tiny Archibald was good at it.

If you have guys who talk a lot of trash, trying to distract their opponents from their game, we'll remind ourselves to keep tabs on it. M.L. Carr and Cedric Maxwell, when they were with the Celtics, were really into this. We might talk about a guy like Dennis Rodman and how he likes to hotdog it out there. How much is too much? Usually you let it go unless he's enticing a player to come back at him or if he starts trying to show up the official. I remember a playoff game when Rodman was new in the league. He started talking it up against Bird. I told him to knock it off. Bird said, "That's okay, I'll take care of him," and commenced to run off about 10 straight points on Rodman.

We might discuss a guy like Mark Aguirre, who'll drive the lane and use his left arm to ward off the defender, then allow body contact as he's taking his shot, trying to draw the foul. If we have a guy who's adept at faking the defender up, then leaning into him as he shoots, we'll talk about how that's really an offensive foul. David Thompson was great at that. Artis Gilmore was so strong he would actually just hold the defender in place with one hand and wheel up his shot with the other. We'd remind ourselves to watch for that and the way he'd take all these little steps while faking his shot. The floppers are always worth a word of caution. Doug Collins was the master. He'd chest up to the offensive player, then flop over backward, trying to draw the offensive foul. I'm sure he was actually fouled on many occasions that weren't called because after a while referees get gun-shy about being conned.

But some of the officials get too caught up in pregame analysis. The danger is that you'll watch for that and let stuff that's developing go right by. There's a difference between expecting something to happen, almost predicting it, and *sensing* it. In the latter case, you have to feel the game and have confidence in your ability to interpret it. Officials make eighty-five, ninety, one hundred calls a game, and that's probably less than half the decisions they're making when you consider all the noncalls. Those decisions are influenced by the philosophy set forth by each supervisor during his respective regime, but the underlying agenda for refereeing the pro game has always been to let the talent come through. Of course, I think that talent includes the referee.

The present regime has tried hard to sterilize the personalities of the officials. That marks a dramatic contrast to the way things started out under Pat Kennedy. He was the only supervisor in the history of the NBA whom I didn't work under. He came up with basketball during the twenties, thirties, and forties when the referees virtually made up the rules as they went along. Games were absolute rodeos and officials had to be iron willed to have a prayer of controlling the players. Kennedy was so outlandish he stole the show. He would yell so you could hear him in the next county. Sometimes when he called a foul he would run up to the guy and jab his finger at him, yelling, "You, you, you!" He would blast away on his whistle like a mad canary. His antics were pure show biz. He wasn't there just to run the show, he wanted to be the show.

One time, though, even Kennedy was left speechless. In the earliest years of the NBA, Lester Harrison was coach and owner of the Rochester Royals. One of his players hit a jumper and was fouled. As Kennedy blew his whistle, he was bumped, breaking off a piece of the whistle. It got stuck in his throat and he collapsed on the floor, fighting for air. Lester ran out onto the court, got down on his hands and knees right over the stricken Kennedy, and said, "Pat, Pat, before you die, tell 'em the basket counted."

I can't say that I subscribe to Kennedy's brand of theatrics, but the pendulum has gone too far the other way. It's a cinch Kennedy, who wrapped up his career working for the Globetrotters, wouldn't get a sniff by the NBA today, even though he was an excellent official. He was part of the roots of the league, though, and his strong personality was an influence on the guys who came along to shape the way the game would be played in the NBA, guys like Sid Borgia, Mendy Rudolph, and Norm Drucker.

When Jocko Collins, who brought me into the league, became supervisor of officials, he didn't want a whole lot of rough stuff. He had been a top-notch official and he felt the game belonged to the fans, who wanted to see the stars play and didn't want to watch a parade to the foul line. Jocko was asking for a fine line of freedom and safety, and it took an experienced official to carry it off. Judgment was essential. There were many among the dozen regular officials who were working at the time I broke in who could handle it. I wish I could say the same of today's crop.

When Sid took over for Jocko, there was a trend toward more open play. "No harm, no foul" was the line that came to characterize the NBA. Sid had the ability as an official to let things get pretty loose and bring them back under control—if he wanted to. As supervisor he would come down on you pretty hard if you screwed up, but at the same time he would back you to the hilt against the league. So would Jocko. It eventually cost them their jobs. Sid used to watch games, and if he didn't like the way you were working, he'd come down to the locker room at halftime and really unload on you. I'm accused of being pretty demanding of young officials, and I guess I learned that from him.

One thing Sid couldn't stand was cigarette or cigar smoke. It was a saving grace for John Vanak and me one night. We'd stunk up a half in Detroit and we knew Sid was there and he'd be coming into the room to chew us out. So we rushed in there, lit up two cigars, and puffed up a big cloud by the time he got there. He came in, blew his stack as long as he could stand to be in there, and ran off.

When Dolph Schayes was supervisor, Mendy pretty much ran the show. He didn't want fights. He always used to say, "These are the greatest basketball players in the world. They'll play any way you want them to." He thought talent and finesse should prevail. He was suave and he wanted a little dignity in the game if he could influence it. His philosophy certainly had a great deal to do with the attitudes I've developed toward how the game should be played, and therefore refereed. Use common sense, keep the game moving, but don't let the talent get taken out by the butchers.

In 1970, John Nucatola took over. He had been an NBA official until he had a falling-out with the league after he criticized the league for its lack of support for its refs. He went on to become supervisor of officials for the ECAC. It was pretty surprising he ever got back into the NBA. He and Sid had a big hassle in Syracuse one night. They had to be surrounded by players from both teams because the fans were going to kill them. John came back and told Commissioner Maurice Podoloff that they needed more protection and Syracuse ought to be fined for not providing better police protection. He was told to like it or pack it in. He did the latter and came out with an article in *Sports Illustrated* really blasting the league. He wouldn't let any guys work college ball for him if they were working in the NBA.

When they made him supervisor, he brought his college philosophy back with him. He wanted a real hands-off approach. He wanted you to go strictly by the book because above all else he didn't want any protests. Forget about judgment and common sense. He and Mendy had many long arguments about it. It just isn't practical to referee the game to the letter of the rules, and Nucatola made it even tougher by lobbying to have the rules committee take out the "force out" rule. There are so many times where a guy goes up for a rebound, another guy bumps him, and he falls out of bounds. Before, you could say it really wasn't enough contact for a foul, give the team who had possession the ball, and get on with the game. That's just common sense. So many times two guys get to the same spot at the same time. The defensive man cuts off an offensive man driving the baseline. They don't really bang each other, they just get to the same spot at the same time—it's a tie—and the guy with the ball falls out of bounds. Now, since they changed the rule, you have to call either a foul or a turnover. You should just give the offense the ball and keep the game going.

Drucker tried to provide an era of common sense. It was the way he had worked the game, and he knew it was the best way to bring out the best in the players. The problem was, he took over in 1977–78, the year after a major officials' strike, and there was a lot of union politics that kept many of the guys from concentrating on refereeing. He tried to get more interpretation into the calls. Use rules as a guide, rather than by the book. In contrast to the present-day Garretson regime, Drucker was more personal in his approach to the officials themselves. He didn't allow politics to dictate assignments. He dealt with people in private. He never set out to embarrass people. He didn't live by the threat. All that changed when Garretson took over in 1981.

Beyond the politics and intimidation—and I'll have a lot to say about that later—what bothered me most under Garretson was the insistence on taking the personalities of the officials out of the game. We were to be as anonymous and regimented as could be achieved with living, breathing human beings. It was as if corporate America had swallowed a whistle. Everything was to be standardized: standardized signals, standardized techniques, standardized mechanics. We had a checklist we had to send to the league office for every game. We could be fined if we didn't discuss each of these things with our partners. We were not to initiate any conversation with anyone—coaches, players, fans. We were told exactly where to position ourselves on the court, exactly where the eyes were supposed to be aimed, virtually every aspect imaginable was defined in exacting terminology. Officials were to be like interchangeable parts. And even off the court we were to have virtually no contact with anyone other than other officials.

This ran so much against my nature and the way I came into the league. In those days you saw the teams much more frequently. We were supposed to avoid flying with the teams if we could, but flight frequencies were much lower and you kept bumping into the players as you traveled. We could stay in the same hotels as the teams in the old days; that was great because you could work a game, have a run-in with a player or coach, and see that same guy in the lounge later that night and talk the night away without any hassles. Today, you can't do it. The league wants as much separation as possible. I can see the intent behind this in a lot of ways. Players and coaches seem to feel things more personally after a game than they used to; things just seem to get carried over in their minds, and if you do run into them, the beef can start right up where you left off. Maybe it's because there are so many more teams, players, coaches, and officials, or maybe it's because they're all making so much money, but there isn't that fraternal "we're all in this together" feeling anymore.

Early in my career, Mendy and I had a game in Cincinnati a couple of nights before Christmas. We ended up staying at the same hotel as the Celtics. There was this piano bar down in the basement called the Coal Hole, a dingy little place. We all ended up there after the game. Red wasn't there but a lot of ballplayers were—Cousy, Loscutoff, Heinsohn, Ramsey, all these guys having a beer. This piano player was there doing a half-assed job. He went on a break and Mendy went over and started playing Christmas songs. He wasn't a bad piano player. All the players and I gathered around and we were singing and carrying on. It was great, two Jews leading a bunch of Celtics in Christmas carols. The piano player finished his break and announced, "Okay, I'm back."

Loscutoff and all these big, brawny players told him, "Hey, screw you, buddy. We got a piano player, take a hike." He got upset and said it's his job and ran off to get the manager: "These guys won't let me have my piano back." Loscutoff told him, "Hey, we'll give the bum his pay, just leave the piano alone. We got our guy." The manager looked at the size of the Celtics and turned to the guy. "Yeah, why don't ya just take the rest of the night off?" And we went right on our merry way with Mendy at the keys. That sort of thing happened often. You'd run into the players who were traveling and end up having a couple of pops with them in the hotel bar or sitting with them at the airport or on flights when we happened to fly with teams. We'd sit around the

hotel lobby laughing and telling stories, go out on the floor
and scream and cuss at each other, then come back and
laugh and tell more stories. That's just the way it worked in
those days.

Bill Fitch was kind of a ha-ha guy in his early years at
Cleveland. Then they started becoming a factor and he became a real hard-ass on officials. I had him one night when
the Cavs were just stinking it up and he was on us hard. With
twenty seconds left, one of his players got laid out with an
elbow. Fitch came over and started ragging me about finally
giving his team a call. I said, "Don't give me that bullshit."

"I am going to give you that bullshit," he said. "You think
because you've been around twenty years you don't have to
take anything."

"Not tonight I don't." And I tossed him.

The next morning I ran into him at the airport. He asked,
"You want to talk?"

"I guess it depends on what you've got to say."

"The trouble with you is that you always think you're
right."

"Well, most of the time, I am," I told him.

"Yeah, well, maybe that's what pisses me off. I still have
something to say once in a while."

"As long as you're willing to pay for getting tossed, that's
your privilege." We then headed off to have a cup of coffee.
No hard feelings. We'd start fresh the next time out.

Part of working the game is establishing who you are with
these people. If they only see you as a nonhuman whistle
machine, you have far less chance of establishing a rapport
that will encourage mutual respect. The pro call isn't just
sensing the game, but also having a sense of who these people are who are playing and coaching it. Today, it's all
treated as if it's a matter of life and death. The officials are
always looking over their shoulders, afraid someone's going
to pitch into them to the league office for being a human
being. We've got some referees who won't even stop in an
airport if they bump into a team. I don't think you best serve
the game by taking it to that degree of regimentation. I

know I was the last of the old breed where the referee was part of the show. I don't mean you should be the show yourself, like a Pat Kennedy, but when I make a call in a game, I want to sell it, much like Sid Borgia, Mendy Rudolph, Arnold Heft, and Norm Drucker. We each had our own personality, our own flair on the court. And it paid off. You couldn't take a Mendy Rudolph and put him out there on the floor and expect him to be a robot like they want today. He simply wouldn't have been as effective an official. I always gave it a "tweet-tweet" when I made a call, but Garretson promised there wouldn't be any of that double-whistle stuff after I was gone. What the hell's wrong with a little individuality? Who really cares anyway?

If you have a bang-bang play and there's not a real clear picture of what happened, you have to take charge. If you're nonchalant and unemotional in your call, guys on the floor and the folks in the stands are going to think you're just not really working at it, not really in control. You have to jump in there and show 'em you've got it totally in command. You saw it all, you've got your call, and there's no discussion, gentlemen. That's the only way you can stand in there against all the opinions and challenges. I always tried to give it that extra boost, a little schmaltz, a little extra colorful treatment when I had a call that needed to be sold. I don't think I went overboard, and I don't think I tried to be the center of attention on every play. But there are times when you've got to get your point home. Someone once said the best referees are part actors. Maybe that's true.

You don't have to go flying through the air to make your point. Sometimes it's just a matter of getting everyone focused on your call that sells it. An example of this approach is noted in a newspaper account of the end of a game I had in Seattle a dozen years ago: "Milwaukee's Alton Lister had tipped in what appeared to be a game-tying shot at the end of regulation play last night in the Kingdome. But as hoarse throats were giving way to upset stomachs in a gallery of 23,062, Strom calmly pivoted from his midcourt position and strolled toward the official scorekeeper. He shook his head from side to side, then waved his arms slowly in front of him, signaling 'no shot.' " What's wrong with a little drama? After all, pro basketball is billed as part of the entertainment business. And a referee can take his role very seriously and still have some fun. It's all part of the pro call.

chapter 3

LIVIN' ON THE FAULT LINE

The first twelve years I worked in the NBA I also worked in customer relations for General Electric in Philadelphia. It was a simple matter of "don't give up your day job." The league could bounce you pretty much on whim, and I needed the security for my family. As a result, I did a lot of scrambling getting to and from games. I was usually pretty short-fused when I worked the games, and when I did make it home, I was usually too pooped to catch up on all the family life that I had missed. It wasn't as bad when I was eventually able to drop the job with GE, but even today there is no way you can have a normal lifestyle with a job like this. The pro basketball referee often travels alone, never has a home game or a supportive crowd behind him. Hell, there are times when he can't even stand the other referee he has to face the world with that night. When I broke into the league in the 1957–58 season, there were eight teams, the farthest west being Minneapolis. In my final season, 1989–90, the league had grown to twenty-seven teams, spread from Boston to Los Angeles and Seattle to Miami. I traveled 160,000 miles by air my last season.

In the old days, I didn't even have time for a hotel room on many occasions, scrambling between games and my job. I could work games in New York, Boston, Philadelphia, and Syracuse, for example, on weeknights, then head out to cover the Midwest teams on weekends. I was scheduled to work a game one Saturday afternoon in St. Louis and left work Friday evening to fly out from Philadelphia. I was sitting on the plane, a TWA, waiting for us to taxi out onto the runway. Some guys came onto the plane, went up to the cockpit, and a couple minutes later the pilots came walking back down the aisle with these guys. A couple minutes later, a stewardess got on the PA system and announced, "The flight engineers have gone on strike and this flight is canceled." I rushed over to the North Philadelphia train station and caught a train to Chicago.

I changed trains in Chicago and was heading out across the countryside in the middle of the night when the train ran into a cow. That stopped us for a while. The next morning I went into the dining car. It was just crummy, filthy, dirty, greasy. No one else was in there. That should have been a tip-off on the food, but I tried to eat some eggs and greasy potatoes. I couldn't stand it, so I got up and left. When I was about a car and a half away, there was this big explosion. The damn dining car had blown up. Some grease line had caught on fire and blown the thing up. One of the waiters who was between cars was thrown right out into a snowbank.

We had to hang around until they could get the dining car off. I changed into my uniform on the train, and when we got to St. Louis, I jumped into a cab and rushed to the arena. I got there right before the end of the first quarter. Some local guy was filling in for me. I worked the remaining three quarters and went back to the train station, then got on the same damn train on a turnaround back to Chicago. When the conductor saw me, he said, "What are you, some kind of a train freak?"

When I told him I had come all this way and gone through all this bullshit to work three quarters of a basketball game, he said, "Well, it could have been worse."

"How's that?"

"You could have been in the dining car when it blew up."

Yeah, the adventures of travel could be endless.

I was to work a game up in Providence one night, Boston was playing there. I worked a half day at General Electric and went to the airport. It was foggy as hell and all the planes were delayed. The airlines said there was a plane out of Newark that was coming in from Detroit. I could take a train up to Newark and catch that. Before I left I called my wife, Yvonne, and told her what I was doing.

By the time I got to Newark, the fog had settled in there. They expected it to lift soon and the plane would be coming in from Detroit. I called Yvonne to chat and told her I was standing by in Newark. The plane finally arrived, we boarded and headed out to the runway. The fog closed back in and we sat on the runway for an hour. It was four o'clock going on five. They took us back to the terminal. Now I find out Providence is fogged in. I called Dolph Schayes, who was supervisor of officials at the time. He told me to forget about trying to get up there and go on home. I called Yvonne and told her I was going to catch a train back to Philly and I would be home in a couple of hours.

Just as I was ready to go out and get in a cab to the train station, there came an announcement that there was a plane taking off for Philadelphia in fifteen minutes. I jumped out of the cab and ran back into the terminal. I called Yvonne and told her not only was I coming home that evening, but if she wanted to hold on, I'd be there for dinner.

We got on the plane and took off. It's only about a fifteen-minute hop from Newark to Philly. We were just ready to land and the fog rolled back in. We couldn't get down. Our alternate was Washington, D.C., so we flew over Philly and landed in Washington. I called Yvonne.

"Guess where I am."

"Where?" she asked suspiciously.

"Washington."

"At the rate you're going, you'll be in Miami by morning," she said with some irritation.

To hell with all this, I figured. I was tired and I was ticked off. It had been nearly twelve hours since I left the office and I was farther from home than when I'd started and I'd missed my game, to boot. I had a couple belts to calm myself down and got on the train for Philly. When I got in, I figured it was stupid to drive home, but then I didn't want to call Yvonne again and wake her up, so I just drove to Pottstown. I got in about four-thirty A.M. and was up at six-thirty to head back to work.

I did make one smart decision when it came to travel in those days. Officials are always supposed to travel on flights different from the one a team flies on. The exception to that used to be when they had the Sunday afternoon game of the week on TV and we were to fly with the team if we worked their game the night before.

I was with Jim Duffy in Minneapolis on a Saturday night. The Lakers were to play the next afternoon in St. Louis, and since they had their own plane at the time, we were to fly with them. They had an old DC-3, a real patched-up job. We dressed in a hurry after the game and rushed out to the airport. I took one look at the plane and said, "Whoa." I was only a young official at the time, and Duffy had been around. We were talking about the plane and walking around it, and I didn't like the looks of the tape on the fuselage and the patches on the wings. I said, "Well, Duff, if you want to travel with these guys, fine, but I'm not getting on that plane."

"Well, we've got to," he said. "It'll be all right."

"Bullshit. I'm not going." At that time I wasn't too fond of flying anyway. This was more than my limit of tolerance. "There's an early-morning flight out for St. Louis and I'm going to grab that." Duffy took another look at the plane and decided to join me at the hotel for a drink. We got up the next morning, flew out to St. Louis, landed, bought a paper, and saw this big story about how the Lakers' plane had gone down in a cornfield in Iowa. Luckily they got into the field with the furrows in the right direction and didn't flip over. They tell me half the guys were on the floor crapping in their pants, and I'm sure I would have been among them if we'd flown that night. They canceled the game, of course.

As I said, I was a little touchy, maybe even a little grouchy on occasions. And over the years I did earn a reputation for being pretty aggressive when challenged, especially when a player or coach tried to embarrass me. That carried through the years, even after I was able to leave GE and devote full time to refereeing. I had a game with Joey Crawford in Kansas City against Chicago. Joey's father, Shag Crawford, worked as a major league umpire. He was a real fiery guy, never backed off. Phil Johnson was coaching at Kansas City then and Joey had a beef with him. It was a real bang-bang thing; two T's and he was gone. At halftime, I told Joey, "The first T he had coming. But you've got to get away. Turn and walk away. Don't stand there and challenge the guy. Everybody's all steamed up and you can't expect them not to have the last word. It's up to the ref to swallow it a little bit." Joey said he saw what I was saying and agreed to work at it.

In the second half I called a foul on Tommy Burleson, the Kings' 7'3" center. I was walking down the lane after giving the signal to the bench when I thought I heard him say, "Motherfucker." I wasn't positive. I turned around and said, "Look, you big SOB, I don't know if you called me a motherfucker or not. But if you do it again, I'm gonna throw you out and I'm gonna flatten your ass on the way. And I know how you can fight, so I'm not afraid of trying you. Let that be a warning." And I walked away.

Chicago guard Norm Van Lier, who was always a real fiesty little guy, told Burleson, "Hey, he's crazy enough to fight you out here. Don't fuck with him." I was still steamed after the game. Joey said, "Well, Earl, I guess what you're trying to say is, don't do as I do, do as I say."

"What do you mean?" I asked him.

"I didn't see you exactly swallowing it and walking away out there."

Generally, the great players don't give you the heat. It's much more often the marginal players who are struggling to

keep up with the stars and keep getting themselves into
situations that might be embarrassing—getting a shot
blocked or the ball swiped, getting beat on defense, getting
outplayed on the boards. That's when they start turning on
the referee, trying to plead their case. Walt Bellamy was a
good journeyman center who spent the sixties in the shadow
of Russell and Chamberlain. Actually, he'd give both those
guys all they could handle; he just had a tendency to lose that
intensity against the rest of the league. One night "Bells"
turned to me—he liked to refer to himself in the third person—and said, "You don't call a foul on Wilt Chamberlain or
on Bill Russell. But you call a foul like that on Walter. If Wilt
stayed in the lane for an hour, you don't call it. But you won't
let Walter even walk across it."

He could test your patience. In another game he was mad
after a call and let the ball roll down to the other end of the
court. I told him to go get it. He said, "If it was anyone else
but you asking, Walter wouldn't do it."

"Fine," I said. "It just happens nobody else is ready to
throw Walter out of this game."

Some guys just don't know how to let up, even in victory.
In the case of Bill Laimbeer, it was the ultimate victory as
Detroit swept Los Angeles for its first NBA title in 1989.
Laimbeer was standing in the hallway outside the Pistons
dressing room, sharing in the bubbly celebration, when I
walked by. "Great game, Earl. But why did you do us the
way you did in the first quarter?" I couldn't help laughing to
myself. Here's a guy who said he liked the way I gave him
warnings on the court, telling him to keep his hands off, to
watch the key, to quit sagging into a zone; he'd tell me,
"Keep talking to me. It helps me, Earl." So I didn't think
he'd mind if I told him, "Can't you just enjoy your win? This
is one time you really don't need to get in the last shot."

On every call you know you're going to have somebody
upset at you. But there are times when even the guy you'd
think would be the most appreciative turns on you. I mean,
you try to make the guy a hero, and well, I can't help but
chuckle when I think about poor Tom Boerwinkle. He was

a first-round draft pick for the Chicago Bulls in 1968, a huge guy, about 7' and 270 pounds. Near the end of the season Chicago was fighting for a playoff berth and needed every win desperately. They were playing Los Angeles and down 1 with twenty seconds left. The Bulls worked it around, and finally, with three seconds left, Boerwinkle had to take a shot. Jerry West hit his arm and knocked the ball away. I called the foul and Boerwinkle went to the line with three chances to make two.

As I turned to give him the ball for the first shot, he looked as tight and mechanical as a robot. The crowd was on its feet. He looked back at me and said, "This is a helluva spot you've put me in." His first shot went up to the board like a line drive to center field, hit the backboard, and came back nearly to his hands on the fly. He knew he had to let up, took something off the next shot, and it knuckleballed its way not even to the rim. The third shot went up, hit the very top of the board, and bounced over. The Lakers controlled the ball for the remaining three seconds and the Bulls were dead. As we headed off the floor, Boerwinkle hustled alongside me and said out of the side of his mouth, "If you ever do that to me again, I'll punch you out, Earl." Fortunately, he didn't mean it.

I have to admit I always enjoyed seeing how guys perform under pressure and didn't mind adding a little edge to it at times. Bill Bradley had the golden-boy image, but he could be very sarcastic. When he came into the league with the big salary, he was looked on as sort of a prima donna. I guess I'm always curious to see what a guy like that is made of. I was working a game in his rookie year, and it came down to his shooting a couple of key free throws at the end of a game. I handed him the ball and said, "Here you go, Bill. Let's see what all that money does for you now." Such a look he gave me. In his book he said, "I don't think a referee should say things like that."

If he had come into the league a decade earlier, he'd have gotten a hell of a lot more than that out of referees' mouths. In my second year in the league, Richie Guerin was playing for the New York Knicks. They had an exhibition game up in Hartford. I'm working the game and he's giving me a whole lot of shit. I warned him and finally gave him a T. He kept it up and I gave him another one and tossed him. He was really after me then and he came up and got right in my face and said, "You gutless son of a bitch. You think you're pretty tough, but I wonder how tough you'd be without that shirt and whistle." I told him to wait by the bus after the game and I'd show him how tough I was. He said he'd be there and turned to walk away.

I said, "And remember, be there by yourself."

"I will be," he said.

"I know you will, because I ain't coming," I shouted at him. It broke him up, fortunately.

Even if you aren't out there challenging players, you can get in harm's way. We don't have the major fistfights that we used to, but an official has to learn to protect himself anytime these guys start swinging. We had a fight a few years ago in L.A. when Houston was there. Jess Kersey got mixed up in it and ended up on the bottom of the pile. He came up, his face all red and his hair mussed up. Bill Fitch, Houston's coach, was pulling the guys up. He looked over at me and said, "Where the hell were you?" and I said, "Taking names, baby."

If you can get to them early and get a word in before they start swinging, do it. But once they square off and start toss-ing punches, don't get in there and catch one. They might just be looking for a chance to nail a referee. I got in between two guys once. The Warriors were playing in Hershey, Penn-sylvania, against the Knicks. Richie Guerin and somebody got into it. I jumped in and caught one square and started to go down. Carl Braun was playing for the Knicks and he caught me and was holding me up. I said, "Let me down, I don't want to get hit again." That felt pretty lousy.

When I tried to see how guys would react to pressure, it might have been a little payback from when I first broke in. Coaches will test you and pick at you from the moment you step out on the court. My first game was an exhibition in

Coatesville, a little town west of Philadelphia. I was working with Willie Smith and Philly was playing Syracuse. By the luck of the draw I had to face one of the league's toughies in Syracuse coach Paul Seymour. Hearing about someone's characteristic misbehavior doesn't really help you prepare for dealing with him in person. Actually, it makes you more edgy—it's like waiting for a gun to go off.

The game got underway, and after a few trips up and down the court I started to relax a little and get into the flow of the game. One time as I went by the Syracuse bench, Seymour leaned out and yelled at me, "Hey, ref, your fly's open." Knowing his reputation as a wise guy, I looked over and said, "Let's knock it off."

I came back up the court a few seconds later and he yelled at me again. "Hey, ref, I'm tellin' ya, your fly's *open!*"

I turned to him. "The next time I hear you say that I'm going to run you out of here."

"The hell with ya then," Seymour answered. "If you want to embarrass yourself and let it hang out all over the court, that's your business. But, I'm tellin' ya, your fly *is* open."

I was just about ready to hit Seymour with a technical when Johnny Kerr, who played for the Nats, ran by and said, "Hey, buddy, he's not kidding. Your fly is open."

What could I do? I had to look down, and sure enough, the zipper was broken and the fly was wide open. Totally embarrassed, I ran off the court and into the locker room, changed into my civilian pants, and came running back out. There was a time-out when I got back onto the court, and Seymour called over to me, "Hey, rook, you're gonna have to learn when we're kidding and when we're not."

It didn't take me long to figure that when you're dealing with the folks at the edge of the court, you can be pretty sure there isn't much kidding in anything they dish out toward referees. When it came to courtside manners, Seymour was among the most aggressive, especially in the early years of the NBA when coaches might bump you and you'd just bump them back. Seymour would always try to get right up on you and grab a pinch of your stomach so he could really get in your face. I never had enough of a gut for him to grab, but we'd stand toe to toe and shout at each other. As hard-assed as Seymour could be, there was another coach who I have to admit brought out visions of violence in me on more than one occasion.

Only twice in the thirteen years from 1956 to 1969 did the Boston Celtics finish an NBA season without the league championship. When St. Louis did it in 1958 and when Phila-delphia did it in 1967, the same man was coaching: Alex Hannum. He was a big guy, 6'7", who had played for half a dozen NBA teams. Those two championships were pretty dazzling accomplishments for him, but the main distinction he carried with me was as my No. 1 nemesis in the NBA.

As we've already discussed, I could get mad as hell at somebody one night and be ready to start with a clean slate the next. I tried to do that with Alex, but he made it awfully difficult. That's exemplified by all those articles and pictures that showed up over the years with the two of us in one hassle or another. They all seemed to have the same image: me standing there yelling up at this bald-headed guy who was yelling back at me, both of us pointing fingers in each other's face. What usually followed seconds later was Alex's taking an early exit to the locker room.

Alex gave me a lot of heat when I was breaking in. I probably brought a lot of it on myself. We just didn't have much use for each other. A coach may get along fine with one official and have a continual war with another. It's just a matter of personalities. Sometimes it only takes one inci-dent to establish an animosity that will go on for years. I never carry grudges, but maybe a particular blowup with a player or coach will make them think I'm out to get them, so there'll be tension from then on. Alex was always a master at turning the crowd on a ref. When he was in Syracuse, he used to stand up in front of the bench, put his hands on his bald head, and turn to the crowd like, "God, this guy is crucifying us!" It always brought the crowd to a boil.

The one night that might have broken it for Alex and me was a playoff game between Boston and Philly in Philadelphia. Boston was kicking the crap out of the 76ers, and Alex, whom I had been into it with a couple of times already that season, started in on me. He was trying to use me as the scapegoat for his own embarrassment. He kept on, calling me everything he could think of to ridicule me. I finally tossed him near the end of the game. By the time we got him out of there he had stirred the fans up so they were throwing things at me and swearing pretty foul stuff. As I was leaving the court, the police had all they could do to keep the fans off me, and someone dumped a beer on my head.

My wife was there that night and saw all this happening. She had never been very comfortable sitting in the stands listening to fans yell at her husband, but she tolerated it as best she could. There was a night when a group of guys in leather jackets hung around the exit in Philadelphia and threatened me. We were with another couple. The arena guards kind of held them at bay while we ran for the car. That's a great way to live, isn't it? Running for your car because some punks think you're a lousy ref. I guess it bothered me all the more because my wife and friends were subjected to this abuse. Well, after the night I had the run-in with Alex, my wife just quit going to my games.

The next day in the papers Alex was really on me. He said he would take me any night away from home, but he didn't want me at home. Maybe he figured he could intimidate other officials with the home crowd behind him. He knew he wasn't going to gain any edge with me that way. Okay, fair enough, he said some things in the papers, no big deal. But when the seventh game of that playoff series came around, which was to be played in Philadelphia, I wasn't named to work the game. I had worked every big game that was to decide a series or a championship during the previous five years. I had been working either with Mendy or Norm Drucker. But Alex had created a situation where they didn't think it would be good for me to work the game.

This hurt me deeply. It wasn't so much a matter of ego that he could do this to me, but it was like missing out on the best party of the year. The Celtics and the 76ers were in the seventh game of the Eastern finals, and I wasn't going to be there. I was probably resentful of Alex from then on, though I tried never to let it get in my way of calling a fair game.

It's funny how perspectives change depending on whose payroll you're on, or who's working for you. Alex coached several seasons at Syracuse when I first came into the league, and he was always harping about how Wilt took steps when he got the ball in the post. "He's walking! He's moving his feet!" Alex would scream every time Wilt touched the ball. I ran into Alex the summer he was named to coach the San Francisco Warriors, who happened to have Wilt at center. Things hadn't gotten so bitter between us yet, even though he had given me enough grief from day one to have me looking to goose him whenever I got the chance. I couldn't resist giving him a shot. I acted as though I hadn't heard about his new job. "Alex, you know, I keep thinking about what you've been telling me over the years about how Wilt walks all the time, and . . ."

Alex started to protest, holding up his hands and shaking his head. "Now, Earl . . ."

"And I went to look at some film, and by God, I really need to watch that more closely."

"No, no, no, Earl, I think you're right all along."

"I'm not so sure, Alex. I'll sure be checking him out. So, what's new with you? Going to be up in Syracuse again this season?"

We had a good laugh once he figured out I was putting one over on him. Too bad it got so ugly between us, although we did eventually patch things up after he retired.

A referee, by the very nature of his role, is standing between two factions that want the same thing. There really isn't anyone he deals with whom he can count on to be as objective as he's supposed to be.

The referee's two worst enemies are ignorance on the part of fans, coaches, and players, and the built-in prejudice each of them possesses that keeps them from even trying to be objective. The prejudice starts right in the arena. Some of the PA announcers are pretty straight, but a lot of them are nothing more than cheerleaders. A guy in Indiana used to be terrible; he'd say things like, "And that was a beautiful basket by so-and-so on a spectacular feed from so-and-so." And when you'd call a foul on the Pacers, he act as if you were committing murder. "Oh, no, they're calling charging on our George McGinnis. They've now hit him with four personal fouls." You just kept waiting for him to say, "We're not going to take it anymore, are we? Let's hang the bum!"

A guy in Syracuse named Jim McKechne was the worst. He'd announce a foul against the Nats in the form of a question. "And that was a foul on Dolph Schayes?" Or he'd say, "That's *our* sixth team foul and Boston has only one."

Despite the battles I've had over the years, I can take a lot from fans. They pay the freight and you expect them to let off some steam at the refs. But sportswriters and broadcasters have no right to be anything but impartial. A lot of them don't know the game, and they're quick to follow the perspective of a player or coach who has a biased viewpoint. I expect more from someone in that kind of a role, but it isn't very often fulfilled.

As a former player, Rick Barry should be knowledgeable enough to be above that kind of behavior, but then, as a player he certainly didn't work very hard at understanding the ref's perspective. He was working as an announcer in the 1977–78 finals between Washington and Seattle. Game three, being played at Washington, came down to the final three seconds with the Sonics leading 93–92. The Bullets had just scored. Sonics forward Paul Silas took the ball out of the net, stepped out of bounds, spun around, and wound up to fire a pass to Fred Brown, trying to beat the Bullets' full-court press. I blew my whistle. It seemed as if the whole world shouted, "What?"

"He stepped over the line before releasing the ball," I said. "Washington's ball." I moved in to grab the ball. You always want to get the ball back into play as quickly as possible so they have to concentrate on playing defense instead of complaining to the referee. Silas didn't complain, but I could hear wailing away at courtside. I noticed the clock had slipped to two seconds. I ordered it reset. The ball came in to Washington forward Bobby Dandridge. He rose and fired from the corner. His release was in time, the shot was off the rim. Game over.

Barry went into an almost hysterical harangue when I made the call. "What a shame if Seattle loses on a call like that," he screamed to the national TV audience. "What a shame if Seattle had lost on a mistake like Strom's," he said after the game. How a guy can sit at midcourt and second-guess a call on the baseline is beyond me. Barry has a pretty good understanding of the game, and I think he'd make a good coach, but when it comes to reviewing the referee's work, he's like so many of these people, he doesn't understand the rule or he's made a call with an untrained eye.

After the game, Elvin Hayes told the media, "Everybody knows Earl Strom is a road official." The fact he played for Washington and the call had gone *against* the Sonics on the road didn't get in the way of his logic. Jack Madden and I ended up working the seventh game of that series in Seattle. Early in that game Madden hit Hayes with a couple of quick fouls. Dick Motta was coaching Washington. He didn't go at Madden, but instead, he shrugged his shoulders and said, "Earl, what are you going to do about this? You're not that kind of official." Then Hayes came over to me and said, "I didn't mean all that stuff they said I said about you in the paper." I wasn't going to give him the satisfaction of knowing that I had even read it. I said, "I don't know what you're talking about," and I got away from him. When the game was over, a total of 31 fouls were called against the Bullets and 28 against Seattle. The Bullets attempted 38 free throws, Seattle 43. The Bullets won 105–99. The "Road Ref" had struck again.

I have Harvey Pollack to thank for that nickname. He has to be the most amazing stat freak in the history of the NBA, having worked as the Philadelphia 76ers' publicist for decades. He was hardly a meek accountant. One night he was carrying on and on from his place along press row. I told him to shut up and keep to his pencil. Norm Drucker was working with me and eventually threatened to eject Pollack from the premises.

"You can't throw me out. I'm keeping the statistics," Pollack protested.

"So what?" Norm said. "You can make 'em up after the game, nobody will know the difference." Norm had thrown out a sportswriter a few years earlier, and Pollack knew enough to back off.

Pollack has been with the Philadelphia organization since the founding of the league in 1946–47. He did a statistical analysis one year in which he showed that I had the highest percentage of visiting-team victories among all NBA referees. In games that I worked, the visiting team won 42.9 percent of the time. That compared to the league average of 30 percent. Milt Cooper and Mel Whitworth, each working a half schedule (41 games), were the only other officials above 40 percent. They were both fired at the end of the season for incompetence. John Vanak was next below me among the regulars with 38.4 percent, followed by Joe Gushue at 37.2 percent. Garretson was in the middle of the pack at 32.9, and Jake O'Donnell had only 24.7 percent visiting teams winning. Bernie Fryer, the former NBA player, was on the bottom with 19.7 percent. That survey brought me the nickname Road Ref.

Other officials would try to play it down, kid about it. They'd pick up a paper and see that Los Angeles won at Chicago in a close one and say, "Strom must have had that one." Or they'd say, "Why the hell am I working? All I have to do is go bet the road team every game Strom works." Steve Hawes, who played center with Atlanta and Seattle for a number of years, had a pretty interesting perspective on it when he said, "When you're at home, you expect things to lean your way, because when you're on the road, you don't get those calls. You can resent it when you aren't getting all the breaks at home." Of course, a team should never feel it's getting or giving anything. It should feel it had a fair chance to win based on how well it played.

Hal Lebovitz, a columnist for the *Cleveland Plain Dealer*,

wrote something after a playoff game I had there before 20,000 fans: "When Earl Strom called three technical fouls on the Cavs . . . I wanted to rush out and congratulate him. The Cavs deserved those three T's. They were baiting the crowd. It took a man to call those T's, one who wasn't afraid of the mob. Strom took control, maintained discipline and as a consequence the Cavs started to play basketball again." As much as that might come across as tooting my own trombone, I put it in here because it really nails the issue. If I can get teams to forget about looking for an edge and just play their best, I've provided the best environment possible for that game.

I wasn't particularly fond of the title "Road Ref," to tell you the truth, because it drew attention to something that I always tried to avoid: *any* sort of trends or tendencies. Some people have accused me of going out of my way to help the visiting team. They'd say that I was so caught up in not letting the home crowd intimidate me that I would actually make calls to favor the visiting team. That's like calling me a liar and a thief. That's challenging my character. Still, while I hate to say it, more than a few officials just don't have the guts to stand up for what's fair. They cave in to the home crowd, let it influence them when the pressure's on. I suppose every official has a subconscious desire to be liked and to have 15,000 fans roar when you make a big call. Maybe that's as big a part of calls favoring home teams as officials just not having the balls to stand out there on their own and make the call that has to be made, even if it's going to bring those 15,000 fans right down on your neck.

The league has never called us in and said anything about the high percentage of home wins, even when the press was making a big deal about it a few years ago when it got up over 70 percent. If they got a complaint, the NBA could send out an observer scout to chart an official, see how many calls you're making against the home team and the visitors and under what circumstances and how legitimate they are. But no one ever called me in to talk about it.

They used to call us in when players were getting hurt.

They had meetings and they'd say, "The fans are coming out to see the Pettits and Baylors and Robertsons. They're all getting hurt. Are the hatchetmen running these guys out of the league?" They weren't saying to protect the stars, they were just making sure the game was played fairly. And that's all I ever wanted, to make sure the game was decided by what happened between the two teams on the court. Whoever plays the best ball that night wins. That's the way I was taught by the Mendy Rudolphs, Sid Borgias, and Norm Druckers. I tried to impress that on the young guys who came along later.

I had been in the league almost a dozen years when I had a game with Ed Middleton, who was a rookie that year. Chamberlain was playing with the Lakers in Baltimore. It was a wild one. The next day's *New York Post* said I was observed egging on the crowd by motioning with upraised hands. I can't imagine I would ever actually provoke a crowd. I mean, Sid Borgia loved to do that kind of thing just for sport, but I've always been a much more controlled person than that. I was probably just waving to somebody I thought I should know.

Anyway, I had scouted Eddie and brought him into the league. He was really a good, strong-looking kid. He was sharp right from the start, but he was catching all the usual flak a rookie gets. That night we'd had a pretty rough first half, and as we were walking down this hallway with the Baltimore team, Jack Marin started in on Eddie. I told him to knock it off.

"I'm not talkin' to you," Marin told me.

"Well, I'm talking to you. Knock it off."

"Ah, screw you, Earl."

"Okay, if that's the way you feel, don't come out for the second half. You're gone." As soon as I had ejected him, Bob Ferry, who was an assistant player-coach, started in. "You've been on his ass all night. You guys are screwing up and you know it," Ferry yelled at me.

"Well, if you feel so involved, why don't you just stay in the dressing room and console him in the second half? You're gone, too." So he was out and everybody was screaming in the hallway. Along came the trainer, a guy named Skip Feldman. He started yelling at me. "We don't need you either," I told him. "So just stay in the room this half, too." Gene Shue, who was coaching the Bullets, was really upset. "What the hell do you think you're doing, Strom?"

"Hey, I just unloaded three of your guys. You wanna try for four?"

He knew it was time to shut up and he led the team into the dressing room. When we came out to start the second half, I went to the PA announcer and told him, "I just threw three guys out at halftime and L.A.'s going to start the second half shooting six technical fouls."

He was shocked. "How can I announce that?"

"Very simply. You just push that little button to ON and say, 'The Lakers will start the second half shooting six technical foul shots.'" Of course, the crowd went crazy and they started throwing all sorts of trash and coins at us. Johnny Egan went to the line and was potting all the shots.

The game came down to the wire and Baltimore was coming back on the Lakers. The crowd was really stirred up, and Kevin Loughery came sailing in with a shot that tied it, but he wiped out the defender. Eddie and I hit our whistles simultaneously. I thought if I could get to the play first, I could take the pressure off the kid and let the call come down on me. But Eddie was right there and since the play was coming right at him, he made the offensive-foul call, disallowed the goal, and everybody was on his neck. Loughery was jumping up and down and screaming, and the fans were throwing everything but the chairs.

With a few seconds to go, there was a time-out, and I was concerned about how we were going to get out of there. Wilt came over and said, "Don't worry, you guys. It looks like you might have some trouble, but we'll help you get off the court." The horn blew and the Lakers were so happy they had won that they just ran off the court whooping it up. Completely forgot about us. Mendy and I used to take our belts off, roll them up, and stuff them in our back pocket. Just an idiosyncrasy, I guess. Eddie saw me doing this as we were getting ready to run through the crowd, and he took off his belt and rolled it around his fist. Gus Johnson, who was playing for Baltimore, saw this and started to challenge him. "Who you gonna use that on?" A bunch of cops surrounded us and we pushed our way through. Just as we got into the hallway, here came Wilt running back out of the Laker dressing room. When he saw us, he said, "Jeez, Earl, I'm sorry. I forgot about you."

"So I noticed."

Sometimes the deck seemed as if it were just stacked against the officials. I was working a game in San Francisco. It was a sellout crowd and San Diego was whipping the Warriors. About the middle of the second period, Nate Thurmond went in for a lay-up and thought he was fouled. He started cussing and I hit him with a technical. He ran by me and called me a motherfucker, and I threw him out of the game. We had a little trouble getting off the floor at the half, and when I came back out and went over to the scorer's table, the PA announcer said we could start the half as soon as he read an announcement.

It was written by Franklin Mieuli, owner of the Warriors. It said the fans could hold their ticket stubs and be admitted to another game free because the star Thurmond had been thrown out and they were being robbed of seeing a top-notch game. I blew my stack. I told him if he read the statement, the game was over. Mieuli and I jawed about it and finally he backed down.

I worked what turned out to be Frank Layden's last game as coach of the Jazz. He was always seen as such a fun-loving guy, but he was dying inside from the fans' getting on him about his heavyset physique on top of all the customary pressures of the job. He figured people's spitting on him and calling him names was beyond the call of duty. It's a good thing he never wanted to be a referee.

If there was ever a coach who you thought was finding a way to have fun in this pressure-cooker business, it was Frank. He was quick with the bits and one-liners, but he did

get after officials pretty good and got nailed with a couple of
hefty fines for bashing officials in postgame comments to the
media. When he first took over the Jazz, they were pretty
bad and he just tried to lead them along with good humor.
The next year was pretty much the same. One night he was
getting on me and finally I said, "Hey, Frank, I'm getting sick
of this. Let's knock it off." He said, "Jeez, Earl, we're just
trying to win and put some people in the seats, and you won't
give us a break." I said, "If you want a break, go to McDonald's." He said, "That's pretty funny, Earl, but we really
should get a break. Pretty soon these people are going to get
up and leave because of you." Near the end of the game I
called a foul on the Jazz and people were hitting the aisles
to leave. Frank jumped up and yelled at me at the top of his
voice, "There they go, Earl. I warned ya."

Several years ago in a playoff series between Utah and
Golden State, there was a pretty serious fight. Utah came in
to play at Golden State a couple nights later. George Karl,
who was coaching the Warriors, was saying how Utah better
be ready because Golden State wasn't about to back down
to anybody and this was going to be war. Layden was out
watching the warm-ups, then he disappeared right up to the
time of the introduction of the players. He came walking out
wearing these glasses with the bushy eyebrows and big nose
on them. He had his jacket collar turned up and he had on
an Oakland A's baseball cap. He came sauntering up the
sideline waving to the crowd, then he stopped and put his
arms around George. As he walked by me, I said, "You think
it's funny now, but wait'll the commissioner fines you." He
just shrugged, figuring it was worth it. He did get fined, I
guess, but it was a funny bit and it took some of the tension
out of the situation. The game went off without any problems.

Jerry Reynolds seldom beefed at officials when he was
coach of the Sacramento Kings. That still wasn't any insurance against getting a technical. The night he jumped up
from the Sacramento bench and then blacked out, falling

onto the court, Blane Reichelt nailed him with a T before he figured out that Jerry had passed out from stress.

Pat Riley is a guy who concentrates on coaching his players. I've always felt that the more you're screaming at the referee, the less you're able to analyze the things that are happening between your players and the opponents. Certainly Riley would stand up to you if he thought you'd kicked one, as I did one night when the Lakers were playing Atlanta. I missed an out-of-bounds play. It was obvious to everybody in the place but me. He got on me and I told him, "Don't tell me how to referee." "But you missed that." "Don't tell me I missed anything." There was a time-out and I stuck my head in his huddle and was yelling at him. He said, "Get out of my huddle." I went over to my partner: "Can you believe him getting on me like that?" He said, "Earl, you did miss it." So, I turned around and went back into the huddle and said, "I just want to apologize for kicking that play." They all cracked up.

I'm glad Dick Vitale only had a short stay as coach of the Pistons before going off to make big money with his mouth. He was always so wound up. He'd chip away with things like, "I can't wait until we grow up to be the Celtics so we can catch a break." He told this story in his book, *Vitale:* "I had one game where I jumped right on Earl Strom from the get-go. 'Your shirt doesn't say CYO, Earl. It says NBA. Let's blow the whistle like you know you're in the NBA!' He was laying for me and he let me know it. 'That's one,' he said, making the big T. 'I'm not taking any bullshit from some junior high coach.' " I don't remember any of that, but I'm glad he chose another line of work. He's a character, but characters at courtside I don't need.

Everybody's always working the edge. Shooters think they're getting hammered all the time, but they forget that when they have the ball so much, they're going to draw traffic. A lot of times they're creating the contact by jumping into people, going up under the defensive man after faking him into the air. There's some contact on virtually every shot. You have to use judgment or you'd never finish a game.

Walt Frazier and Earl Monroe were the kind of guys who never said a word earlier in their careers. But when they got older and slowed down and needed to hold more to keep up defensively, they started to complain about the fouls on them. Mike Newlin was typical of the way guys try to con you. If you made a call in his favor, he'd come by and say, "Good call, good position, good hustle." I'd tell him, "I'm the ref and I'm getting paid to have good position and make good calls. You play and knock off the bullshit." Dave Cowens, a no-bullshit kind of guy, had a couple of ticky-tacky fouls called on him one night with Boston playing at Houston. Newlin tried to chase down a loose ball, and Cowens hit him like a truck, sent him crashing over the press table, then turned around and said, "Now *that's* a foul!"

Frank Ramsey, the first of the fabled sixth men in the Celtics dynasty, was so proud of his bag full of tricks to draw fouls—flopping, falling over to draw a charge—that he wrote an article about how he fooled officials. It came out in the middle of the season in *Sports Illustrated,* with drawings and everything. The day I saw the article, I had the Celtics in a game against Philadelphia as the top half of a doubleheader in Madison Square Garden. I was reading the article and I was thinking, what a son of a bitch this guy is to come out with something like this that is totally aimed to embarrass officials and imply what fools we are. I reread it on the train on the way to New York, and by the time I got into the dressing room I was pretty peeved. Norm Drucker was working with me. We talked about it and he said, "Well, what are we going to do about this?" I said, "I don't know, Norm, but he's kind of playing us for chumps, don't you think?" "Yeah, it sure seems like he doesn't think we're very bright at all."

Philly had a bunch of butchers: Andy Johnson, Woody Sauldsberry, Joe Graboski, all these big, tough guys. Ramsey came in off the bench sometime in the first quarter, and of course, the Philadelphia players figured the officials might be a little upset at Ramsey. He went for a shot and they went after him like a bowling ball in search of pins. Andy Johnson hit him with a shot that knocked him three rows into the stands. I looked at him as he was pulling himself out of the crowd, and he asked me, "What's the matter, didn't you see that?"

I said, "Yeah, but I couldn't tell if you were fooling me or not."

He gave me this funny look and went on. Next time down the court Sauldsberry nailed him. We just kept looking away. We went into the dressing room at halftime and we weren't even discussing it. There was a knock on the door. It was Auerbach.

"Can I talk to you guys for a second?" he said real nicely.

"Sure, Red, what's up?"

"Now, goddamnit, are you guys gonna let him get killed out there?" He started yelling.

"Who are you talking about, Red?"

"You know goddamn well who I'm talking about. You gonna let him get killed?"

Norm said, "Well, Red, it's really hard for us to tell if he's just fooling us or if he's really getting hit. For the most part we think he's fooling us."

Now Auerbach really blew up. "I'm going to the commissioner! This is murder! You're gonna have blood on your hands!"

When Auerbach stormed off, we decided Ramsey had probably had enough. As we came back out onto the court, Ramsey came over to us. "I know what you guys are doing to me and I probably have it coming. I shouldn't have written the article, at least not during the season. I'm sorry and I want to apologize. But please let me get out of here in one piece."

Of course, we had to, even though he didn't deserve it.

There was no question I was on the ragged edge most of the time in my early years. I was worn-out and uptight trying to do both jobs. There was a lot of tension just getting to games. Many times I would change into my uniform on the plane, and as soon as I hit town, I would jump into a cab—or sometimes they would even have one waiting with a police escort—and I'd go rushing off to the arena.

A few times I would come running into the arena, hand my clothes to a guard by the door, and run onto the court after the game had already started. "Yo, I'm here," I'd signal my partner, and away I'd go, wound like a spring. Afterward I'd maybe end up sleeping on the bench at the airport for a middle-of-the-night flight and get back into the office in time to shave in the washroom and get to my desk. Sometimes I'd have something hanging at the office and that would add to my worries about getting back on time. Often I slept on the couch in the lounge and had the guard wake me up in time to get cleaned up and at my desk by eight. That sort of living puts you on edge, no doubt about it.

I was very quick with my family at that time, although Yvonne would never let me get away with it, fortunately. If the kids did something and I snapped off and it wasn't warranted, she'd say, "You're not on the basketball court. Just act civil or don't talk to us at all." My ego started to grow pretty fast in those early years, and yet she was never afraid to knock me down to where I belonged if I got too obnoxious. When I did make it home straight from work, it seemed as if I was always just beat. Dead tired. I always tried to stay awake so I could find out what everybody was doing with their lives, but I'd end up falling asleep on the couch in the TV room. The kids would say, "Mom, make Dad go to bed so we can watch TV." I'd lie there making this kind of puffing sound, not snoring, but moving my mouth like a fish. Yvonne would nudge me and say, "Why don't you go up to bed?" I'd always say, "Aw, I like it here. I like to be around my family."

That got to be kind of a standing joke in our family. Here was the old man trying to get close to his family by sleeping in front of them, and here they were telling him to get out of the room and quit making that *uhhhhhh-paaaaaah* sound. Drove 'em crazy, poor kids.

My five children teasingly used to call me "Uncle Daddy" because I was so seldom home. I couldn't be there to share many of the special occasions, the first prom, birthdays, holidays, and the array of crises that pop up in a young person's life. I wasn't there to develop the relationship that would enable me to counsel my kids when they made decisions about joining this or quitting that. When you're around the home that irregularly, you aren't part of the normal pattern of discipline and communication. I don't think the kids were pleased by that when it was happening, but now when people relate to me and refer back to events, they seem proud. We all missed a lot for not being able to share more as the years passed and the kids grew. I'm sure they each suffered in some ways for my not being around. But I suspect I suffered the most for what I missed out on. You can never get that time and those occasions back. It's the one major negative to my career.

Sometimes it seemed as if it were courting frustration even to try to be part of the major events with the kids. When my daughter Susan was going to get married, I called John Nucatola in September to tell him I needed a weekend off in November for the wedding. He told me fine, he'd take care of it. I saw him at preseason camp and said, "I just wanted to remind you about the date I need off in November for my daughter's wedding." He said, "Earl, do you realize how many games we have that weekend? I just don't see how I can give you that off."

I said, "Swell, there's a game that night down in Philly. I'll just give her away and go down and work the game." And I stomped off. He called after me, "You don't have to get sarcastic about it." I said, "Look, I work anyplace you ask. I work Christmas, Easter, I work anytime you want. I asked you in September for this one night and you tell me you've got too many games. How'd you expect me to feel?" He gave me the weekend.

I did try to let the kids have the benefit of a little of the glamour when I could. Eric was the only one of the five who was really into sports and the hero-worship stuff. I bought Bill Russell's first book, *Go Up for Glory*, and took it up to Madison Square Garden one night when I was working a game with the Celtics in to play the Knicks. Before the game

I asked Russell if I could get him to sign it. I told him I had Eric with me, and he said to send him over to the locker room after the game.

Russell's autograph was about as rare as sunshine at midnight, and when Eric went into the Boston locker room after the game and said he wanted Russell to sign his book, Sam Jones laughed at him and said, "You gotta be kidding."

Russell told Eric to bring it over and he signed it. It might have been the only signature he signed after quitting the practice early in his career. I don't know that for sure, but believe me, it was rare. When Eric brought the book home, his brother Stephen couldn't have cared less, but did relate it to some of his friends at school, who immediately said, "Prove it." He took the book to school and showed it around. One friend said, "Gosh, would I love to have that!" Stephen said, "Sure, go ahead. My dad wouldn't care. Heck, he can get all of these he wants." Later on I was looking around for the book and I couldn't believe it when I saw the page with Russell's signature was ripped out. I had him get it back fast.

While I couldn't be home much during the season, I did take the kids on trips occasionally. I'll never forget a time I took my daughters, Margie and Susan, to Syracuse when they were about nine and seven. There were these three heavyset women who would sit right under the basket, and they always seemed to be so nice. When I got to the game that evening, I took the girls over to these women and asked them to keep an eye on the girls for me. They said they'd be glad to. Late in the second quarter, I went down with a twisted ankle. I was lying there on the court and the Nats trainer came out and was working on me. People started hollering things like "Shoot 'em. They shoot horses, why not referees?" The loudest jeers were coming from these three baby-sitters.

The half ended a couple minutes later and I hobbled off to the locker room. A few seconds later, the girls burst into the room crying their eyes out. I asked, "What's wrong?"

"Daddy, they're not going to shoot you, are they?"

"Nawwww, now you just take it easy and go back out there and watch the rest of the game."

"But those ladies kept saying, 'Shoot him, shoot him.' "

It took me the rest of the night to convince them it was all in fun. Some fun. Great people in Syracuse, but nasty fans.

Ten or so years later, I took Margie and her fiancé and two of my sons, Jonathan and Eric, up to Madison Square Garden for a playoff game between the Knicks and Baltimore. Before I went into the arena, I told the kids I wanted to meet them afterward by the employees' entrance. We had a lot of problems during the game, and afterward Bob Rakel and I were in the dressing room when a cop came in and said they had some people milling around outside and they wanted to take us out the back way to avoid any confrontation.

I told him I had to go out the other way because I had to meet my kids. As we came out of the tunnel heading toward the train station, the kids were getting a little edgy because the crowd was starting to get on me. This guy in his twenties came running by and said, "Strom, you suck!"

I don't tolerate people talking like that to me in front of my family. I threw down my bag and started after this guy. A cop was there, but I ran past him and chased the guy through the crowd. I caught him and was shaking him and telling him never to talk to me like that in front of my family. The cop finally caught up to us and pulled me off the guy. We started back toward the train. I saw Margie and Rick and Eric, but I didn't see Jonathan. Then I looked up a ways and saw him, about half a block ahead. When we caught up to him, he was walking fast with his hands stuffed into his pockets and his head down. I asked him why he had taken off.

"Are you kidding? If they knew I was with you, they'd have come after me."

Generally, I was in a great mood if I got enough rest, but when I didn't, I was hell to be around. I grew up very passive, I wasn't a fighter at all. I can count on maybe one hand and a couple of extra fingers all the scraps I had while growing up. It wasn't important to me to have to fight to prove anything. I was pretty aggressive as an athlete, but I guess people who knew me then would have described me as a pretty mellow guy. The first years I started working in pro ball, that changed. I became explosive as a result of the pressure, and I felt as though I had to fight back to survive. It really came down to an understanding that I had to take charge, or they'd take charge of Earl Strom.

chapter 4

HOW THEY PLAYED THE GAME

There were about eighty jobs in pro basketball when I came into the league. When you consider there hasn't been much of an increase over the last thirty-plus years in the number of colleges playing basketball, it's not hard to envision how intense the competition was for those jobs. A dozen years later you had roughly 250 roster spots spread over twelve NBA teams and eleven in the new ABA. Today there are twenty-seven teams in pro basketball, representing some 325 jobs. Sure, seven-footers today are doing things only six-foot guards could do thirty years ago, yet I always think about players in the context of when they played and how they measured up against those standards. Maybe it's just a matter of pure competition, 80 jobs versus 325, but the stars of yesterday left the greatest impression on me. I'm not saying the average journeyman of today doesn't have greater technical skills than the greats of long ago; I'm just saying that I'm influenced considerably by those intangibles of performance under pressure, of excelling in the most intense rivalries and against the keenest performers, and that belongs to the earlier eras.

Rod Hundley has been around the league as long as I have; he broke in as a rookie the same year I came in. He now works as a radio broadcaster covering the Utah Jazz. One night I was in Salt Lake City and ran into Rod and some of his friends at a lounge. We were sitting around talking about the good old days. He said, "I'm going to show you guys how we old basketball minds think." He took a piece of paper and wrote some names on it. He folded it up and handed it to a buddy of his. Then he told me to name my all-time NBA team. I told him, okay, I'm going to pick Jerry West and Oscar Robertson at guards, Bob Pettit and Elgin Baylor at forwards, and I should probably pick Wilt, but I'm going to pick Russell at center.

Rod said, "Okay, now of today's players, who would you pick as your third guard?" I told him Magic. "Now, what about your third forward?" I told him Bird. "Center?" I decided on Kareem. So he told his friend to open up the piece of paper and read off the names. It was identical. "It just goes to show you," Rod said, "how guys who have been around the game and seen the old-timers and the contemporary players sort it out the same way."

Come on, Strom, Pettit over Bird? Well, I might give you that one, but don't sell Pettit short. He just did so much himself. Bird makes everyone around him play better, but he has so much more talent around him than Pettit did. Pettit wasn't as much of a free-lancer as Bird, but I guess that's where you get into trouble trying to compare players in different eras and with different styles of play. I think they played better team defense in the earlier days. They had to because the game was slower. Today, you don't see as much halfcourt set offense. When I came into the league, Bob Pettit was without a doubt the strongest and best-shooting, best-rebounding forward in the league. He revolutionized offensive rebounding and made the St. Louis fast break go with his defensive rebounding. He would be considered a strong forward in the language of today's game, but he was truly a strong player period since he often had to guard opposing centers. He couldn't put the ball on the floor for more than a couple dribbles without risking problems, but he didn't have to since he was deadly from twelve to fifteen feet. He didn't have great speed, but his quickness got him good position under the boards, and his strength enabled him to hold it. He played often with injuries, including one playoff series with his arm in a cast. When he played Los Angeles, he'd go up against Baylor. Those were some great matchups. Bird doesn't go up against any particular guy, he's all over the place. Granted, he has that innate sense to be where the ball is. That's a gift. But he doesn't play as much tough, face-up defense as Pettit had to, and I don't think he could.

When you talk about the skill level overall, you think about what a big deal people made out of the way Cousy played. Now, if any player who has to put the ball on the floor can't execute to that level, he won't make it in the league. You take that little reverse spin move that Earl "the Pearl" Monroe used to put on guys. He couldn't get away with that now. They'd strip him every time he tried it. But two decades ago he was a star player with that move. Now, it's through the legs. If you put the Celtics of thirty years ago in against the Celtics of today, today's group would have all the advantage for overall skills. They're better runners, better leapers, better shooters. I won't say they're better passers. And for my money, those advanced individual skills wouldn't guarantee them the edge in a seven-game series against their forefathers, either.

For as long as I have been around basketball, Oscar Robertson is inch for inch the greatest all-around player ever to touch the ball. He was invaluable as a scorer and at 6'5", was the first of the big guards. He loved to get his man up in the air with that head fake of his and then drive for the lay-up. His strength was a big factor in gaining position for rebounding, especially on the offensive boards. He wasn't as spectacular as, say, Bob Cousy in the passing department, but he always managed to find the open man for a better percentage shot. He was better than anyone I've seen at making a pass after getting an offensive rebound. Defensively, he was able to play smaller and quicker guards well. He wasn't particularly fast, but he was quick. He knew how to get where the ball was going, and when he got it, he never seemed to lose control of it. As great as he was with the ball, he never liked to showboat.

He came into the league with Jerry West in 1960. Both of them were on the Olympic team that won the gold in Rome. He played in Cincinnati for ten years where he averaged nearly 30 points a game. Then he went to Milwaukee and teamed up with Kareem when they won the title.

He was all-time in the bitch department, too. He wasn't apt to cuss or shout. He didn't try to show you up, but in his own inconspicuous manner he was always griping. He'd gripe about plays when he hadn't even seen what had happened. His favorite saying was "Aw, doggone sheeeet," and he'd serve it up every time the whistle blew against his team or didn't blow when he thought it should have. He went beyond that one night in a game we had in Hershey, Pennsylvania. He fired a pass at a teammate, who missed it. "Sheeeet, motherfucker," he hollered out. He was right next to me as I retrieved the ball from the stands. "I don't have a real problem with what you just said, but see that woman over there?" I asked him. "That's my wife, and I'm afraid she heard that. I don't talk like that around her and you're not going to either." He got the T and the message.

Jerry West gets the ball if the game goes to a last-shot situation. I am sure if anyone ever kept track of last-second heroics in a career, the guy they called Mr. Clutch would top the list. I regard his 63-footer against the Knicks to send a playoff game into overtime as probably the most spectacular shot I ever witnessed. He was a big guard, at 6'4", who could take advantage by going inside to post up smaller defenders. He was surprisingly strong, although injury prone. He invited that with his determination to drive the lane against big forwards and centers. When he first came into the league, he wasn't a great dribbler and had to work hard to develop that skill. Once he accomplished that, he could drive around any defenders who dared play him tight, but you had to play him tight or he'd kill you with his jumper. It was a good example of working on a weak phase of your game to make the strongest part, in this case his shooting, all the stronger. His one shortcoming, if he had one, was his passing. He usually managed to get the ball while in his shooting range, and that eliminated his need to give it up. His value was evident when he and Elgin Baylor would take on the Celtics in the championship round with less than adequate help from their teammates. Often they would score 75 points or more between them in these games, forcing the series to six or seven games before they would invariably lose.

Baylor was such a dazzling player, I'm sure I don't have enough superlatives in my vocabulary to describe what he could do on a basketball court. He always went up against bigger forwards and outscored and outrebounded them consistently. Baylor-Pettit matchups were some of the greatest confrontations in all of pro ball. Baylor had an uncanny ability to control his body while in the air. He would go up and hang and twist and lean and get his shot off and in the basket in ways that you thought surely impossible on this planet. He was an excellent passer and made some mediocre teammates successful as a result. He was often double- and triple-teamed and still managed to get the job done.

When you had eight teams in the league, guys were playing each other a dozen or more times during the season. This bred familiarity and plenty of contempt. They knew each other's habits and abilities. As a referee you were always aware of the matchups in ways that only matter now during a playoff series. Oh, there were some great matchups: Al McGuire against Bob Cousy, Jerry West against Oscar Robertson, Bob Pettit against Elgin Baylor. But there was never a rivalry to match Philly against Boston, and there was no other individual matchup in the history of the league to rival Russell against Chamberlain. Wilt always maintained that he held all the records so it wasn't right to rate Russell as the greatest center. There's no question Wilt had the greater stats for rebounds, scoring, and assists. But Russell would do things in spurts; he'd get you the one rebound you had to have. He took a good team and made it a great team. Wilt came to good teams and they stayed good teams. His teams didn't win eleven out of thirteen championships.

If the teams were reversed, I think Russell could have done the same things and helped Philly win a lot of titles. Wilt came into the league as a big scorer, and I doubt he could have helped Boston the way Russell did. Wilt kept hearing that Russell was a better defensive player, so he tried concentrating on that and his scoring dropped off. But Philly needed him to score. Wilt could do whatever he put his mind to—he could concentrate on winning the rebounding and assists titles and do it, but he never seemed to be able to take all those things and put them together at the same time. I think what hurt Wilt the most over his career was always having to be compared to Russell. He just kept reacting to people's comments instead of playing his own game.

There was such a competitive thing between them. I remember when Wilt got a contract for $100,000 and Russell came right back at $100,001. According to Mr. Stats, Harvey Pollack, Chamberlain and Russell played against each other 142 times over a ten-year period. Wilt averaged 29 points and 29 rebounds, Russell 15 points and 24 rebounds. Boston won 85, Wilt's teams—Philadelphia, San Francisco, and Los Angeles—won 57.

Harvey didn't mention how many of those I worked, but it was a lot. And I do know this: I worked the first meeting, and I worked the last.

The first one was in Boston in November of 1959. Wilt had spent a year with the Globetrotters, and Russell had been in the league three years, winning two championships. It was my job to toss the initial jump ball. The main responsibility of the official who's tossing is to get the toss straight and to make sure it's higher than either man can jump. They are required to tap the ball at its apex or on its downward flight. I tossed the ball and both jumped. The ball got as high as their elbows and they clamped it right there. The looks I got from these two behemoths just about drove me back to the

Pottstown City League. They really went after each other and played splendidly; you couldn't tell who got the better of it. Wilt had 30 points and 30 rebounds, Russell had 22 points and 35 rebounds. Boston won by 9.

There were so many close calls between Russell and Chamberlain, Boston and Philly. If they had evened out, as odds would dictate, these teams and these two players would be heralded as a matched set of greats—instead of one being called a great champion and the other a celebrated choker. They still call Mendy Rudolph "the franchise mover" in Philadelphia for his goaltending call against Chamberlain on a last-second shot by Tom Heinsohn that gave Boston the victory in the Eastern finals in 1962. Eddie Gottlieb wanted to move the club to San Francisco, but there would have been some problems doing so if the Warriors had gone on to win the NBA crown. It was just one play in one game, one interpretation by one official, but it went the way it always seemed to—against Wilt.

Of course, he brought a lot of pressure on himself when he developed his horrible hang-up about free throws. It got so bad it seemed as if it weren't even worth his going to the line, which made it all the more tempting for people to foul him, since he was a cinch to slam it through anytime he got the ball underneath.

I was in a sympathetic mood one night and tried to help him out. The Knicks were playing at Los Angeles. Wilt got clobbered. I didn't call it. As we were heading to the other end, Wilt said, "Earl, didn't you see me get fouled?"

"Yep."

"You didn't call it."

"That's right."

"Why the hell not?"

"You want me to put you on the line so you wind up missing thirteen straight free throws and embarrassing yourself even more?"

Wilt shook his head at me and went on about his business.

Wilt's reluctance to go to the line could lead to some fierce intimidation—and some very funny moments. He was playing for the 76ers in the 1965–66 season, and Philly needed a win against Baltimore to beat out Boston for first place in the Eastern Division. Boston had been on top ever since Russell had come to the Celtics a decade earlier. As always seems to happen in those sorts of circumstances, Baltimore blew Philly out early and was still up late in the second half. Then the 76ers came to life and finally got up by 1 with eight seconds to go. Paul Seymour was coaching the Bullets. It was Philly's ball to inbound, but Baltimore called a time-out. As the time-out was signaled, Wilt turned to Jim "Bad News" Barnes, a big, tough kid who was checking him, and said, "If you put a hand on me, I'll knock you out." Wilt knew they would be fouling him and he didn't want to have to go to the line with the division title in the balance.

Barnes just looked at Wilt after the warning and went into the huddle where Seymour said, "Okay, News, as soon as they throw the ball in, you grab Wilt. He's life and death to make even one. When he misses, we get the rebound and call time. We've still got a shot at this." Barnes just looked at him as if he were crazy. At the end of the time-out, Wilt came out to Barnes and told him again, "Remember what I said, it's lights out if you touch me."

Barnes came over to me and said, "Look, I'm not going to grab him. I'll just look like I touched him and you call the foul immediately." I said, "News, that's no foul. Everybody touches players. You gotta really grab him." I had overheard the threat and I knew damn well Barnes wasn't going to grab him if he treasured his life. "No, I'm not going to grab him. I'm just going to touch him and you're gonna call the foul immediately."

Philly threw the ball in and the clock started ticking down. Every time Barnes would start to reach for Wilt, Wilt would glare at him. Barnes would drop his hands. Seymour was over on the bench screaming, "Grab him, News! Grab the big guy!" Barnes couldn't make himself do it. The clock ran down and the horn went off. Baltimore players were falling all over themselves with laughter. Barnes got out of there in a hurry.

While Wilt was a master of direct intimidation, Russell's dominance was more subtle. He revolutionized the defensive game in the NBA. There always was good individual defense, but Russell brought into the game a sense of team defense. His teammates were able to take chances on defense, and if they were beaten by their man, they knew Russell was behind them, providing a final major obstacle. He was and still remains the biggest intimidator the game has ever known. His offense was adequate. I say that in the sense that he wasn't required to play as well offensively as most centers since he was on a team of super offensive players. When Russell came to the Celtics, they were already the highest-scoring team in the league. He just made everyone that much more productive with his defensive play and rebounding. He always seemed to know what everyone was doing at all times. He had great athletic ability, but he made himself all the more valuable by his cunning and ability to psyche out other players. Blocked shots were just blasted away before Russell came along and developed a unique knack of keeping the blocks in play, usually setting up the famous Celtic fast break. He was mentally tough and could focus himself on a single game or a single play better than anyone I ever saw. But he could also crack the ceiling with that laugh of his when he was so inclined.

In one of his last seasons, when he was player-coach, the Celtics were to play Seattle in Vancouver, British Columbia. I was to work the game with Charlie Marino, who was about 5'7", from Los Angeles. Italian. Very intense. In those years the league used to bring guys in toward the end of the regular season to work a few games and get a sense if they could do the job or not. It was pretty much trial by fire. They'd get assigned a game that didn't figure to be real important and be given a tryout. Charlie was really determined to make it in the NBA.

I was lying down the afternoon of the game when I got a call at the hotel from Russell. He said he had some concerns and if we didn't get matters resolved, he wasn't going to let his team play that night. He wanted me to go over to the arena, so I jumped into my clothes and headed over there. When I walked in, there were these workmen painting out the court on this cement floor. They were putting down the free throw lanes and the center line and so on. When I got down to courtside, Russell was standing there with Dick Vertlieb, then general manager of Seattle. "What seems to be the matter?" I asked innocently.

"We aren't going to put our players out on cement!" Russell said.

"Look, they just didn't get their court shipped in on time," Vertlieb said, "but jeez, we've got to play this game. It's sold out. We can't afford to miss this game tonight."

I told him I tended to side with Russell's concerns about player safety. Vertlieb said he knew of a court that the Globetrotters used to use when they came in for their annual games. Russell thought that would probably be okay, and Vertlieb set out to get it put down in time. It turned out to be an old thing made up of square wood blocks nailed into two-by-fours. The thing was uneven and the lines looked as if they'd been painted on by a drunk, but at least it was a wood floor.

So Charlie and I went out and we're working the game. Russell made sure he got the Celtics up big right away and took himself out. He replaced himself with his backup, Wayne Embry, who was a large man, 6'10" or so and probably at least 260 pounds. Charlie, being the intense competitor he is, was working the game in earnest and both teams were on him pretty good, since he was the new kid on the scene. Embry went up for a defensive rebound, and when he came down, he went right through the floor. His foot got caught between these broken boards and he kept tugging to get loose. I was watching and Charlie was just standing over him staring and staring. Finally, Wayne pulled loose and took a few steps in the process. With that Charlie blew his whistle. I figured he was going to use some common sense and stop the game and get the floor fixed. But no—*he called Embry for traveling.* Well, Wayne went nuts. He's yelling down at Charlie, who was more than a foot shorter, and Charlie's screaming at him. I went over and said, "What've we got, fellas?"

Embry was beside himself. "Earl, are you gonna let this guy get away with calling me for traveling after my foot got stuck in the floor?"

I said, "Well, if he hadn't called you for traveling, I was going to call you for a ten-second violation in the backcourt."

Embry went even more nuts for a few seconds until he saw Russell over on the sidelines doubled over in laughter. Then he realized how crazy the whole thing was and started laughing himself. Of course, Russell would have changed his expression in a hurry if Wayne had gotten himself tossed so Russell would have had to play the rest of a game he obviously wanted nothing to do with.

There might not have been a more dramatic confrontation in the Boston-Philly rivalry than the Eastern finals in April of 1965. The Warriors had gone to San Francisco in 1962, and Syracuse had become the Philadelphia 76ers a year later. At the all-star break in the 1964–65 season, Wilt was traded to the 76ers. Now he was ready to lead them into the seventh game against Boston.

Meanwhile, Baltimore was in the Western finals against Los Angeles. On Friday night, April 13, L.A. eliminated the Bullets 117–115 in the sixth game. I worked that game, but as I was leaving the court, an angry Baltimore fan hit me in the face with a wadded-up paper cup. I went after him and nailed him with a punch. I hurt my hand, but Norm Drucker finished the guy off.

That night my thumb was killing me. I took some pain pills, but that didn't help. I went to the hospital the next day and they said the thumb was broken. They put a pin in it, and when I came out of surgery, Yvonne was in the room and very upset.

"I can't believe that Walter Kennedy. He called and wants to talk to your doctor. He says he wants you to be at that game tomorrow in Boston. I told him no way."

"Why not?" I asked.

"You've got your hand in a cast, Earl. For God's sake, use your head."

I went on arguing with her, trying to convince her I could work the game. Then I heard this basketball bouncing in the hallway. Two doctors came in with a hacksaw and a ball. They cut the cast down so the ball would fit well enough for me to hold it. It was still a pretty large mitten of plaster. I had Willie Smith, who was to work the game as the alternate, come down and give me a ride to the airport. Richie Powers would meet us there.

I wasn't going to miss this one for the world. All six games of that series had been close. This was what it was all about, Wilt vs. Russell in a seventh-game showdown for the Eastern Conference title at Boston Garden. The 76ers were down 30–12 early, but Wilt brought them back to where they trailed 110–109 and had the ball with five seconds left. They flubbed the ball away trying to get it in to Wilt, and it was Boston's ball out-of-bounds under the Philly basket. Russell threw it in, but the ball nicked an overhead wire supporting the basket. Richie, working out front, didn't see it. I did. I blew the whistle. It was Philly's ball.

Russell dropped to his knees with his head on the court, pounding the floor in despair. He later said of that moment, "All I could think of was that we had lost, and all summer long people would be coming up to me saying, 'Why'd ya hit the wire?'" The crowd was in a fury; fans were surging up to courtside while Red and the rest of the Celtics screamed at me. The 76ers huddled around Dolph Schayes to design a play.

It figured they'd go inside to Wilt. But you knew Russell would clobber him before he could get off a good shot, making him face his nemesis, the free throw line. Maybe Philly would decide not to chance it. Hal Greer lined up to toss in the ball. Russell leaned on Wilt, fronting him to protect against a direct pass. Greer lobbed over K.C. Jones and the ball came out toward the right side of the free throw line. John Havlicek, who had been lurking with his back to Greer, covering Chet Walker, whirled and deflected the ball to Sam Jones. It was all over. Johnny Most, Boston's fabled radio announcer, kept screaming his most fabled line, "Havlicek stole the ball! Havlicek stole the ball!" Russell didn't have to answer any wire wisecracks. In the championship series, Boston went on to whip L.A. in five for their seventh straight title, and I got out of Boston Garden with my life.

I honestly wonder what might have happened to me if Philly had pulled that out. I might have been the first guy buried under that old parquet floor. It really was one of the most dramatic episodes in NBA history, one of those things that makes the winners' reputations bigger and the losers a little more brokenhearted. I still have an article Jack Kiser wrote about it in the *Philadelphia Daily News:*

> In the Celtic dressing room Red Auerbach was smashing oranges over heads and setting fire to Sam Jones' hair, acting like a truck driver on a binge. Across the way Dolph Schayes sat stunned, softly and politely explaining over and over without protest about what was supposed to happen that didn't. . . . Wilt Chamberlain . . . finally going over and extending a big paw to Dolph. "It was a great effort, coach, it really was." . . . Too bad other 76ers weren't around to see it, too bad it came too late to change some of their attitudes toward Wilt. . . . Hal Greer huddled in a corner, staring down at his hands, the hand that had thrown a bad pass. . . . "I've never played a worse game in my life," he mumbled, his lips quivering. . . . Larry Costello, playing his last game and still hoping for his first NBA title, slamming a fist into his heavily taped thigh. "I just couldn't move fast enough," he groaned. . . . Bill Russell, a man in victory and defeat, admitting, "This was the first game in my life that I went into scared, really scared. I honestly was afraid of Philadelphia and what they might do to us." . . . Ref Earl Strom, who had spent the night in the hospital to have a metal pin inserted in a broken thumb, taping up the cast and working a magnificent game, making some big anti-Boston calls despite Auerbach's screaming protest. Athletes have no monopoly on guts. . . . And maybe someday Philadelphia will beat Boston."

Philly finally did end Boston's string of nine straight Eastern Division titles the next year, but the Celtics came back

once again to win the playoff finals. Schayes was fired and
Red retired, turning the reins over to Russell. Finally, in
1967, Philly broke through. A lot of people have called that
team the best one for a single season ever. I'm inclined to
agree with them. They blew through the regular season with
a 68-13 record, although only 4–5 against the Celtics. But
there was no stopping them in the playoffs. They wrapped
it up in five games and won the final one by a score of
140–116. The Philly fans were chanting "Boston is dead.
Boston is dead." Philadelphia went on to defeat the old franchise, San Francisco, for the title.

Boston won the title back in 1967–68, but then struggled
in as the fourth-place team in the Eastern Division at the end
of the 1968–69 regular season. Wilt had gone to Los Angeles
to join Elgin Baylor and Jerry West on a Laker team that
everyone was calling the greatest talent ever put on one
team. With Russell in his final games as player-coach for the
Celtics, Boston whipped Philly and New York to advance to
the finals. It came down to the final game. It would be the
last meeting between Russell and Chamberlain. I worked
that seventh game in Los Angeles.

Here they were, one last time with everything on the line.
They were playing in Jack Kent Cooke's new Forum. In the
fourth quarter, Wilt got hurt and took himself out of the
game. For someone as big and strong as Wilt was, he was
very injury prone. There were times he played when he
shouldn't have, granted, but there was a lot of controversy
about his coming out of this game. The Lakers were making
a rally when Wilt went out with about five minutes left in the
game, and they kept clawing back while he was on the
bench. Mel Counts was in there doing a pretty good job. Wilt
wanted to come back in, but Butch van Breda Kolff was
ticked at Wilt for coming out and wouldn't put him back in.
Counts was playing well for Counts, but Wilt should have
been back in there, if you ask me. Butch was tough and I
think he cut off his nose to spite his face that night. Boston
won it by 2 and Butch was gone.

So Russell retired at the top. He always rose to the challenge. He would pace himself, even take a night off on occasion. But he had the most intense concentration of anybody who ever played the game. Neither he nor Wilt ever gave me much trouble as an official. Wilt once made a statement in the papers: "With few exceptions, I could referee a game better than most officials. Earl Strom would be one of those exceptions." That naturally made me feel good, because it came from a man who had been on the firing line, who had really taken a lot of pounding on the court and a lot of abuse from the media.

There was only one time I ever saw Wilt and Russell get upset with each other. Wilt was playing the role of the peacemaker in a fight. It was always great to see him wade into a battle because when he said, "Knock it off," they almost always stopped immediately. This time Russell grabbed one of the Philly players to try to pull him off a Celtic, and Wilt said, "Hey, don't grab my man." It was customary to grab the other team's players. If you grab your own and he gets hit, he gets a little upset at his teammate for giving the other guy a clean shot at him. Wilt and Russell discussed it and tossed a few threats back and forth, but they never swung on each other—which was lucky because they were both awfully strong and tough.

I had a game in Chicago when Russell coldcocked Jimmy Krebs. Knocked him out. The only guy Wilt ever hit was Clyde Lovellette. It was late in one of the playoff games between Boston and San Francisco in the 1964 championships. Boston had this one in the bag, and Auerbach was taking the Celtics out one at a time so they'd get their standing ovations from the Boston Garden crowd. Finally, with about a minute to go, he took Russell out and the place came down. Lovellette came in for Russell. This was Clyde's last year and he started bumping Wilt around. Wilt said to him, "Hey, the game's over, you've won, we're embarrassed enough. Let's knock it off." Clyde kept it up.

"Look, the next time, you're gonna pay, buddy," Wilt warned him again. Nobody had ever seen Wilt punch anybody; you were almost afraid to think what might happen.

San Francisco got the ball with about twenty seconds to go. Wilt took a pass under the basket. I was standing on the end line. Clyde banged him with an elbow. Wilt just stopped. He put the ball down. I thought to myself, "Oh, my God, here it comes." Wilt threw a punch that I swear didn't travel over six inches. Right on the button. Clyde started to go down in sections. The place went nuts. Now Wilt was standing over Clyde, who was flat out cold on the floor. All the players came running over, but nobody was going after Wilt.

Auerbach came charging over. He and Wilt had never had that much time for each other. Red yelled at me, "You saw him do that. Throw him out! I want him out of here!"

I said, "Come on, Red. We've got twenty seconds left. Get Lovellette picked up and get somebody in here so we can get this thing over with."

Mendy was working with me and he was hard-pressed to keep from cracking up. Red said, "I'm not putting another man in here until you throw him out."

Wilt walked over and looked down at Red. "If you don't shut up and get out of here, I'm gonna put you down there with him."

Red had that victory cigar sticking out of the corner of his mouth. He looked up at Wilt and said, "Yeah, why don't ya pick on somebody your own size?"

So Mendy came over and said, "You got any more seven-footers who want to volunteer, Red?"

Russell was just sitting over on the bench with a towel around his neck, cackling his head off.

Russell was a good partner for Red's devilishness. In the last season before Russell became player-coach of the Celtics, Norm Drucker and I had Boston at Philly. During a time-out, Russell strode slowly toward us at midcourt. Soon as he spoke, I sensed something was up. "Mr. Auerbach wants me to ask you a question about the rules. Will you answer it?" I said, "Okay, what is it?" He said, "I don't know, he didn't say. I'll have to go back and ask him."

They were just stalling for rest time or trying to break Philly's rhythm. Russell never had much to say to officials during his years as coach. He does tell the story about a game in which he would call out periodically to one of the referees things like "It's a shame isn't it?" and "It's really sad" and "I guess I can't blame you." After nearly a dozen of these comments strung out over three quarters of the game, the ref came by and asked, "Russ, what the hell are you talking about?"

Russell looked up at him and sighed, "Oh, just the fact your mother and father never got married."

chapter 5

SOURSTROM

I live in a house about eight miles from where I was born and raised in Pottstown, Pennsylvania. Sounds pretty stable for a guy who's spent more nights in hotels than the Gideon Bible. Pottstown is located forty-five miles northwest of Philadelphia, kind of sandwiched between the coal fields to the north and Pennsylvania Dutch country to the south. It was an industrial city, a real workplace with a melting-pot atmosphere that made me feel right at home in the NBA. I grew up in a neighborhood that was like the League of Nations. My folks were very devout Jews, my mother having emigrated from Hungary and my father from Poland. Our family name was Sourstrom. Years later, a lot of coaches, players, and fans would probably have thought they had me perfectly named before it was shortened. There were four Jewish families in the neighborhood and others from Italy, Czechoslovakia, and even Gypsies.

My neighborhood had the stigma of being what they called the other side of the tracks. My father was a foreman in a bakery, and during the Depression he would "borrow" the flour and other ingredients and bring them home so my mother could bake bread. Then he would take the bread around to all the families in the neighborhood. This was all some of those families had to eat some days. Everybody loved my father, of course. But he was an alcoholic and eventually lost his job.

I had four brothers and two sisters, all older than me. They had to quit school and go out and get jobs so we could live, because my father kept losing jobs. I never had that close a relationship with him. I guess I figured he was unfair to my mother and the kids for not getting his act together and providing for us. I felt he could have controlled his drinking if he had any regard for his family. Years later I came to understand that type of problem and realized there was no place for him to get the kind of treatment he needed. But his abdication was hard on us all and left my mother to be the disciplinarian, the strong one who held the family together.

My second-eldest brother, Len, was an excellent basketball player. Nat Holman wanted him to come to the City College of New York when they had their real good clubs, but Len had to stay home and work to help support the family. Of course he resented my father for that. When World War II broke out, all my brothers went into the service within six months. Len and Izzie were in the South Pacific, and Ben and Mort were in Germany. They were all in the thick of it and that brought our family closer together. I was still in school until the war was over, then went into the Coast Guard for a couple of years. I came back and everyone in the family had gone off and gotten married. It wasn't the sort of family situation you would cling to.

Sports was the only activity any of the kids in my neighborhood could afford, so we played all the time. In grammar school we had our own little teams. Each of the playgrounds had its own teams in the various sports. We didn't have uniforms or anything, but we'd hop on our bikes and play against other playground teams. We had a basketball team, called ourselves the Rangers, and we borrowed money from one of the teachers to rent the community rec center. The

bakery where my dad worked before he got fired was right
around the corner from where we lived, so we'd spend all
our time either sitting on the bakery porch talking sports or
off playing sports. I was tenacious, but not very accomplished. Was I the arbiter, always trying to settle arguments
and preserve fairness among my fellow athletes? The answer
is no. In fact, I was the pain in the ass who always started the
arguments. All the way through school and into semipro ball,
I was the typical marginal player looking for excuses for my
less-than-glittering play. It was never my fault; it was always
the official's fault.

I was known around town as Yogi, my future brother-in-
law having hung that nickname on me for no particular
reason. When I was in the Coast Guard, I played in a baseball
game against a team that had Yogi Berra on it. I kept thinking how neat it was that the folks in the stands kept saying
things like "Way to go, Yogi," until I figured out they were
addressing the future Yankee, not the wanna-be. My desire
to be a star athlete couldn't match his abilities.

There were a couple of pro basketball leagues going when
I was a teenager, and sometimes I'd go down to Philadelphia
with one of my brothers to see the Sphas, the South Philadelphia Hebrew Association. Looking back, I can see that I was
watching the developments that would lead to the founding
of the National Basketball Association, and certainly a lot of
the names that would become part of my career were getting started as players and coaches. But frankly, I didn't
really follow it that closely. The sport didn't get much press,
and we were much more into playing than watching.

I loved sports and sports was what I gave myself to. I was
scrappy more than really talented, but I played on the Potts-
town High School teams in football, basketball, and baseball.
I was a marginal athlete—oh, maybe even below marginal—
but I worked hard. I was the best practice basketball player
Pottstown High ever had. I was unstoppable in practice. But
I'd get into a game and I was brutal. I couldn't make a basket.
Why? I don't know. Never could figure that out. I was skinny.
I had guts and did a pretty good job as a center in football.

But as soon as I'd get on a basketball court, I'd freeze. ("Some things never change," I can hear Red saying.)

I was one helluva good fielder in baseball. I think I could have been a professional player if fielding was enough. But I was the worst hitter that God ever put on this earth. One year I had my picture in the local paper for leading this semipro league in hitting. I was hitting four something, but I didn't get more than one or two hits the rest of the season and wound up at .096.

There was this bird dog, a guy who was like a scout for scouts, who came around Pottstown and tried to find players for the pros. He was with the old St. Louis Browns and he came up to me once and said, "You know, you amaze me. You have a major league glove, but you can't hit. But we're having a tryout camp and I want you to come on up." So I did, and they had an infield drill and I'm grabbin' everything that comes my way. "Hey, number forty," they yelled at me, "come on in here and grab a stick." Well, that was all she wrote. The guy threw about fifteen pitches past me. I didn't get a loud foul. "Okay," the guy said, "come here." I walked out to the mound, he turned me around, jerked the number off my back, and said, "See ya later, kid." If I could have had one wish filled in my life at the time, I would have chosen to be a major league baseball player.

Here I was madly in love with sports, but lacking the talents to make it anywhere playing any of them. I lived to play even if I couldn't play to live. I was a typical mouthy fringe player in basketball, but I was aggressive enough to hang around on a semipro team. I had played a couple seasons while at the Coast Guard base in Groton, Connecticut, and when I got out, I was playing here and there around Pottstown. Since I was a marginal player, my coach, Ed Good, used to have me referee little kids' games between halves of the varsity games when I was in high school, and I had worked some church league games. I thought I knew a lot about being a referee and didn't mind telling my two-bits' worth to officials when they worked any game I was playing in.

One night I was playing in this semipro game against a pretty good team. Jack Ramsay, who would become one of the winningest NBA coaches, and Jack McCloskey, an NBA assistant coach, and Bucky Harris, who had a lot of real good teams at Philadelphia Textile, were all on the other team. There was a scramble for a loose ball and I thought we were scrambling for a pretty long time. I looked up to see why there hadn't been a whistle, and I saw this referee standing down at the other end of the court with his arms folded.

"Yo, the game's up here!" I yelled at him.

He threw me out of the game. I went over and sat on the bench and kept after him. Finally he came over and told my coach that if they didn't get me into the locker room he was going to forfeit the game. Our owner was sitting there and would have had to cough up $175 if we forfeited. He told me to get my ass in the showers. After the game the referees were dressing in the same room. The guy who had given me the boot came over and said, "Look, you're not much of a player and you've got a pretty good mouth on you, so why don't you think about taking up refereeing?"

I said, "Yeah, if you can make it, I guess I can."

But that incident got me thinking more seriously about refereeing, and I started trying to work my way up from the few biddy league games I was doing now and then. The referee that night was Pete Lewis, and this just goes to show you how success stories, if you want to call it that, are dependent on meeting nice people along the way. Lewis and another Pottstown referee, Walt Foley, were instrumental in my breaking through those first political barriers all referees have to deal with.

Foley was a former minor league baseball player and worked a lot of games in the Eastern Pro League. He was very outspoken, and I think his personality had a lot of influence on my attitudes about dealing with people. If you have something to say, get it out and be done with it. Foley had wanted to try to make it in the NBA, and he finally got a chance to work an exhibition game. Jocko Collins was the supervisor of officials, and after the game he walked into the locker room and told him, "Walt, you did an excellent job. You're a very good referee. Who's your sponsor?" In those days an official had to have a team push for him to be accepted as a pro ref. Foley was infuriated by the politics and said he refused to get involved in a situation where he would be indebted to some team just to get into the league. So that was the end of his NBA hopes.

He then got into a hassle with the College Basketball Officials Association. They wanted him to boycott some schools they were trying to get into the fold, and eventually he got blackballed for not cooperating, and they wouldn't give him any top college assignments. Before he quit refereeing altogether he really pushed for me to be accepted by the CBOA. I was just starting to work high school games then. The first two years he recommended me they turned me down because I hadn't made myself popular enough with the guys. The third year he got up at the preseason meeting and said, "I'm recommending Earl Strom." Abe Goodman was president of that association. He said, "You've been recommending Strom for three straight years, how good a referee is he?" Foley yelled back, "I'll tell ya how good he is. He's a better referee than anybody in this room with the exception of you and me, and I'm not too sure about you." That's the year I got in and Foley got out. That was the 1954–55 basketball season.

At the end of that season, I got a call from this high school that had a playoff game and they wanted me to work it. I asked whom I was working with and they said, "Pete Lewis." I said, "Do me a favor and don't tell him I'm coming." I walked into the locker room before the game and he was sitting there with his feet propped up and a newspaper in front of his face. He was a really nice old guy, and it was kind of a dirty trick the way I quietly came up on him and dropped my bag. He looked up with a start, saw me, and nearly fell out of his chair. It turned out to be a pretty tough game, and when we came back to the room afterward, he said, "I think you're ready for college ball." I told him I'd like to try it, but didn't know how to go about it. "Don't worry about it," was all he said.

Lewis was athletic director and coached at Norristown High School. His boss, a guy named Dr. Gygus, was Asa Bushnell's right-hand man. Bushnell was the man who made up all the officiating assignments for the East Coast Athletic Conference, which represented about all the major college basketball programs in the East except for the Ivy League and ACC. A week after that game with Lewis, I got a letter from Dr. Gygus asking me to fill out an application. Those guys really took me under their wing and pushed me into a top-notch college schedule. Lewis and I became very close friends.

You never get anywhere without some breaks. You could be the greatest referee in the world, but if there isn't someone out there who likes you and helps you open those doors, forget it. There are plenty of guys out there right now who should be working in the pros and who want it desperately, but they haven't gotten that break. Maybe they had a beef with someone higher up and are being held down purposefully, or maybe they just haven't been in the right place at the right time. If I hadn't had that opportunity to work with Pete Lewis that night, or if Walt Foley hadn't gone to bat for me with the CBOA, I might still be struggling to get a decent college schedule. The same thing happened when I broke into the pros.

I had some other things going for me that fit into the ingredients for success as a referee. I don't know what makes one man want to run the fastest race while another chooses not to get out of bed even to watch, but I really wanted to make it. I had that hunger to be the best that I could. Maybe it was to achieve some success that I hadn't found as an athlete or in any other aspect of my life. I never really worried about figuring it out. I just saw that if you worked your butt off and tried to learn everything you could about the business from anybody you could, you improved your chances of moving up. Part of being a good referee is knowing what the hell you're doing out there on the court, and the other is being able to convince others that you do. I had kind of chiseled facial features, even when I was young. I was just under six feet tall and had a pretty solid, muscular build. My voice was strong and I came across with what I guess they call a command presence. These things all worked to my advantage. And I refereed every chance I got.

I was working a solid schedule of high school football and basketball games when Pete Lewis opened the way for college games on top of that. I had spent a couple years at Pierce Business School in Philadelphia and then began working for Jacobs Aircraft in Pottstown as an inspector of reconditioned engines. In 1952, I married my high school sweetheart, Yvonne Trollinger. We lived in a little Cape Cod house on the north side of Pottstown. In 1953, Margie was born, then Susie came a year and a half later. In 1956, I took a job in Philadelphia working for General Electric, which added a couple hours of commuting into the schedule. I ran the Pottstown softball league during the summer.

One night I dropped a note to Jocko Collins, supervisor of officials in the NBA, asking him what a fellow had to do to work a few pro games. I sent him my refereeing schedule and told him to let me know if the NBA might be interested in me. I was nearly thirty years old and wanted to make my move.

I had a game one night in Philly and was planning on just going over to the Palestra, which was near the GE office, after work. But I got sick at work; I was throwing up and finally my boss told me to head home. Yvonne was in the hospital having our third child, Stephen, and we had a woman in to take care of the two girls, Margie and Susie. I drove home and went to bed after calling my brother to tell him to come over later and drive me back to Philly. I didn't feel any better when I got up, and I still felt sick when I got to the Palestra.

I was working with Johnny Stevens, who later became supervisor of umpires for the American League. Duquesne had their great team with the Ricketts brothers, Dave and

Dick, from Pottstown, and they were playing Temple. We got through it and I thought I had done a terrible job. About all I could say for myself was that I had at least stayed on my feet. After the game I was down in the locker room throwing up again. When I came out of the toilet stall, there stood Jocko Collins. He introduced himself as supervisor of officials for the NBA and said, "Gee, Earl, don't you feel well?"

"No, but that's no excuse for the way I worked tonight. It wasn't a very good effort on my part," I told him. He said he liked my judgment and the way I hung in there. We talked a bit more, I thanked him and went back to being sick.

The next day Collins sent a handwritten letter:

Feb. 16, 1957

Dear Earl—

Please fill out the enclosed data sheets and return. . . . As I explained last night the big thing other than ability is an official's availability for travel to be in the NBA.

Also, as a tip, I would suggest you be more EMPHATIC with your VOICE (make it loud and strong) and give BETTER and more DECISIVE SIGNALS. (Study the book signals.) You run good and your judgment looked good but you must strive for ABSOLUTE CONTROL of players and coaches. This is a very important requisite for NBA officials. Awaiting your reply.

Sincerely,
Jocko

Jocko lived in Philadelphia and he had chosen to come over to the game to have a look at me. If he had shown up and found out I wasn't there because I was sick, he would no doubt have wondered how tough I was. Would I fold up out on the road somewhere? This way he saw that I could get through a game even when I was ill. Right place, right time again. Still, after receiving that letter my reaction was mixed. I wasn't too sure I was even good enough to work pro ball. I thought, jeez, here I am with a decent job at GE. Everything's going along well at home and I'm working a good college and high school schedule. Do I want to rock the boat? I filled out the forms. Then I got another letter several months later.

                                                              May 8, 1957

Dear Earl—

   If you were offered a chance to work in the NBA next season what would be your availability as to travel, etc.?
   Would you rather work pro ball or college? Whom do you work for? Would your wife be agreeable for you to work in the NBA? Let me know the answers to the above questions at your convenience.

                                                    Best Wishes,
                                                    Jocko Collins

   I wrote back and told him I would be interested in working a pro schedule, however, I would like to work it around my college schedule. He thought that would be okay, since at that time you had a lot of part-timers working a mixed-level schedule. Yvonne wasn't all that enthralled about my being gone even more than I was already. At least when I was working college and high school games, I would get home sometime during the night; with pro games out of the area I wouldn't get home sometimes for most of a week. Still, she knew it would help financially, and knowing how much I wanted to give it a try, she didn't complain.

chapter 6

INTO THE BIG SHOW

The NBA had been going for eleven years. Boston had picked up Bill Russell and just won its first of that long string of championships. Now it was time for the 1957–58 season, and I was going to be part of it. I received a nice initiation, as I related earlier, in my first NBA exhibition game when Paul Seymour got on me and I almost tossed him before realizing I indeed had a broken pants zipper.

Part of the glory of working in the NBA was to be on the same court with the heroes of basketball lovers everywhere. In my first regular-season assignment I worked a game between Minneapolis and Philly. I guess if I had a favorite player from the early years of the NBA, it was George Mikan, who had retired and was now coaching the Lakers. I came out onto the floor and I thought, "Jeez, here's George Mikan and I'm right out here making my living with him. The player of the decade. This big, powerful man. This guy I used to read so much about, and now we're working side by side." It didn't take long to get the gee-whiz cleared up. Mikan started in on me pretty good. I was a little reluctant to do anything about it. At halftime Mendy Rudolph told me, "If you want to hang around this league, you better straighten this guy out."

"Well, how do I do it?"

"Just tell him you've had enough. These guys will take all the rope you give them. You might as well cut it short."

We came out for the second half, and before we even started play, Mikan came up to me and said, "Hey, rook, this ought to be your last game the way you're going." I really exploded at that. I nearly lit into him and Mendy had to come over and pull me away. I told him, "I'll be around a long time after you're gone, and if you give me any more heat, I'm gonna run your ass right out of this joint.' A few minutes later he gave me some more crap and I nailed him with a technical. He jumped me again and I tossed him. Good-bye hero worship.

The pressure built on Mikan in the following months. Hot Rod Hundley was a rookie on that club, and he was supposed to bring the Lakers back to their championship days. Hundley tells a story about the night Mikan came into the locker room before a game pleading with his players to pull out of a horrible losing streak. "Look, fellas, things are going bad and my job's on the line. You guys can do something to help me. We've got to have this one tonight, and if we get it, I'll buy you all a steak dinner." According to Hundley, the Lakers fell behind by some 25 points, and at the half the players sat around the locker room with their heads hanging as Mikan stormed into the room. He went right down the line: "Hundley, you're going to save this franchise? You couldn't play in most church leagues." Mikan always called his center Foost instead of Foust. "Foost, I could stuff you in the basket you're so weak out there." He moved over to a man who would one day coach the Indiana Pacers, Bobby Leonard. "Leonard, if I could get you sober enough to play, I might find out how bad you really are." And on it went, but to no avail. They didn't eat steak that night and Mikan was fired before the season had run its course. I was still around.

The first game I worked in Boston Garden I was awestruck. The place wasn't full of all the championship banners

that would come over the years, but they had Russell and
Cousy and Red, and it was certainly the big time of pro
basketball even then. I had read about these guys and seen
them on TV. Before we went out to work the game, Mendy
said to me, "This is only a part-time job for you. You draw
your parameters early. You let them know you're only going
to take so much and no more. These guys are going to really
test you here, but just ignore the little stuff and nail them if
they go too far."

Before the game, when we went out to talk to the captains,
Cousy was out there. He had found out where I was from and
he said, "Well, Earl, how's everything in Pottstown, Pennsylvania? Good to have you in the league. Good luck." I was
thinking, jeez, what a nice guy. Mendy whispered to me,
"Watch him, he's getting you ready for the kill."

The game turned into a rout, and after a while the fans
were sitting on their hands and things were pretty routine.
Cousy, of course, was the forerunner of the fancy passers and
dribblers who are so routine nowadays. He had great periph-
eral vision and arms that hung down like an ape's. He would
use his flashy play when it was necessary to make a particular
play, or if he felt the place had gone to sleep and needed to
be wowed a bit, which was the case as this game went along.
He understood about show business.

Midway through the fourth period he came down the
court on a fast break. I was under the basket as he came at
me. He went up in the air and went behind his back not once
but twice. Russell came rolling in on the wing. Russell's man
tried to take Cousy, who flipped the ball to Russell for a big
slam dunk. The fans went nuts, screaming and yelling, until
they heard my whistle. Then it went quiet as a church. I
called traveling on Cousy.

Mendy was well back up the court. Cousy started toward
me. I thought, oh, no, what do I do now? He said, "You know,
Earl, in the Pottstown YMCA that might be walking, but in
Boston Garden, when I do that, it isn't walking." I thought,
well, since we're on a first-name basis, I'll just set this
straight. "You're right, Bob, in the Pottstown YMCA it's

walking, and when I'm working in Boston Garden, it's walking here, too."

"You're full of shit."

"Get out of here or I'll nail you with a T."

"You don't have the guts."

I hit him with the technical. Now the place starts to get pretty noisy. Before Mendy could get to me to tell me to get the hell away from Cousy before things got worse, I said, "Now get away from me before I run your ass."

"I know you don't have the guts to do that."

I hit him with the second T and said, "Get out of here."

That was sort of like throwing the Pope out of Rome. Everything that wasn't nailed down was heading for me on the floor. Boston won by over 30 points and still we needed extra police protection to get out of there. Mendy got on me for not walking away after I'd challenged him with the first T, but I did actually gain Cousy's respect from that night on.

The next year we had a playoff series, and we're in St. Louis one night and had to go to Boston the next night. This was during a time when it was popular to throw eggs and oranges onto the floor. The game was televised back to Boston, and the garbage was being tossed. Mendy said to me, "Earl, whatever we get here tonight, they'll try to outdo it tomorrow night, so we might as well get used to it."

Sure enough, not more than a couple minutes into the next night's game here came a couple of eggs. We called a time-out, wiped it up, and a few minutes later, here came some more. Pretty soon, it was out of control. Eggs were coming from everywhere and landing everywhere, with one exception. Cousy was standing under one of the baskets next to the Boston bench, and there weren't any eggs landing near him. I walked over and stood next to him. We talked about what a mess it was and what a shame it was to treat the game this way. He walked over to the bench where the guys were huddling. I walked over with him. Red was giving them some instructions and I listened in. Cousy walked down to get a drink and I went with him and got a drink. He turned to me and said, "Earl, what the hell are you doing?" He had

picked up a towel and I wiped my hands off on the other end
of it. "Look, Bob, they're throwing a lot of eggs, but none of
them are coming anywhere near you, so I can't think of a
safer place for a referee to be, can you?" He shook his head
and smiled.

It didn't take me long to realize that for all the taunts and
jabs served up by coaches, players, and fans, the number of
times anyone was trying to be helpful was the same as the
number of basketballs that can be shoved inside a referee's
whistle. When I was talking earlier about my physical attrib-
utes and how they suited the authority a referee needed to
convey, I failed to mention my ears. If I didn't have such a
dominating jaw, they would have looked like jug handles.
Still, they worked far too well when it came to picking up all
the things that were shouted my way during a game. The
way I reacted to these "overheard" opinions earned me the
title of "Red Ass," as in, "Look out, Strom's got the Red Ass
tonight." "Red Ass" is the athletic world's way of describing
the sort of disposition you would expect of a man whose
afterburner has been flushed with Tabasco sauce for, say,
four or five days.

When a guy has the Red Ass he gets touchy and he snaps
back under pressure. Take, for example, the pressure of
working a foul-filled game in January of 1960 between the
Minneapolis Lakers and the Detroit Pistons. Larry Foust,
center for the Lakers, was incessantly riding me. With 8:02
left in the fourth quarter, he said, "You're in Baltimore tonight, Strom." I whirled on him and ejected him with,
"You're in the shower, Foust." Or, there was the continual
pressure of coaches and players nibbling at you, trying to get
an edge. No one gave you the slightest consideration, and if
you went looking for mercy, watch out, they'd bury you.
There was a game between Syracuse and Philly in my second year when Mendy Rudolph couldn't get there and I had
to work it by myself. I had the compassionate Seymour
shouting out things like, "Strom, you're blind!" and "Strom,
you're crazy!" and "Strom, you don't know nuthin'!"

It was tougher for an official to break in then. It's tough at any time, but it was tougher then because the league didn't have so many rules governing conduct, and the owners really ran the show. There were hard, tough guys playing and coaching, and they would cost you your job if they could. Being right on a call wasn't enough. They wanted to see if they could break you, because then they would own you. There was only one way to gain acceptance, and that was by how you stood up to them and what kind of judgment you used in making your calls. Consistency was a big factor. But even so, they wouldn't give you any encouragement even if they respected you.

When you're a ref, you're all alone. There aren't too many roles in our society that are so totally denied support, even just to the extent of being told you did the job well. A referee gets attacked on all fronts by people trying to intimidate him. Everybody is taking their frustrations out on him. There is no acknowledgment that he made the correct call, let alone a gutsy one. The game of basketball doesn't lend itself to absolutes; most of the calls are close and involve razor-fine judgment. There's always room for someone to argue, and they always do. To always be challenged and provoked, especially when you're trying to prove yourself at the highest level of competition, promotes a great deal of tension. When the heat comes, you don't want to seem so sensitive you can't take it, yet you can't let them think they're putting something over on you, that you can be conned. Someone, and I wish I could remember who, once said of sports officials: "Ideally, they should combine the integrity of a Supreme Court justice, the physical agility of an acrobat, the endurance of Job, and the imperturbability of Buddha." In the process, refs often develop the Red Ass.

I often had the feeling that they were coming at me in waves. I was working a game in Philly at the University of Pennsylvania, where the court runs right up to the edge of the stands. There was this big, loud, mouthy guy who always used to get on me pretty good when I worked games in Philly. One night a couple years earlier, he was giving us all kinds of crap at courtside. Mendy came over to me during a time-out and said, "Stand over there in front of that guy like you're going to catch the ball. Leave your hands wide enough apart that I can get the ball through." I walked over and positioned myself. This guy's chirping away, acting quite offensive. Mendy signaled play was ready to resume and whipped the ball toward me underhand. It zipped right through my hands and smacked this guy right on the chops, flattened his cigar into his face, and toppled him and his folding chair over backward. I grabbed the ball, flipped it to the player on the sideline, and told him to put it in play. We didn't hear much from the loudmouth the rest of that evening.

This night at Penn he was sitting in the first row under one of the baskets, and one time when I went to move off the end line, I found I was stuck. This guy had wrapped his legs around mine and was holding me there. I tried to shake loose and finally just started kicking the hell out of his shins until I was free.

I immediately stopped the game and asked the police to have this fellow removed from the arena. The guy refused to move, so Jack Ramsay, who was general manager at the time, came over and talked to the guy. He asked me, "Earl, would you mind if we just left him here? He's a season-ticket holder and we hate to lose him." I told Ramsay to move him or the game was over. So what did they do? They gave the guy a seat next to Irv Kosloff in the owner's box. They made a hero out of him.

The next day I picked up the paper and this guy is saying he's going to sue me. He was a Korean War veteran and said he had shrapnel in his legs. The article didn't even mention that he wrapped his legs around me. Eddie Gottlieb, the club adviser, talked him out of the suit, fortunately. But every game for a couple weeks after that this guy brought a large paper bag to the game. Nobody could figure out what was in it. Finally, I came back in there to work a game, and as I walked out onto the court, I heard this roar go up and all these photographers were running to the other end of the court where this guy was sitting. He had pulled a pair of catcher's shin guards out of the bag and strapped them on. I had to laugh. His picture must have run in every paper in the country the next day.

My situation wasn't helped any in those days by the general wear and tear of the lives I was leading. I was working full-time as a specialist in customer relations at GE in Philadelphia and not getting much sleep at all. There were a lot of weeks when I might get home no more than one night. That first year I was working high school, college, and pro games, sometimes on successive nights. I would work NBA games in the East on weeknights and in the Midwest on the weekends. Near the end of that first season, I was having pain in my legs. Doctors diagnosed it as nerves pinched by ruptured discs. They wanted to operate, but I wanted to make it through the season. Sometimes I had to stand up on flights because it hurt too much to sit down.

One night I was working a game at Muhlenberg College and I collapsed at the end of the game. Luckily a neighbor and my brother-in-law were with me and they drove me home. They carried me into the house and put me to bed. Of course, Yvonne was upset. I stayed in bed and didn't go to work the next day. I had a game that night at Annapolis. I called Yvonne into the bedroom that afternoon and asked her to call the guy I was to work the game with. I wanted him to meet me at the train station. She told me I was an idiot to work. I told her to make the call.

"If it's that important to you, you get out of bed and make the call yourself," she said, hoping some sense would be forced into me. I was cussin' and carrying on and she was yelling right back at me. Finally, I was so mad I shoved back the covers and jumped out of bed and just folded up on the floor. I have never felt pain like that before or since. Yvonne was crying. She said, "Now can I please call the doctor and tell him we're coming to the hospital?" There was nothing I could do but go. I was lucky I hadn't wrecked myself for life by going on as long as I did. They performed the operation, fused the discs, but I had to give back my schedule for the rest of the season. What really burned me up was that I had finally been scheduled to work a high school state championship game.

Collins asked me to drop my other schedules for the next season and commit myself full-time to the pros. I didn't have to deliberate long. I liked the idea of being in the big time. There were pictures of me in the paper, breaking up a fight between Bill Sharman of the Celtics and Ron Sobie of the Knicks, ejecting Paul Seymour, sometimes just a face in the background as Russell dunked or George Yardley canned a jumper. They didn't always mention my name, or they called me "Art" Strom and Earl "Strum," but I was out there on the court. There was a picture of me with Yvonne and the kids when I was recovering from the back surgery. People would say, "Hey, Yogi, how're things in the bigs?" I guess I was starting to feel a little like somebody special, like I was good at something people thought mattered. Gottlieb told the press, "Strom is sometimes an arrogant, cocky, short-fused type of guy. He's also too hard-nosed for his own good. Other than that, he's a helluva referee." Other than that, hell—that's what it takes to be a good referee, to take charge of a game full of big men and big egos.

Of course, it didn't take long in any game to get challenged. There were many times, especially in tough places such as Syracuse, that early on I wished I could just disappear. I'd think, "God, I've got to go up to this place where nobody likes me and they're going to come at me with everything but guns." But once the game started rolling, I figured I wasn't going to go down as some gutless jerk who was afraid to make the tough call.

Remember, refereeing in the NBA at that time was an avocation, not a vocation. At $40 per game plus reimbursement for out-of-pocket expenses, I would make maybe $4,500 a season including the playoffs in those early years. That, combined with my salary at GE, gave me about $15,-000 annually in the late fifties, which was pretty good bucks in those days. But we needed it as the family grew to five kids.

Sid Borgia was the best-known NBA official of his era. He

might have been the toughest of all time. He certainly was the most rambunctious. Sid was fearless when it came to clashes on the court or in the stands. I swear he was never happier than when he had 10,000 fans howling for his head. But he hated to fly. We were flying a prop job out of Minneapolis one night. As we were waiting to taxi out on the runway, they kept revving up the engines, and every time they'd give it the gas, Sid would nudge me and say, "Gee, Earl, how does that sound to you?" What I knew about mechanics and engines you could write on the head of a pin, but I kept trying to reassure him that everything sounded fine. I didn't like flying all that much, either. I'd try to lean back, close my eyes, and sleep if I could. Sid tried to do the same thing, but he always had a window seat and he'd sleep with one eye open to watch the engines.

So I was trying to doze and Sid's strapped in next to me as we taxied. All of a sudden, as one of the engines was revving up, a spark caught the exhaust. The whole wing and engine was illuminated as if it were on fire. Sid had never seen this before. He thought the whole plane was going up in flames. He flipped off his buckle, leaped over me, and jumped into the aisle. "What the hell are we waiting for, let's get the hell out of here, the plane's on fire!" he shouted, and with that, he ran down the aisle to the back of the plane.

Of course everybody on the plane was startled by this. Before outright panic set in, the stewardess grabbed Sid and tried to calm him down. He kept yelling, "The plane's on fire!" and she kept telling him it was just an exhaust fire. Finally she got him to look out the window again. When he saw no flame, he just turned around, walked back up the aisle, climbed over me, snapped himself back in his seat, and leaned back as if nothing had happened.

Another time we were flying to Los Angeles from Chicago's Midway airport. It was a little after midnight when we got to the airport for a flight that was supposed to go out at one A.M. There was a DELAYED sign on the flight announcement. We looked out at this four-engine prop job and could see two mechanics up on a ladder working on one of the engines. Sid says, "What the hell do you think's wrong?" I said, "You ask me that every time we have some kind of a problem with a plane, and I still don't know shit about planes."

After about an hour they made an announcement that they were going to board the plane. The guys were still up on this ladder working on this engine as we walked out to the steps. It was cold and very quiet. Sid kept looking over as we went up the steps, looking at the engine. As we got to the top step, this one mechanic says to the other, "Ah, the hell with it, button it up." Sid spun around and started pushing his way back down the stairs past the other passengers. "Get the hell out of my way." He hit the tarmac and ran over to the ladder and climbed right up to the two guys and yelled, "To hell with what? You fix this goddamn thing right or we ain't going anywhere." They were so surprised, I couldn't help but laugh. They reassured him there was nothing seriously wrong and he reluctantly boarded.

Sid was fainthearted for flying, but I'll tell you, he had balls as big as his head when it came to taking on crowds. How he loved to stir 'em up. He couldn't stand to see fans sitting on their hands. I think he considered it an insult to his personality if there wasn't some sort of commotion going on in any game he worked. If nothing happened on its own, he wasn't above making a couple of calls to get everyone in a furor. One night we had a game in Syracuse between the Nats and Boston. When those two met up there, you usually just tried to survive, let alone worry about a lack of excitement. Yet this particular game was going very well and we were down to the last three or four minutes. There hadn't been any fights, and the pushing and shoving had been pretty well controlled. There was a time-out and Sid strolled over to me and said, "This is pretty rare to see these people so calm up here. We gotta get 'em off their hands."

Within a minute he made a series of calls that had the place in an uproar. The players were ready to square off. A couple of fights broke out in the stands as guys gestured wildly at Sid and banged their neighbors in the process. Now there was another time-out. Sid never stood in one place, but kept circling, shaking his legs to keep loose. I was down on the other end of the court dodging pennies and drink cups. I could see Sid making his circles bigger and bigger, getting closer to the sidelines. Some guy was yelling at him from the stands. I saw this guy get up, take off his jacket, and put it on his seat. He walked onto the court and Sid hit him. The guy went down. He got up and Sid decked him again. Sid was tough, really a strong little guy. He didn't fool around with anybody. Of course, the crowd was ready to riot by this time. The ushers dragged this guy off the court and we got through the final seconds of the game. Syracuse had lost and the fans wanted our scalps. Sid was loving it as we rushed off the court for the locker room.

The crowd was focused on us now. We had a detective friend up there who used to work as a standby official. He came into the locker room and said we couldn't get out through the lobby. We looked out the door and there were three or four hundred fans milling around waiting for us. He took us down some back stairs and got us out into a squad car. We crouched down in the backseat while they drove us out of the parking lot to his car, which was a few blocks away. From there the detective took us to the airport. It was snowing like crazy and we barely made it out of Syracuse because of the storm. Sid was his usual nervous self, but we didn't have any problems as we eventually got into better weather. It was clear and calm over New York City when we got there. They put on the no-smoking sign and told us to fasten our seat belts for landing. But we continued to circle over La Guardia. Finally I said to Sid, "You know something's wrong."

"Whaddyamean?" he asked, looking real worried.

"We've been circling too long. Something's wrong."

"Aw, you don't know nuthin' about planes. Whaddya tryin' to pull?"

Now the captain came on the intercom and said we had a problem with the landing gear. He said either the right wheel wouldn't come down or the indicator light just wasn't working. We were going to go in and try to land on the left side, then drop down on the right and see what happened. They said if the wheel wasn't down, the wing would touch and we would spin around, but there was plenty of fire equipment around, so not to worry.

Sid was worrying like mad. He reached in his pocket, pulled out his rosary, threw it at me, and told me to say a prayer. I told him I wasn't Catholic. He told me to say a prayer anyway. We came in with our heads tucked between our legs and pillows over our heads. It turned out that the wheel was down all the time.

The next morning Sid called me at work. He was screaming into the phone. I could barely understand him. The commissioner, Maurice Podoloff, had called him. "He's gettin' on me about the fight and I tell him about how we almost got killed. He says I'm in trouble because of the fight. I tell him, 'Forget the fight. Earl and I damn near died in the line of duty last night and we don't even have any travel insurance.' Podoloff starts laughin' when I'm tryin' to tell him all this. I tell him, 'You wouldn't think it was so goddamn funny if you'd been sittin' there on that plane. And besides, I almost converted one of your kind.'"

As a result of that, the officials did get flight insurance coverage. It turned out Sid also got sued for the fight. It seems the fan had said, "Borgia, if you had any guts, you'd call a technical against Russell." Sid told him he could try his guts anytime. That's when the fan stepped on the court and Sid hit him. He loosened a few teeth and the guy sued him for $35,000. Eventually Sid had to settle out of court for $500, which was a good chunk of dough back then.

If we were rowdy refs, maybe we were inspired by all the rowdy players. There were some dandys back then. Shellie McMillon played with Detroit when I was first in the league. He was a decent player, but could probably have been a better light-heavyweight boxer. A tough customer. One night he picked up four quick fouls, just bang, bang, bang, bang. You only got five then before you were out, so they put him on the bench. He complained to me, "Earl, don't you want me to play tonight? I haven't been in there a quarter and you've hit me with four. What's going on?" I told him he needed to back off a little out there. In the middle of the second half he came back in, but he was gone ten seconds later with his fifth foul. As he was walking off the court, he grabbed the ball. I said, "Let's have it."

"No." He kept walking toward the sidelines.

"Come on, Shellie, let me have the ball."

"Nope. If I can't play, nobody's playin'," he said, and took off for the locker room with the ball.

Shellie goes on my Hall of Maim team. These are the tough guys, the policemen. These guys traditionally were expected to get to the other team's stars or take out the policeman who was trying to get to *his* star teammates. They aren't as much a part of the game anymore, and rightly so. You don't need all this high-priced talent getting laid out by a bunch of hatchetmen. People talk about Detroit's championship team as being a bunch of bad boys, but that was more fiction than fact. They played hard, sure, and Rick Mahorn liked to push people around, but if Bill Laimbeer had 101 fights, he'd lose 100 of them.

Besides McMillon on the all-time tough-guy team, I'd have to go with Andy Johnson and Joe Graboski of Philly, Jim Loscutoff of Boston, Wally Osterkorn of Syracuse, Al Attles, and Walter Dukes, who played for New York, Minneapolis, and Detroit in the fifties and sixties. He fouled out of something like 20–25 percent of all the games he ever played in the NBA.

Dukes was a strong, 7'0", tough guy, but lanky ol' Ray Felix really put one over on him one night. Actually, Felix, who was about 6'10", had a way of getting into it with tough guys. Boston was playing Los Angeles once, and Loscutoff grabbed Felix around the neck and wrestled him to the floor. Nobody was having much luck getting them separated, and then you heard Felix's voice gasp, "Come on, let me up. I'm a boxer, not a wrestler." Loscutoff broke into a laugh and let him go. So anyway, Los Angeles was playing Detroit and Felix got into it with Dukes, and despite Ray's claim to be a boxer,

Walter hammered him pretty good. Since Dukes had instigated it, we tossed him and let Felix stay. At the end of the
half, Felix raced off the court and instead of going to his own
locker room, he went up the hall to the Detroit locker room.
As he ran into the room, Dukes was sitting on a bench pulling
his jersey up over his head. Felix couldn't resist the tempta-
tion and planted one right on his nose, knocking Dukes out.
As soon as the Detroit players saw Dukes lying on the floor,
they turned around and started chasing Felix back down the
hallway. We were coming off the court, and here came this
tall bean pole racing down the hallway with all these Detroit
players screaming for his hide. As he went tearing past us,
he yelled, "I had to do it, man. I had to do it!" The all-time
cheap shot.

There were plenty of growing pains in those early years.
In my second year I was assigned a Knicks-Pistons game on
a neutral court in St. Louis. I was assigned to work with
Marty Cribbins, who was not rated among the elite of the
refereeing corps. Warren Pack, covering the game for the
New York Journal American, figured we were a couple of
junior-grade officials and blamed us for the Knicks' blowing
a 27-point lead and losing 106–105:

"Some of the fouls called were fantastic. And not all of the bad
calls were against the Knicks. Just two out of every three. Ray Felix,
Selvy, and Kenny Sears all fouled out in the wild fourth period
when the Pistons were slamming away to get the ball. Just to list
a few of the stunning moments: Selvy was bringing the ball downcourt and Slater Martin hit his arm and grabbed the ball. Strom
blew the whistle and called a foul on Selvy. A few minutes later
Sears was charged with a fifth foul when he himself was fouled.
. . . Perhaps Jocko Collins couldn't assign top-grade officials because
the money-hungry owners are taking their teams to such out-of-
the-spot places as Houston, Texas; San Francisco; Portland, Oregon
and elsewhere and the National Bush League wants to put on a
good face in the new towns. . . . So the Knicks are here tonight to
play the Pistons and they're hoping that Messrs. Strom and Cribbins will be somewhere else. It's unfortunate that somewhere else
isn't the minor leagues."

Yeah, well, everybody's entitled to his opinion.

It was a struggle to gain acceptance. Many nights I came home and told Yvonne, "Jesus Christ, I made a call tonight and I got all kinds of crap. It was a good call. Two seconds later, Mendy made the same call and nobody said boo." She'd come back, "Well, you dumb jerk, don't you realize he's been around for ten years? Your time will come."

Sid's toughness was a big influence on me. A game I worked with him one night in Detroit in my third year in the league had a profound effect on my subsequent concentration. If Sid had something to say to you or if he didn't like the way you were doing something, he would let you have it. Out on the floor, he'd come over and tell you to bend down and tie your shoe, and then he'd chew you out. It was constructive criticism, but it was in strong terms. This one night Boston was playing the Pistons, and I just couldn't get with it. I was having a bad night, and as a result Sid ended up taking a lot of crap because I wasn't handling certain situations. I was kicking the hell out of plays and guys were getting on both of us. I was almost losing confidence in myself as the game went along, and I started backing off from calls. I had started to gain acceptance, and then I just threw in this terrible night. If I had been a player, they'd have benched me. But there's no such mercy for a referee.

Naturally, Sid had to move in and try to keep the game from coming totally apart. It was one thing if he was stirring up the trouble, but in this case, I was embarrassing him as an official. That he couldn't tolerate. He was throwing guys out for Boston and throwing guys out for Detroit, all because I couldn't keep control. This was in the old Olympia and after the game we were down in this old hockey dressing room. He slammed the door behind us, bolted it, and really lit into me. He let me know in no uncertain terms that if you want to referee in this league you've got to hold up your end and you've got to assert yourself and you can't take any crap. You've got to have guts. You've got to show these guys you're going to be fair, but that you're tough, too. He told me to shape up or he'd run me right out of the league.

From that moment on I never backed down like that again. I've had my share of problems, but at least I didn't bail out again. As the years went along, I'd hear a player who had been around tell another who was giving me some heat, "Stay away from him. Don't mess with him." You have to be right and know the rules, but you also have to have the balls to back up your calls or they'll swallow you.

Richie Powers and I came into the NBA in the same year. We were lucky because we had so many strong guys like Sid and Mendy Rudolph and Arnie Heft, Jim Duffy, Norm Drucker, and Willie Smith to show the way. These guys were real good at giving you enough rope so you could learn, yet they'd still step in and cover your ass if you got into a jam. They didn't like it when you screwed up, as Sid's lecture dramatized, but at least they didn't leave you out there to hang; unfortunately that attitude doesn't always hold true with today's officials.

Richie and I came up the ladder pretty fast because of the help we got from the older refs. There were only a dozen officials working at that time, compared to nearly four times that twenty years later when we first went to the three-man format. The lead officials were known as "A" officials and the others "B." When we broke in, we were, of course, called B's.

One night up in Syracuse—not everything happened in Syracuse, it only seems that way—the Nats were playing Boston. That usually spelled trouble, as I've said, but because some other officials had gotten sick and injured, there was no "A" official to work the game. They had no choice but to send Richie and me up there and hold their breaths. We made it through without any trouble, and that broke the barrier for us. Both of us were then accepted a lot quicker than we might have been. In fact, at the end of our third year in the league we were both working playoff games, which was unheard of at that time. Richie and I got along well enough, although he had a way of getting on a guy's nerves by carrying on and on about anything that happened to be bugging him.

As much as I credit Sid with helping shape my career, my

hero was Mendy. I tried to pattern myself after him from the day I broke into the league. Sid was notorious; Mendy was prestigious. Sid ruled with sort of a bullring toughness; Mendy seemed to be so in command that toughness wasn't necessary. You don't take a swing at the maître d'.

Mendy came into the league in 1950 and became an immediate power referee. He started working playoff games within his first two years and was immediately one of the most prominent referees because of his style, courage, and judgment. He had excellent judgment. He made the call regardless of the pressure, whom it involved, or where it was. His mechanics revolutionized the game. His hand signals were classic. They always say a referee should exude confidence and poise in making a call, and Mendy showed it by the way he handled himself on the court. I never emulated his style because you would have to have his personality to get away with it, but he always made a very definite expression or move to demonstrate the call.

He taught me that if you have a call that could go either way, you have to sell that call by the way you make it. You don't have to use a whole lot of histrionics, but you do use a little more action and strength in making that call than you would a more obvious one. And if you do it for one team, you sure as hell better do it for the other team. Don't play to the home crowd. To give a big show of flair for the home team's call and be much milder for the visitor is bush. Mendy probably had the most to do with my really concentrating on giving the visitor a fair shake. It became very important to me to know that the visiting team wasn't going to be at a disadvantage just because they didn't have a crowd there to intimidate the referees.

I knew I had arrived when, at the end of my fourth season, I was chosen, along with Mendy, to work the entire championship series between Boston and St. Louis. This was the only time two men have worked an entire finals in NBA history. The two teams hadn't been able to agree on any other officials, so they used us for all five games. Boston won the series 4–1, picking up their fourth championship in five years. Working that series really gained me acceptance with the players and coaches. I don't know if it's the confidence or the acceptance that comes first, but I think that was a major stepping stone in my career.

After those finals were over, I got to thinking that since I was obviously pretty hot stuff to work the entire series, it was time to capitalize on it. I had started out at $40 per game and each year we received $5-per-game raises. I figured they owed me more than another $5 raise for the next season. Maurice Podoloff was the commissioner, a nice little old man, but he was tough with the buck. Mendy, who was probably making $100 a game then, was the fair-haired boy with Podoloff, so I said, "Since I worked the whole final series, don't you think I really deserve a bigger raise next year?"

Mendy said, "Well, what do you think you ought to have?"

I said, "I don't know, maybe twenty or twenty-five dollars. Yeah, I'd like to go from fifty-five to eighty dollars a game. I don't think that's unreasonable."

"Heck, no," Mendy said. "I'm sure you can get it. You gonna talk to Podoloff?"

"Yeah. I'm going to go over and see him."

"Good. Now you just stick to your guns and I'm sure you can get it," Mendy told me.

I guess I was kind of in awe of Mr. Podoloff, and when I walked into his office, I started to tremble. I started having second thoughts about even being there. "Earl, how are you?" he said to me. "You had a fine season, you had a fine series, I'm real happy for you. Now, what's this meeting all about?"

I stammered around a bit and told him how I thought since I'd been selected to work every game of the final series and everything that I might deserve more than just another $5 raise. Like, well, I would really like to go from $55 to $80, to get a $25 raise.

He sort of sat back in his chair and looked at me in his own special way, and after a minute he said, "Well, Earl, you did have a real good year and I agree you should get more money. You're thinking twenty-five dollars a game more and I'm thinking more like fifteen dollars . . ."

"I'll take it," I said. I jumped up, shook his hand, and ran out of there like a thief.

As I headed down to the train station, I was thinking, boy, I sure stuck to my guns. I called Mendy and told him I got a raise. He said, "You get the twenty-five dollars?"

I told him I only got $15, but I was happy.

He said, "You dumb ass, you could have easily gotten the whole twenty-five dollars if you had hung in there."

I really didn't care. I'd gotten rewarded for what I was doing, and things were going extremely well for my career in the NBA. And it wasn't my only career responsibility; in fact, I had to work extra hours at GE during the off-season to make up for the time I sliced into my work there during the NBA season. It worked to GE's advantage to have me refereeing because they could utilize my contacts for public relations, but they still expected me to carry my load. I was a liaison between the Air Force and our quality-control engineers. I was in the missile and space department, and when there were units that didn't pass an Air Force acceptance inspection, I would have to coordinate their complaints with our engineers so that corrections or adjustments were made. I wasn't technically oriented, but I was a go-between for technicians. As things developed, I handled a lot of PR, taking Air Force representatives to dinner and ball games and generally keeping the path of communications as smooth as possible.

The double life was still a burdensome price to pay. Our standard of living was above average, but working at GE was the only way I could provide for medical insurance and build a pension. There was no security from one season to the next in the NBA. There were horror stories about officials much more established than I was getting the boot for running afoul of an owner or league official. Jocko Collins had worked in the league since the start and succeeded Pat Kennedy as supervisor of officials in the 1954–55 season; he was an honest, dependable man with a high degree of integrity, but an episode one night in Boston triggered his eventual firing by the owners.

It was one of the bushest things I ever saw. I was supposed to be working with Richie Powers, who more than once found himself late for a game. This night he missed the train out of New York because of bad weather. The game was delayed for a long time, nearly an hour, and the fans were stomping their feet. There was a former referee living in the area named Jim Gaffney. Jocko called him to come over to the Boston Garden and work until Richie could get there.

Carl Braun was coaching the Knicks and he raised all kinds of hell about Gaffney's working the game. He didn't want Gaffney because he had been fired from the league for incompetence. Braun was a hard-nosed, obstinate sort of guy, and he wasn't in the mood to help anybody get through our predicament. He got on the phone to his owner, Ned Irish. Irish had it in for Jocko, so he wasn't about to cooperate either. They refused to play with Gaffney, and they refused to let me work the game alone until Richie got there.

By this time, poor Gaffney had come in, put on his uniform, and was ready to work. Jocko was beside himself. So while Jocko was trying to tell Gaffney he couldn't work the game after all, Walter Brown, owner of the Celtics, came up to Jocko. This was in the middle of the lobby with all these upset fans stomping around. Brown started screaming at Jocko: "You're horseshit, Jocko . . . you always were horseshit, you'll always be horseshit . . . you're doing a lousy job . . . we're going to have your job, Jocko!" Within a year he was fired.

He had done a good job of trying to back his referees and still keep a rapport with the owners, but it was just about an impossible job. He was always trying to find new referees who were competent, but unlike baseball where an official can work his way up through the minors, the NBA was—and still pretty much is—a place where a guy got his first and only exposure to professional basketball. The owners weren't very sympathetic. They just raised hell and complained.

Collins was replaced by Sid Borgia in the supervisor's hot seat. Sid worked as an active official in addition to his supervisor's duties until a Ben Kerner cannon shot eliminated his work on the floor. In the 1963–64 season the race for the Western Division title came right down to the final weekend between San Francisco and St. Louis. Borgia assigned Mendy Rudolph and Richie Powers to work back-to-back games involving the 76ers and the Warriors on the West Coast and assigned me to work with him in a back-to-back series between Detroit and St. Louis. We tried to talk Sid into taking himself off the games because we felt it was leaving himself open for possible problems with Kerner—who was very powerful in the league—if the Hawks didn't win. Norm Drucker was at a teacher's convention in Toledo, and we tried to talk Sid into using Norm at least for the final game in Detroit, but Sid wouldn't hear of it. He wasn't about to back off from anything.

It came down to where St. Louis had to win at Detroit to have a chance for a tie. We again asked Sid to use Norm. He said no. Detroit kicked the hell out of St. Louis in the first half, up by 20. Sid was saying at halftime, "See, nothing to worry about. Not even a game." But the Hawks started to scrap back with Bob Pettit firing in everything he put up. Midway through the final quarter St. Louis was right back in the hunt, and Pettit went up for a shot. The ball fell loose. Sid didn't think there had been a foul. Pettit screamed at Sid and started calling him names. Sid hit him with a T. Pettit came after him. Sid hit him with another T and tossed him.

This finished off the Hawks and their hopes for the division title. Kerner was furious. He came down out of the stands and started running up and down along the sidelines, screaming at Sid. "You're through. You'll never work another NBA game if I have anything to say about it. You've finished yourself off, Borgia!" Of course, one owner didn't run the league, but if he wanted to get an official, he could solicit the support of the other owners and they'd back him, figuring they might want the favor returned someday. As it developed, Sid worked just a couple of playoff games that year, and they forced him to work solely as supervisor from then on.

Walter Kennedy succeeded Podoloff as commissioner in the 1963–64 season, and Sid continued to have problems. Kennedy finally shoved him out in 1966. It seems like such a crime that a man who dedicated his life to basketball, just loved the NBA, could be treated so shabbily. When I saw what happened to Jocko and to Sid, I knew there was no security nor real respect for a man just because he had courage and integrity. Still, I guess some of us never learn that to back down and not fight the system is the best way to avoid trouble. It just never quite works that way for some people—some people like me.

I had a game with the Hawks and 76ers in Memphis, where St. Louis used to play some of their games before the ABA came along. The game was televised back to the Philly area and Yvonne was watching. There was a play at the very end of the game with St. Louis behind by 1. Richie Guerin stole the ball for the Hawks and went in for the winning basket, but I called him for palming the ball and wiped out the shot. Philly got the ball back and held on for the win. As I was going by the scorer's table after the game, Irv Gack, who was the assistant general manager of the Hawks and also ran the 24-second clock, yelled something at me. I didn't understand it and asked him to repeat it.

"You're a gutless bastard," he said.

With that I leaped over the table, grabbed him around the neck, and wrestled him to the floor. Fans poured down around us and there was all kinds of commotion. I didn't realize it, but all this was going out over the TV coverage. The announcer was saying, "It looks like referee Earl Strom is involved in some kind of a problem over there, but our time is up. We'll see you next Sunday on the *NBA Game of the Week.*" As the picture is just about to go off, here comes Wilt Chamberlain stepping over the table and grabbing me.

Well, poor Yvonne didn't know if Wilt was coming to squash me or what. And the picture cut away.

What it was in fact was Wilt coming to my aid. He picked me up and carried me clear across the court and out of trouble. He set me down and said, "You owe me one, Earl."

That was that. I decided to call home as I usually do after a game and the operator said, "Will you accept a collect call from Earl Strom in Memphis?" Before she could finish, my wife was yelling, "Will I!" and before I could even tell her I was healthy and everything was cool, she started in on me for what a fool I was to go looking for trouble, and what right did I have to go worrying my family like that, and she went on for fifteen minutes. She was absolutely right, of course.

The next day I called Kennedy and told him my side of the story, figuring Kerner and Gack would already have gotten in their side. Kennedy seemed pretty calm about it and I didn't have much thought about any problems. The next day Sid called and said he was going to fine me a couple of ball games for what I had done. I told him I expected that and asked which games I was being pulled off. He said I was coming off the St. Louis game I had there the next week.

There was a policy, and still is to some degree, that they try to keep officials out of spots or away from teams they've had a recent problem with. It makes sense not to go inviting trouble. But Sid always challenged the owners and tried to send guys right back into the hot spot. He didn't want anyone telling him what to do or who should be working where. But in this case the orders were coming from Kennedy.

I told Sid if they took me off the St. Louis assignment, they could have my resignation. Kerner wasn't going to have his way with me. I called Kennedy and we went back and forth before he finally relented and said I could go back into St. Louis. Kerner wasn't too happy about it and he really got after me during the game. He would sit in the front row with his lawyer and accountant and family and they'd all come down pretty hard. His mother kept yelling in Yiddish. I couldn't control myself and I yelled back once in a while, but though Kerner said he'd have my job he never got it.

Kerner kept Mendy out of St. Louis for over a month after they had a run-in. Kerner was constantly writing the league office to complain about officials. And his words, as you can see, didn't go unheeded. He really did a number on Jim Duffy, a guy I regarded as one of the better officials in the league when I broke in. In the 1961 playoffs, St. Louis was playing the Los Angeles Lakers in the Western Conference finals. Mendy and I had been working the Eastern finals between Boston and Philadelphia, while Duffy and Sid worked the Lakers-Hawks series. They worked the first six ball games, but when the seventh game came around, the Lakers decided they didn't want Duffy to work it.

It seems that Duffy was about to be fired the year before and Kerner was behind the move. Podoloff, realizing the league couldn't afford to let a good man go, decided to keep him on. Well, Kerner was shrewd enough to know he might as well be in the good graces of the guy if he was going to be in the league, so during the exhibition season he threw a Jim Duffy Night in St. Louis. This was unheard of for an official—and the guy wasn't even retiring. They showered him with gifts and really turned it on.

This didn't go over very well with the other owners around the league, and when it came down to that seventh and deciding game against Los Angeles, the Lakers decided not to test how appreciative Duffy might have been to Kerner. So Podoloff removed Duffy from the seventh game. With this, Sid went through the roof and refused to work the game. They called in Mendy and me and we worked it without a hitch, which is almost always the case; if there are a lot of complaints about officials and they're taken off the game, the replacements are usually given no heat from the players and coaches. They don't want to make it look as if they can't get along with anybody.

The following year they fired Duffy. The pressure had finally gotten to him. He was one of the best, but in the end he lost the edge. There were some grounds for criticism of his work. I remember one night I had a game with him and we had a really tough first half. When I got to the locker room during the intermission, he never showed up. I went out for the second half and he was up in the stands. He sold cars in addition to refereeing, and he was up there making some deals. I ended up working the second half by myself.

Kerner was really a tough customer. One time when Boston was playing in St. Louis, Cousy went over to Auerbach during warm-ups and told him that he thought one of the baskets was too low. Red went to the officials and complained. They brought out this pole that shows the exact ten-foot mark where the rim was supposed to be, and the rim was indeed too low. While they were all standing there looking up at the basket, Kerner came charging out onto the court; he was apparently just coming out to find out what was going on, but Red thought he was coming out to raise hell. When Kerner got within a couple steps of him, Red turned and punched him right in the mouth. They damn near had a riot before the game started.

When things finally quieted down, Kerner was still fuming, of course. He was looking for someone to unload on. He spotted Boston's radio announcer, Johnny Most, at his usual seat along press row. Kerner decided he wanted him removed from courtside. Most refused to move, so Kerner hauled off and slugged him. The way things were going that night, I wouldn't have wanted to be Johnny Most's dog when he got home.

The owners in those days were really something. You look at the money modern-day owners throw around for player salaries and you have to wonder about their sanity, but these guys were classics. Lester Harrison, who owned the Rochester Royals, was a case in point. If his team lost, the officials working the game would actually have to sprint back to their dressing room to get into the shower before Lester had the hot water shut off. It was rumored he was so cheap that he and his brother actually scalped tickets. I'm not kidding. When their teams were going good and a sellout was expected, Lester and his brother would supposedly hold back a bunch of tickets, then go out front just before the game and scalp them.

The owners were just like little boys who threw tantrums if they didn't get their way. St. Louis was at Los Angeles one night, and with the Lakers up by 1, Pettit took a shot at the buzzer. It didn't go in and everybody was celebrating for L.A. But I had called a foul and Pettit was to be on the line. He hit both free throws and St. Louis won. As Richie Powers and I were walking to the dressing room, everyone was giving us a lot of heat, naturally. When we got in the room, there was a knock on the door. It was Bob Short, owner of the Lakers, informing us that Richie and I would be going to New York to explain that call. He wanted the commissioner to hear us talk our way out of what he deemed a ridiculous call. I told him I wasn't one of his puppets and I didn't have to go anywhere to explain anything.

"You'll go," he warned me.

"Don't count on it," I told him. We shouted back and forth for a few minutes and he left. A few days later I got a call from Kennedy, and he informed me that Short had called him and explained that after viewing the films he was in error. He apologized. That was a very rare outcome to most of those types of hassles.

In 1966 the league seemed to conclude that the best way to avoid problems with their supervisors was to quit filling the job with tough-willed referees. Besides, the NBA had a very embarrassing problem. In the 1965–66 season, the Dolph Schayes–coached Philadelphia 76ers finally won the Eastern Division title, ending a nine-year reign by Boston. Dolph was named coach of the year. But after the Celtics roared back in the Eastern playoffs and eliminated Philadelphia in five games, Dolph was fired and Alex Hannum was hired to coach the team built around Wilt Chamberlain. The NBA hired Dolph, their fired coach of the year, to succeed Sid, who had been fired as supervisor of officials.

Dolph was regarded as one of the great forwards ever to play in the NBA. He was all-league half a dozen times, but he was a political pawn in this case. He wanted to implement a "let 'em play" player's approach to refereeing, but he really never got a chance to perform in the role. Eddie Gottlieb once said, "Referees are referees and we can get them anywhere . . . we can take guys off the street . . . we can take the sweepers out of the stands and they could become referees." They looked at us as necessary evils and didn't seem to realize that the problems the league had with low respect for officials was of their own making.

It was sad how they treated Schayes. At the same time they hired Dolph, they made Mendy referee-in-chief, and he handled all matters pertaining to mechanics, techniques, and rule interpretations. Norm Drucker and I were assigned as crew chiefs. The staff was divided in half, and each of us was in charge of scouting our crew, rating the referees, and developing their skills, in addition to working our schedule of games.

Kennedy used to ridicule Dolph, make life miserable for him. Just to show what kind of shabby support he had, there was an incident that occurred when Dolph asked me to go to San Diego to run a clinic for young referees. They were supposed to be sending the twelve best officials from around the country. I was to come up with some candidates for our staff. I told Dolph that I couldn't possibly go away for a week in the summer without my wife; I saw her little enough as it was during the winter. I told him I wasn't in a position financially to take her on my own. Dolph said, "Go ahead and take her and we'll see that her expenses are paid." So I did. A week later I got a call from Kennedy.

"Earl, what's the idea of charging your wife's trip to the league?"

"Wait a minute, Walter. I thought it was with your approval that Dolph told me to do this. I don't want Dolph in any trouble, but he told me to take her and keep track of her expenses."

"Well, Dolph's an idiot and he had no right to do this, and he's going to catch hell but good."

I couldn't believe he would run down my supervisor that way in front of me. He told me to combine the expenses and turn them in on one report. Actually, I was surprised he was making such a big deal about the expenses since they had

always been good to me that way. For instance, if I had a
game in Cincinnati on a Sunday night, they would let me fly
farther west to Chicago, then come back to Philly from there
because I couldn't get to work Monday morning on any
direct connections out of Cincinnati. Though they were always good about expenses with me, Sid told me he once got
a letter from Podoloff telling him to quit staying in a hotel
that was costing $6 a night because there was one down the
street that was only $4.

The league had held at eight teams since the midfifties.
Fort Wayne had moved to Detroit and Rochester to Cincinnati the year I entered the NBA, 1957–58. The next year
Elgin Baylor joined the Lakers in Minneapolis, and the following year Wilt Chamberlain hooked up with the Philadelphia Warriors. The following season, 1960–61, the Lakers
threw away their snowshoes and left Minneapolis for Los
Angeles. That was also the year Oscar Robertson joined the
Cincinnati Royals and Jerry West came in with the Lakers.
It was a dramatic cast to add to the talent pool just as my
career was getting launched. The next season the league
added its first team since 1950, the Chicago Packers, and still
another noteworthy name entered the show as they picked
up rookie Walt Bellamy. John Havlicek came in for the
1962–63 season, and Philadelphia became the San Francisco
Warriors. The next year Syracuse moved to Philadelphia to
become the 76ers, Chicago became the Baltimore Bullets,
and Walter Kennedy replaced Maurice Podoloff as commissioner.

This marked a significant infusion of talent that would
elevate the level of play. But it was still a slam-bang world.
Al Attles was very competitive, but also very quiet as a
player with the Warriors. Still, he had this reputation as a
wild man for a fight he had one night when he and Wilt were
playing for Philly. Bob Ferry was playing for Detroit and
somehow bumped or elbowed Wilt. I don't know if it was
intentional or not, but it sort of stunned Wilt. Wilt turned
around, but didn't know who had done it. Attles saw it and
took out after Ferry, who outweighed him by about fifty

pounds. Attles picked up Ferry and threw him to the floor and proceeded to pound the hell out of him. Everybody was trying to get him off. Finally, Wilt went over and was the only one who could get him up. "I think he's had enough, Al," Wilt said as he lifted Attles up. Ferry said he'd never had so many punches thrown at him. He wasn't sure they were coming from just one guy. That fight earned Attles the nickname Whirling Dervish, and whenever a fight would break out they'd say, "Grab the Whirling Dervish and don't let him get started."

I had a pretty good rapport with him and had him come up to Pottstown one time to do a little Chamber of Commerce bit as a favor to me. One night after that he was in a game in Chicago, playing then for San Francisco. We got into a little jawing just before the half, and he thought I was being smart-assed. "Don't talk to me like that," he said.

"Oh, all of a sudden I can't talk to you." We went back and forth as we were going down the steps to the dressing rooms, which are under the court in Chicago Stadium. Finally I said, "Aw, knock it off Al and stop being such a little boy." I meant he was being childish, but it had a deeper connotation to him. He started toward me. George Lee was the coach then and he and a couple players grabbed Attles. He was yelling, "Let me go. Let me go." I told them they were all going to get T's if they did and ducked into the locker room. People have said I was crazy for getting into fights and doing all kinds of freaky things, but I wasn't so crazy that I didn't know when to duck and run.

After I had been in the league half a dozen years, it developed that either Mendy or I had to be working every playoff game from the semis on through the finals. If a series came to a seventh game, we were both supposed to be there. This was really gratifying for me because it was a vote of confidence and it meant I'd be where the action was. In the pressure games, that was where everyone was really tested. That era was noted for great matchups and personalities, great rivalries, and much better team play. The individual had to be more complete in his skills. He had to be able to pass, set picks, rebound, and play defense as well as find the basket with regularity. There are more pure shooters now, in fact shooting percentages are dramatically improved over the past thirty years. But there was so much better ball movement when I came in. It was cut and bump and pass and scramble.

They depended more on pattern play and set offense. Hitting the open man, setting screens. It was cut and pass, cut and pass, until someone shook open. There was much less one-on-one play then, and with all the missed shots, there was so much more hammering on the boards. They played man-to-man defense and you played your man. If the ball was lying on the floor behind you, you might not see it because you'd be glued to your man. That's not a total exaggeration.

My wife knew basketball and followed it back then. She used to say the only team she would ever pay to watch was Syracuse because they played such beautiful pattern basketball. They all did to some degree, except Boston once Russell arrived because they could dominate the boards and beat you with their fast break.

Things were evolving in the NBA. There was more glamour among the stars, bigger crowds, more media attention. Still, the wars were fought in the trenches and some fans still measured their evening by what they could get on the referees. I was working a Boston-Philly game in Convention Hall. This was right in the middle years of what was about a ten-year rivalry between these two teams, and the fans came with blood in their eyes whenever they met. So it kind of surprised me when the ball rolled out of bounds just before the half and a fan got up, picked up the ball, and walked it over to me. I thought, jeez, that's a nice gesture.

"Here, you fuckhead," he said to me as he handed me the ball.

I looked at him and I was thinking, you can't do that to me. I looked around and nobody else heard him so there weren't any cops coming over or anything like that. I was mad, but there was nothing I could do. I couldn't put it away. I was getting hotter and hotter as time went along. Just before the half the ball was rolling toward him again. Mendy started after it. I said, "I'll get it." I went over and the guy started to get out of his seat to go for the ball again. I said, "Maybe you'd like to come over in the back of the stands and repeat what you just said."

"I'm not going anywhere with you, you fucker."

With that I just blew. I grabbed him and pulled him out of his seat and hit him. I saw his glasses go flying and I realized that was a mistake, hitting a guy with his glasses on. But now all his buddies jumped on top of me. I was lying on top of this guy and all these guys were on top of me. I was thinking, well, so long world. I kept banging away on him and guys kept banging away on me. Then I felt the load getting off my back. Somebody grabbed me and lifted me up. I turned around and it was Tom Heinsohn. The other Boston players were grabbing fans and throwing them aside, and Russell had this guy whom I'd hit. He had his arm around the guy's neck and was holding him so tightly the guy's eyes looked as if they're going to pop right out of his face. Red was standing there with this mock look of disgust on his face, shaking his head. "See, here we are again, Strom. You start it and we gotta finish it."

That turned out to be true on a few occasions, particularly with the Celtics. But it was a general practice that the visiting team would help the officials when there was a problem, like getting off the court after a tough game. It's harder for the hometown players to take on fans to protect the referee, whereas the visitors couldn't care less if they have to hit some fan. I was going off the floor one time in Syracuse where we had to go under this walkway in the stands. Gene Conley of the Celtics was behind me. He was about 6'9". Some guy reached down from the walkway and swung at me and missed. I didn't even know it. I heard this smack and turned around to see the guy slowly sinking into his seat. Conley wiped his hand off on his shirt and just kept on coming. He didn't even look around.

The day after the battle with the fan in Philly, it was

pictured in the papers. The guy's name was Sid Gurschkou; they identified him as a thirty-five-year-old mechanic. There were quotes from each of us. I had told reporters: "I think he swung first." He said, "I was sitting where I sit every game. Naturally I rib them the whole game. I can heckle all I want to. I just heckled the heck out of him. I called him every name under the sun, like we all do. He walked over and hauled off and I let him have it. I got news for you; if Russell hadn't gotten hold of me . . ." Gurschkou was going to file charges, but Philly owner Eddie Gottlieb talked him out of it.

A couple weeks later I was walking through the Philadelphia airport when, lo and behold, who comes walking toward me but Mr. Gurschkou. He walked up to me. I didn't know whether we were going to start in again or what, but he held out his hand as if we were long-lost friends. "Hi, Earl, remember me? I'm the guy you punched in that game. Sorry for what happened. When I go to games, I lose control of myself." I told him I believed him.

This gets even more bizarre. A dozen years later Yvonne and I were at a Temple–Penn State football game. Yvonne was watching a confrontation develop between some fans several rows in front of us. A man and his son were being squeezed together so the poor kid could hardly sit down. Two couples were trying to fit into one set of seats. It was Gurschkou who was getting squeezed along with his son, and he was trying to make the extra couple show their tickets. They wouldn't cooperate. Gurschkou stood up and started getting hotter. Seeing us sitting a couple rows above him, he started screaming, "Look, don't get me mad. I'm an absolute wild man when I get mad." He pointed at us. "Tell 'em, Earl. Tell 'em how crazy I am when I get mad." I yelled back, "You better listen to him. He's nuts." The people took off. I started wondering if I was ever going to be done with this guy.

Not all the abuse was lethal. In some cases it was all I could do to keep from cracking up on the court. Archie Dees served me one of those zingers. He came into the league as a superstar out of Indiana. Drafted by the Cincinnati Royals, he was about 6'11", all-American, figured to be a big star. Well, he didn't get off to a good start. This one night the Royals were going to showcase him in hopes they could peddle him in a trade. But every time he touched the ball I had to call him for something—palming the ball, three seconds, walking. He was just so uptight. After he'd had four or five violations called on him, he ran alongside me going down the court and said, "Earl, look at me."

"Yeah, Arch, what's the matter?"

"Does my stomach look big to you?"

"No, I don't think it looks big, Arch. Why?"

"Well, you're giving me such a screwing out here, Earl, I just thought maybe I was starting to show."

chapter 7

THE ABA AND FARTHER AWAY

On July 14, 1969, NBA Commissioner Walter Kennedy wrote a note to me expressing his regrets that he would not be able to attend a testimonial dinner being held for me in Pottstown. He had a long-standing family commitment, but explained:

"I greatly regret that I will not be able to be with you to share what surely will be a very delightful evening. I especially regret not being there because I would like to tell your friends of the great regard I have for you, not only as an outstanding professional basketball official, but as a very fine person as well. I know of no one who is more dedicated to his work or more cooperative with those [with] whom he is associated. Those qualities, plus the ability you have as an official, combine with other qualities to make you the outstanding man that you are. Don't let these nice words motivate you towards asking for a raise! Please extend my warmest personal regards to your wife and family. I know that the night of Saturday, July 19, 1969, will be a very memorable one for you."

The occasion that prompted this note was billed as a celebration for "Pottstown's Own TV Personality." It was going to be held at the famous Sunnybrook Ballroom of big-band fame. I guess some of my friends in town thought I was big time because I was in the papers and on TV during coverage of NBA games. The fact that I was usually getting screamed at by some maniac player or coach didn't matter to them. It was a flattering milestone for me. At the age of forty-one, I had been in the league a dozen years and was considered sort of a local celebrity. It was a big night for me, but Neil Armstrong kind of stole my thunder when he became the first man to walk on the moon the next day.

Seventeen days later, Kennedy sent me a letter outlining my contract for the 1969–70 season:

August 5, 1969

Dear Earl:

This will serve as a letter of agreement between the National Basketball Association and you to formalize a verbal understanding.

Since you have previously served as an official for the NBA and if you commit no misconduct during the season, then this engagement is for officiating a full schedule of 82 games to be selected by the NBA during the 1969–70 season, for which you will be paid $16,000. The NBA reserves the right to assign more games to you, in which event you will be paid $190 for each game over 82.

You will, of course, be reimbursed expenses incurred except that, on trips to the east or west coast, reimbursement will be on the basis of excursion rates whenever excursion rates are available.

I hope you have a good season.

Sincerely,
Walter Kennedy

This was the first time I had been offered a salary contract, as opposed to per-game arrangements. This also marked an increase of $2,000 over my contract for the previous season, a jump much higher than the five-to-ten-dollar-per-game raises that had been customary since I came into the league.

It seemed the bidding war that was heating up between the ABA and the NBA was having the slightest of influences on even us lowly referees. Still, there was no pension plan, no family hospitalization plan, no long-term disability plan. Those were of importance to me as Yvonne and I raised five kids. That was why I was still working at General Electric in Philadelphia, where I was making about $12,000 then. That was why I had been at least casually interested when representatives of the ABA—which had been launched in the 1967–68 season—started making some curious noises that summer.

It surprised a lot of basketball people that the ABA had survived its first two seasons and was intensifying its war for talent. The NBA had landed Lew Alcindor, but there were rumors flying that such NBA stars as Billy Cunningham, Dave Bing, Zelmo Beaty, Luke Jackson, and Wally Jones were going to jump. The ABA really put everyone into orbit when they committed the unpardonable sin of signing an underclassman, Spencer Haywood of Detroit University.

It might have been Sid Borgia, who was then supervisor of the ABA referees, who first came up with the idea. He knew the influence good officials have on the quality of play at the pro level, and he knew the NBA staff wasn't very deep. Sid always loved the game so much, he just couldn't put up with the people who ran it. He was fired as supervisor of ABA officials at the end of the 1969 season, but I'm pretty sure he planted the idea that the ABA should go after the top NBA referees. He knew Mendy was untouchable because of his ties with NBA management, but he also knew the other four top officials were approachable, or at least worth talking to. They included John Vanak, Norm Drucker, Joe Gushue, and me. With only eight full-time referees in the NBA at that time, to steal the four of us would be a heavy blow for the ABA to land.

Norm had a friend named Ralph Dolgoff, an investment broker who was helping to lure players to the ABA. He was forming what was called the Dolgoff Plan with huge sums of money invested in players' names with big returns guaranteed. I think it was a sincere thing. Dolgoff got in touch with the four of us that summer.

They wanted to sit down and talk, and we all felt, what the hell, it wouldn't hurt to listen. We met with Jim Gardner, then acting as ABA commissioner while also owning the Carolina Cougars, and Earl Foreman, who owned the Washington franchise. We went to this meeting in Washington, D.C., figuring we would make some outlandish demands and they'd most likely say forget it. We wanted a $25,000 bonus for each of us to jump. We also insisted on a pension plan. We gave them some more outlandish figures, like I said I would have had $11,000–12,000 in the NBA pension pool. We wanted a health insurance plan for our families. Each guy came up with his own figures. Norm and I asked for more because we had more experience than the other two. I asked for a $25,000-a-year salary, which came out to a little over $300 a game. Kennedy's offer for the upcoming season had worked out to just under $200 a game. I wanted a guarantee of twelve games in the playoffs at $500 each for another $6,000. We gave our demands to Gardner and he said, "Well, that doesn't look too bad. We'll take it back to the committee and decide."

Figuring the insurance plans and everything, my whole package came to about $150,000 for three years. That was easily double what I was looking at in the NBA, and they didn't have any of the fringe benefits of health insurance and pension plans—although they kept saying every year they were going to come up with something.

We heard back from the ABA—and they accepted our demands. I called the other guys and we all had the same thought: "Wow, these guys are serious." I figured it was time to talk to Kennedy and see what we could do about upgrading our situation in the NBA. I called him:

"I suppose you know there are four of us being approached by the ABA, and I would like to come over and talk to you."

"What are they offering you?" he asked.

I told him. He said, "No way. Nobody pays referees that kind of money anywhere."

"Walter, we sat down with them and discussed this. They told us they are going to give this to us. Now I don't expect the NBA to come up with that much money, but if you could show us in good faith that you are considering improving the referees' position, that's all we're asking. I don't want to jump. But if I have to, I will."

He said he would get back to me. But he didn't, and the ABA was starting to put the pressure on us to find out what we were going to do. Finally, I called Kennedy again and said, "Look, they're going to have a meeting. They're going to have a big press conference to sign us. Is there any chance I can get in to see you?"

"Well, you're coming over for that meeting, so stop in before then and I'll talk to you." I was upset. He still didn't appreciate the fact that we were serious about this. On the day of the scheduled press conference Norm and I went up to the NBA office in New York City. It was about ten A.M. Walter wasn't there; he was at a meeting with Gardner discussing merger possibilities. Finally, he came into the office, in a huff. The pressure of the merger talks was working on his mind. We weren't in the best of moods since we had been waiting there half the morning.

He said, "What the hell are you guys doing here?"

We said, "Good morning."

"Good morning. I can't talk to you right now. But wait." And he went into his office. He took Carl Scheer, then deputy commissioner, in with him. Carl came back out and said, "Look, fellas, Walter's very busy. He's upset and he doesn't have time to talk to you. But he wants to talk to you later."

"We're running out of time," we pleaded. We were supposed to meet the ABA people at one P.M. Scheer took us into his office and we told him what the ABA was offering, just as I had outlined to Kennedy earlier on the phone. Scheer said, "I'm telling you one thing right now, fellas, Walter is not ready to offer you that kind of proposition."

I was getting hot. I said, "Now wait a minute. I told him we didn't expect him to match it dollar for dollar. But if he could just show some sign of acknowledgment of what we're trying to gain for our careers, for the opportunity we have here. Just a raise, take care of the pension plan or some hospitalization or put together some protection for our families. We don't want to jump, but if we're forced to, we will. And it really bothers me that he doesn't think this is important enough to talk to us."

"Well, I'm sorry, he's just so tied up. Maybe you guys could come back at three o'clock. Maybe we could discuss this then. But I'm telling you, he's not going to meet those prices."

I was really upset that Kennedy wouldn't even come out and talk to us. I thought I had a good rapport with him. I know I did. We were close. I was his fair-haired boy. I couldn't understand what was coming down on us, but we were running out of time. As we headed out the door, Scheer said, "Are you going to come back at three?"

"We'll think about it."

The NBA office was in the Empire State Building. We came out of there and went over to the Americana where the ABA group was. Shelly Bendit, our attorney, and the four of us—Gushue, Vanak, Drucker, and I—sat down and talked it over. We had the feeling the NBA didn't have any appreciation for us. Didn't even have the courtesy to discuss the matter with us. Shelly said we were crazy not to go for what the ABA was offering. Gushue had come into the meeting with a big money bag, dollar signs all over it. He said, "Let's let 'em fill it up."

There were some ABA owners and front office people at the meeting, and some of them made some pretty smart-ass remarks. I started thinking to myself, "These guys are just throwing us a bone and a buck, but they don't give a shit about referees either." One guy said, "No matter how much you guys are making, you're still necessary evils, and don't forget you're just merger bait as far as we're concerned." Gardner just glared at the guy. We were peeved at the NBA and wondering what kind of people these guys were. It wasn't a real comfortable feeling.

They laid the four ABA contracts out on a table. Everything we asked for was down on paper. We sat down, the four of us. We looked at each other. "Looks like we have no choice," I said, half wishing someone would think of a choice in a hurry. "Walter's giving us the cold shoulder and here's the moon right there waiting to be signed up." We all nodded. So we did it.

That evening we went out to dinner. Shelly was sitting across from Jim Gardner. Gardner wanted Luke Jackson, who was with the 76ers. Shelly took out a book of matches and wrote a figure on it. He slid it across the table to Gardner's lawyer. This was the price tag for delivering Jackson to the ABA. Gardner and his lawyer went out to the men's room; when they returned, they said, "Okay, we're buying." The next day Jackson went to North Carolina to sign a contract with the Cougars. That was the way things were being done then. The ABA had the money and they meant business.

After dinner the four of us went over to Drucker's place on Long Island. Mendy called. He wanted know what we had done. "We did it," I told him.

"Oh, Christ. I've been trying to get you guys all day. Carl, Walter, and I were prepared to offer you guys the greatest contract in the history of pro basketball," Mendy said.

"Don't give me that crap. You guys had three weeks to do that. Carl said there was no way we could get anywhere near what the ABA was offering, and Kennedy wouldn't even give us the courtesy of sitting down and talking with us. He treated us like dirt."

"Jesus, I can't believe this. We had this deal all worked out."

"It's a little late to be telling us that now. Where the hell were you at eleven o'clock this morning? Where was Walter? He snubbed us."

"God, this is awful. I wish you had gotten in touch. I was really working on it." Mendy was really upset.

"Look, Mendy, we're close friends and I'm not going to call you a liar. But there was plenty of time for the NBA to come up with something, and they didn't. So it's done."

I got off the phone and the other guys had been listening. We started looking at each other like, "What have we done, boys?" I didn't sleep ten minutes all night. I'd get up and go to the bathroom and bump into one of the other guys. I'd start pacing around the place and bump into someone else pacing around. None of us slept a wink. I felt sick. We all were so attached to the NBA, the people and the places. I guess none of us really wanted it to come to this. But I told myself, "You did it. You didn't have any choice the way the NBA reacted, and this is your life for the next three years." I still had my job at GE. I was in great shape financially. And surely a merger couldn't be more than a year away, maybe two at the most.

Despite the pep talk, I wasn't in the greatest of moods the next day when they had a press conference at the New Yorker to announce the signings. The press was running around asking everybody the significance of this and that, and the TV cameras were flashing around. Howard Cosell came marching in with his entourage of cameramen and assistants. He wasn't such a big wheel yet, but he thought he was pretty big stuff. He was a close friend of Kennedy's. He interviewed Norm, who was going to be succeeding Sid Borgia as supervisor of officials, and then he came over to me.

"Earl, why did you do it?"

"For money."

"Don't you have any loyalty? After twelve years, doesn't that mean anything to you?" He was pitching me in this sanctimonious voice.

"Howard, if CBS came up and offered you twice what you're making for ABC, wouldn't you consider it?"

"Well, I'd have to give it a lot of consideration."

"Don't you think I gave this a lot of thought? Don't you think I tried to work something out with Kennedy?"

He looked at me with this condescending expression on his

face and said, "Well, I hope so for your sake. I hope it works out for your sake, but I just can't understand your kind." And he walked away. I haven't had any use for the guy since then.

Or as Muhammad Ali would one day say of Cosell, "Sometimes I wish I was a dog and Howard was a tree."

When I got back to Pottstown, I received a telegram from Kennedy. It read in part: "I was shocked to learn that you had entered into an agreement with another organization without giving me the courtesy of discussing the situation with you as was agreed upon. We had worked out a five-year contract that the NBA was prepared to offer you that in our opinion would have been the best contract ever offered to an official in any sport. . . . If the price we have to pay for signing Lew Alcindor is the loss of four officials, I guess that is the price we have to pay." Kennedy was furious. He went on to call our actions rude, discourteous, and unbelievable.

He came out with a statement that included, "Who needs them anyway. Nobody ever paid a nickel to watch a referee." What he was ignoring is the fact that the quality of the show people pay a lot more than a nickel to see depends a great deal on the ability of referees. I found out later from Mendy and Eddie Gottlieb that when the league learned we were contemplating jumping, Kennedy was given carte blanche to keep us there. Some of the owners wanted Kennedy's scalp for letting us get away. I don't know what his motives were in not telling us, except possibly he was trying to be a big man and call our bluff so he could go back to the owners and say he was able to keep us from jumping and it didn't even cost much extra at that. I was really upset with the statements he came out with. He said we had positively promised to call him back that afternoon and how he had this great package all ready for us.

As soon as we jumped, the NBA went to contract salaries for all its regular officials. Salaries jumped tremendously. They didn't want to lose any more guys to the ABA. The core of the staff was gone, and a lot of guys who really weren't all that experienced moved up to the top rung. They started putting together a medical and pension plan, and they started a monthly expense program to replace out-of-pocket payments. As Norm said, "When we jumped, we did a hell of a favor for the NBA officials. They all got raises."

No one benefited more from our jumping than Richie Powers. Our departure actually gave him a new lease on life in the NBA. He had sat out the year before we jumped. He half quit and half got fired. Before we made the move to jump he had written Kennedy asking to come back into the NBA. Kennedy took the letter to Scheer and said, "Here, you answer this. I don't want the SOB back." So he was out. He had always been trying to get into major league baseball as an umpire, but he didn't make it because he was too short. He incensed a lot of guys over the years by always making comments about "going to the big time" to work baseball.

After we jumped, Norm got a call from Richie saying he wanted to join us in the ABA. Norm asked what I thought. I told him, "Hey, the guy's a great referee when he isn't pulling some crazy stunt. We'd have a great staff with him and some of the younger guys. Sure, grab him."

Norm called Richie and told him they'd take him. He got him a thousand-dollar bonus and everything. It wasn't as much as we had gotten, but he didn't have a very good bargaining position then. Norm and I had an exhibition game in New Jersey and Richie came up. We got together and talked it all out, gave him a rule book and official's manual, and he was ready to sign up. Mendy heard about this and went to Kennedy. He told him, "Hey, as bad off as we are for referees, we've got to have him. I don't care how eccentric he is. We can't afford to let him go to the ABA." So Kennedy backed down and Richie signed with the NBA for a ton of money. He made out like a bandit, and the NBA wasn't even going to take him back until the ABA went after him. Tell me that feud between the leagues didn't change the status of a lot of people.

Unfortunately, it sure changed the status of my morale. My frame of mind went the way of a basketball on a missed dunk. From the three-point shot to the red, white, and blue basketball to the red-and-white-striped referee's shirt, I was confronted with change. I didn't handle it well at all.

The first game I worked was an exhibition between the Pittsburgh Pipers and the New York Nets in a high school gym in north Jersey. There were no superstars and there were no dominating centers. It was funny how wild and loose play was as a result. The first shot went up and ten guys went to the boards. And ten guys went to the deck. Vanak and I both blew our whistles and looked at each other. Who the hell were we going to call the foul on? Take a pick. Everyone in the league crashed the boards, guards and forwards alike. Everyone drove the lane because it was so open without big centers around to clog things up. Plus, you had the three-point perimeter to keep things opened up. When they set picks, they ran over people. It was a real rodeo.

I remember a column Jim Murray of the *Los Angeles Times* wrote. He has always been great with the hyperbole, but he wasn't exaggerating much, I'm afraid: "In the ABA, basketball is not so much a game as a dock fight with backboards. . . . If they did on a street corner what they do under the basket, someone would call the cops. . . . They call a two-shot foul only after rigor mortis has set in. . . . In the rival NBA the refs have a rule—'No harm, no foul.' It's 'No death, no foul' in the ABA."

I sank into a terrible depression. Instead of Madison Square Garden with 19,500 or Chicago Stadium with 20,000 screaming fans, I was working in front of a few hundred onlookers rattling around in high school gyms or other small city arenas. Instead of the great feuds between Boston and Philadelphia and the fans ready to riot, I had collapsing backboards, players quitting in the middle of games. If a decent crowd was assembled, it was usually to watch the second half of a doubleheader—between a couple of major college teams.

Granted, arenas in the NBA weren't as slick as they would later become, but even then the facilities in the ABA were bleak by comparison. Early in that first season, I was working a game on Long Island. The Nets were playing in this old Quonset-type building, kind of like a circus tent. They had this tiny little dressing room. The court was set on a dirt floor, and the fans would kick dirt up onto the court from their seats. The lighting was so bad Abe Lincoln couldn't have read by it, and they had this scratchy old record to play the national anthem. I was out there mopping up rain puddles from leaks in the roof, and Carl Braun, who used to coach the Knicks, walked by, kind of shrugged his shoulders, and asked me, "Earl, what the hell are you doing here?"

My frame of mind went from bad to pitiful. I think I blew the whistle three times in the first half. I just couldn't get into it. Working a game is the same as being an entertainer in your reactions to a crowd. If there's no one out there, who the hell cares what you do? That's not the right attitude to have, of course; it's not fair to the players or the coaches. But that's what was happening in my head then. I always fed off the crowds. The tension and the energy the fans created was what made it feel the way it did to work big games in the NBA. That's why I always loved the clashes between big rivals, the games up at Syracuse, the playoffs. People really got cranked up, and I had been right in the middle of it.

I never was as happy as when I was refereeing. I loved the challenges and the action. I always wanted the games to go on forever. I really hated to see a good, tight game come to an end. That's why I put up with the strain of working two jobs and getting back and forth all those years so that I could referee. I lived for it.

Now that I was in the ABA, I found myself just totally down. I was having trouble getting back and forth to work because the ABA cities were smaller and it was harder to make plane connections. The people at GE were already upset that I didn't have the same prestige as when I was in the NBA, and now I was missing days at work and getting in late because of travel problems. For the first time in my life I couldn't wait for the final horn to blow. Get me out of here.

I had anticipated that the ABA would be an inferior product and that the drama of the NBA would be sacrificed in the move. But I didn't think it would affect me as much as it did. I figured the money would compensate for any lack of luster. Even though the final move had been triggered by the emotions of being ignored by the NBA, I thought I was looking at the full picture of the ABA and would be able to accept it for what it was. My ego proved me wrong. I should have been able to cope. The rational mind said, just do your job. But I guess there are people out there every day who can't bring themselves to do what seems obvious and rational. I sure couldn't at that time.

I became a walking nervous breakdown. The depression just kept building. I wasn't proud of the job I was doing. These guys were pros, and even though overall they might not have matched up with the NBA, they deserved the best in officiating. I was being paid to give them my best and I was shortchanging them. I tried, but I just couldn't get with it. As I went along and I saw all these dumpy little arenas and the ragged style of play and the horseshit travel and all the rest of it—teams folding and players getting traded seemingly in the middle of games—I just couldn't take it. I called Carl Scheer and asked him if he could get me out of the contract and back into the NBA. Would Kennedy take me back?

Scheer got back to me and said Kennedy told him, "Of course I'd take him back. But first he's got to get out of that contract." I called my attorney and told him I wanted out of my ABA contract. I had hung on to the GE job for added security, so I could still survive with less from the NBA. I was willing to give back the $25,000 bonus and everything else it took. My attorney called Gardner's attorney, who said there was no way I was getting out of that contract. I was beside myself. I was like a zombie out on the court. Some of the other officials were bothered by the same things that got to me, but they were able to be bigger men about it. I just got worse and worse as the season went along. It was a sad first year, and as much as I would like to forget it, I will never be able to because I didn't earn my way after somebody really invested in me.

I was bothered by the loyalty issue. I had been close to Kennedy, and even though he had ticked me off when he wouldn't talk, I felt as though I had somehow betrayed him. And with Mendy, I guess I felt I had somehow tossed something in his face. I didn't know exactly what, but it just felt as though I had betrayed my own character. I had never been caught up in counting my bucks. For years I never knew nor cared what we had in savings, as long as Yvonne had enough to pay all the bills. I did figure that in jumping leagues I was giving some additional security and material comfort to my family. I hadn't given my wife and kids the time and attention, but this extra money seemed as if it were a way of giving them what I could. Yvonne had encouraged me to jump. She told me later that she figured it might have been a way she could see if I really loved my family more than I loved the NBA. There was a lot of resentment that had built up in her over the years, all the time gone while she was forced to raise the family on her own. She used to get on me to at least ask for the main holidays off, to at least pull rank after I'd been in the league awhile and ask for Christmas off. But I'd usually leave after we'd opened presents, heading out on the train to Philly or New York to work a game that afternoon or evening.

Yvonne was worried and upset that I was falling apart. She would really lay into me, saying things like, "Who the hell do you think you are? Earl Strom the Almighty? You're not indispensable in this field. Do you think that just because you had done such a great job for so many years that everybody was going to bow down and make sure everything went your way? Doesn't it show that no one gives a damn whether you referee or not? You may be good, but they can live without you." She was angry. I was dragging the whole family down. I didn't want to get out of bed. I didn't want to be around any of our friends. We'd sit around the kitchen and talk and talk and talk. Sometimes I'd be pretty calm and able to analyze things. Other times I'd just completely fold up and we'd sit there and cry together. It seemed as if I were going to spend the signing bonus on phone calls to Norm. "Oh, Norm,

I can't go. I just can't get with it. What am I going to do?"
The guys were supportive, but I remember Vanak telling
me, "Earl, I don't understand how you can be so tough on
the court and so weak off of it."

Norm gave me the all-star game in hopes that it would
shake me loose and get me rolling again. My son Jonathan
was in the hospital with pneumonia. Obviously I should have
stayed home, but I went, figuring by going I'd prove to
myself that refereeing was all that mattered. That's how
convoluted things had gotten.

Yvonne was at her wits end. She got me to see a psychia-
trist. We discussed how I had been this basically shy person
who was very sensitive by nature, and how I really needed
to feel as though I were in control. When a referee gets
challenged from all sides, he's all the more dependent on
having control and being sure he's doing well. I needed the
big time to feel as if I were the best. When Yvonne told me
I'd have to move out to save the rest of the family, I remember saying, "Well, where am I going to go?" Finally, something clicked and I saw how I was acting like such a dumb
ass. I started to get with it again. But poor Yvonne finally
collapsed under the weight of it all. I had dumped so much
on her all those years, the resentment and frustration and all
just finally landed on her. We hung in there together and
things got better. She told me later that what turned her
around and helped her out of her depression was hearing me
on the phone one day tell Norm, "I can't referee tonight. My
wife needs me at home."

We were almost into the playoffs by this time. I was ready
to referee basketball again, to give it my best. At this time
I also took another big load off by getting rid of my job at GE.
They were going through some layoffs and were going to let
another guy in my office go. He needed the job, and I had
things going well enough financially that I could finally let
go of that security blanket. For the first time in thirteen
years of refereeing pro basketball, I could devote myself to
it without having to get back and forth to my day job. Instead
of having to work a game and dash for a train or plane,

catching my sleep on the lobby couch at GE or in an airport waiting room, I could go out and have a couple of belts, eat a nice steak, and laugh at all the crazy stuff coming down around me.

In nine years the ABA had seven commissioners: George Mikan, Jim Gardner, Jack Dolph, Robert Carlson, Mike Storen, Tedd Munchak, and Dave DeBusschere. In 1967, New Jersey had to forfeit its hopes for a playoff berth when its court was declared unplayable. In 1968 the Minnesota coach decked his owner just before the all-star game he was supposed to coach and lost his job. In 1970 the ABA obtained a TV package with CBS—for six games.

In 1971, Rick Barry said he didn't want his kids growing up with a Southern accent and forced the Virginia Squires to trade him to the New York Nets. That was the same year some nosy reporters got into commissioner Jack Dolph's briefcase before the all-star game and found that the ABA had Jim McDaniels and Howard Porter under contract while they were still in college. Their Western Kentucky and Villanova teams were forced to forfeit their Final Four NCAA finishes as a result. When McDaniels jumped from Carolina to Seattle, it was reported he did so because the steering wheel on the Caddy the Cougars had given him didn't tilt the right way. Charlie Scott jumped from Virginia to Phoenix, saying the ABA beds weren't big enough. In 1972, Julius Erving signed with Virginia after the Nets refused to sign an underclassman. That was the year Memphis and Pittsburgh played the bottom half of a doubleheader that featured an exhibition by Muhammad Ali as the opening act. Less than half the crowd of 5,000 stayed for the game.

In 1974 the ABA failed to sign Bill Walton, and New York won the first of two titles in the league's final three seasons. Erving averaged 27.4 points per game, George McGinnis 25.9. In 1975, Dan Issel and Artis Gilmore led Kentucky to the title. In 1976, Marvin Webster and David Thompson were rookies with Denver, which had also acquired Issel.

The Nuggets were upset by the Nets in the finals, and Erving took the final ABA scoring title with a 29.3 average.

Erving was, of course, the superstar of the league. His greatness had been obvious from the first time I laid eyes on him, during an exhibition game between the Squires and Kentucky. After that game I was coming back through the Philadelphia airport when I ran into the 76ers. I told them I had just seen the greatest player alive. One of the writers put that comment in the paper. Mike Storen, president of the Colonels, raised hell, saying I had no business promoting players. Jack Dolph fined me $50. I sent him $100. I said, "The first fifty dollars is for the fine and the second fifty dollars is because I'm tellin' ya' he *is* the greatest." I thought he'd take it as a joke and send back the other $50. He didn't.

Al Bianchi coached the Squires and maybe has to go down in history for frustration levels as he saw financial woes drive the team to deal away Erving, Charlie Scott, Barry and George Gervin. Pittsburgh can probably lay claim to the craziest of all the teams. That franchise was a total joke. One time I was flying with the team from Pittsburgh to North Carolina. The trainer walked by me and whispered, "Wait till you see this commotion. I had to wait until we took off before telling these guys we don't have any meal money for this trip." So he went up in front of the team and told them how they would have to eat at the hotel, charge the meals to their rooms, and the club would pick up the fare—if the hotel would accept the club's check. I thought they were going to throw the guy out at 29,000 feet. Many travel agencies and hotels refused to handle ABA teams after a while, so these guys shouldn't have been all that shocked. They were just upset because they couldn't pocket any of their per diem this way.

You remember how everyone made such a big deal about how zany the New York Mets were on the field when they first started out? Well, the Pipers and Condors lived like the Mets played. They had a league rule that a team could carry eleven or twelve players, but only ten traveled. Pittsburgh was playing some place about twenty-five miles out of town. It was considered a home game, but they were playing in this little high school gym. The eleventh man—I'm pretty sure it was Walt Szczerbiak—thought since the game wasn't at the Civic Arena, he wasn't supposed to go. He never showed up.

That same night, John Brisker, who was one of the league's top scorers and a real pugilistic sort, walked in while they were playing the national anthem. Mark Binstein was coaching the Condors then, and he didn't start Brisker because he had showed up late. They were playing Virginia, coached by Bianchi. Pittsburgh fell way behind and they put in Brisker midway through the quarter. The team was still going bad so Binstein decided to start a whole new team in the second quarter. As we were lining up for the jump, the trainer came over and said, "Earl, this is going to be very, very interesting because Brisker won't come out of the lineup." We were ready to go, except there were six Condors on the court.

Binstein was out there trying to get Brisker to come to the bench. The trainer was out there, too. Bianchi came out and tried to reason with him. Finally, after threatening he would have to be carried out of there, he left the game. But instead of going to the bench, he walked to the dressing room, showered, and went home. A couple other Condors saw this, got up, and left with him.

Jack McMahon coached the Pittsburgh team when it first became the Condors. He was a helluva good coach and fortunately, had a good sense of humor. He was holding practice one day when Brisker got into a pushing match with Walker Banks, who was regarded as something of a tough guy himself. Brisker walked off the court and McMahon asked him where he was going. "To the locker room to get my gun," Brisker hollered. With that, Banks took off in the other direction. "Where the hell are you going?" McMahon asked. "My heat's in the car," Banks yelled back. "I ain't facing him unarmed." That's when all the rest of the team went running out the door. McMahon didn't know whether to stay around and act as a peacemaker or make a run for it. Neither player came back so he never had to find out how brave he was. He did call off practice.

One night, Skeeter Swift of Memphis went running off the court in disgust at a no-call, saying, "If you're not going to give me any calls, Earl, I quit." He refused to come back onto the court, so I had to call a T on Memphis for having only four players on the floor.

Wendell Ladner only played a few seasons in the ABA, for Memphis, Carolina, Kentucky and then the Nets, before dying in a plane crash. He was a wild man on the court, truly a legend. He was about 6'6", a big tough kid. He was the only guy in the league whom John Brisker wouldn't fight. They say the night before he left to start his career in Memphis, he got into a fight with a couple of cops in the little Mississippi town where he lived. He got out early the next morning and stayed away until the end of the season when the town welcomed him back with a parade. A cop stepped up to him and handed him a summons. Wendell took it, signed it "Wendell Ladner, Number 33," and handed it back.

He was constantly diving into the stands after loose balls. One night he took out a water cooler, got all cut up. They stitched him up and back in he came. After the game a reporter said to Memphis coach Babe McCarthy, "Boy, he just doesn't know the meaning of the word 'quit,' does he?" Babe replied, "There are a lot of words Wendell doesn't know the meaning of."

Wendell loved to pound on Rick Barry. One night Barry called him a psycho. When Babe took Wendell out of the game, he asked the ball boy, "What's a 'psycho'?" The ball boy told him to forget it, it wasn't important. Wendell got upset and ordered the ball boy to go get a dictionary from one of the writers. He tried to look it up under C and S and was getting hotter all the while. Finally the ball boy found it and read it to him. Wendell leaped up off the bench, ran out onto the court, and punched Barry right on the button. I don't know if it's true that Barry said, "I told you!"

The Miami Floridians were pretty sad on the court and

had the worst home court in the league when they were playing in Dinner Key Auditorium. Bones McKinney was a Baptist minister who had coached at Wake Forest. He had been a great pro player; in fact, he had been all-league the first year of the Basketball Association of America playing for Auerbach in Washington. He was coaching the Carolina Cougars one night in Miami. Dinner Key Auditorium was a converted boathouse, only seated about a thousand, and was a dank, dingy place along the waterfront. As I stood next to Bones as this scratchy record played the national anthem, he leaned over to me and said, "Earl, I had a couple of belts earlier this evening, but tell me if you don't think that basket is sinking." Sure enough, the hydraulic system had failed on one of the basket supports and it was slowly sinking to the floor. "I'll give you ten-to-one it's on the floor by the time this record's over," he whispered. It took twenty minutes to get the basket up again, and during the delay Bones wandered over and said, "And I'll give you another ten-to-one the lights go out in this joint before we get out of here tonight." Sure enough, late in the first quarter the generator stopped and all the lights went out. Bones knew his way around the ABA and could have made himself some money that night if I hadn't learned to expect anything by then.

The Floridians always got off to a good start because the other team would be so busy looking at the ball girls in their bikinis, but eventually they'd fall behind. When they moved to Convention Hall, that was some improvement, except they used to shoot off fireworks whenever someone for Miami scored a three-point play. Some nights coming down to the wire it looked as if they were holding the Battle of the Bulge in there with all the smoke.

The best thing about the Floridians was these ball girls. Usually there were two of them, but sometimes there would be four. They wore jumpsuits over bikinis, and they'd come out and do a dance, then take off their jumpsuits to some strip-tease music. The place would be full of hoots and hollers. One night they held an ABA doubleheader in Madison Square Garden to try to get some attention for the league.

The press spent more time interviewing the ball girls than they did watching the game. They interviewed the girls on TV and asked them if they had any trouble with the players hustling them. They said, "No, the players behave themselves pretty much, but we get a lot of action from the referees." That went over real well on the home front.

Bones really kept things hopping wherever he was. One night I was working with Tommy Frangella. Bones couldn't stand him. Carolina was playing Pittsburgh, and as soon as Bones came out and saw who I was working with, he came up and said, "Earl, you might as well throw me out right now because I'm not going to stay and watch this guy try to referee. He's terrible." I told him, "Everything's going to be all right, Bones. Just take it easy."

Well, Frangella would make a call and Bones would leap up and holler and carry on. I'd come over and say, "Just take it easy, Bones. Everything is going to be all right." One time the ball rolled over by Bones and he guided it behind his feet under the bench. He just crossed his legs and sat there. I started over to get the ball. He said, "Everything will be all right, Earl. Just take it easy." Before I could do anything, Bones flipped out his cigarette lighter and held it under the bench by the ball. Frangella was still looking for the ball, and Bones yelled to him, "Hey, over here. I think I found it." I thought about throwing him, then decided he wasn't going to get his wish.

Later Frangella made a call and Bones raced out onto the floor and started clapping his hands in Frangella's face. That was it. I tossed him. On the way out he said, "You could have saved yourself a lot of trouble. I told you I wanted to go half an hour ago." He walked out waving a hankie over his head.

I don't think there ever was a more loyal guy in sports than Bernie Beglane, who wrote for the *Long Island Press*. He loved Louie Carnesecca, who was coaching the New York Nets. In Louisville one night after a playoff game that the Nets had taken from the Colonels, we had to leave the court through this narrow aisle that was roped off from the fans. As I went through, a fan reached out and hit me on the back of the head. I turned to get the guy, and Bernie, who was all smiles because the Nets had won, came bouncing along behind me. He saw the commotion and stopped. "What's going on?" he asked me. Knowing how much he loved Louie, I said, "Bernie, that guy right there with the glasses on just punched Louie in the back of the head."

Bernie set down his typewriter and punched the guy right on the jaw, knocking his glasses off. Bernie picked up his typewriter and proceeded to the locker room. While he was in there interviewing the players, two big Louisville cops came in, picked him up, and hauled him out. He was arrested on assault charges. Louie came over to my room later and said, "Hey, Earl, don't do me any favors, will ya? We just had to bail Bernie out of jail." I said, "Yeah, but doesn't it make you feel good to know he thinks the world of you, Louie?"

Referees have enough pressure on them, but black refs have a couple of added burdens. In time, the pressure has eased, but black players leaned on black refs to give them a break. Plus, they had to deal with the general prejudices of society. I was reminded of that one night in Louisville when I was to work a Kentucky Colonels game with John Thompson, a black ref out of Philadelphia. I had gotten John into the ABA. The game was in Freedom Hall and we had a little problem getting off the floor at halftime. A few fans fired a couple of verbal shots at us, and I fired a couple back in turn and kept on going. As we got near the dressing room door, one of the Louisville cops said to me, "You know, you shouldn't talk to those people like that. They're spectators and you're an official, and you should be above that."

"Hey, wait a minute," I said. "If they want to pass those kind of remarks at me, I don't see anything wrong with me giving them a little right back."

He said, "Well, I want you to know I don't appreciate it."

"Well, who needs you? If you don't like it, take your beef elsewhere," I told him, and we went into the dressing room. When we came back out of the room, there was this police captain standing outside who said he heard from his sergeant that we had given him a hard time and been obscene to some fans. I told him that's right and I didn't exactly appreciate his comments to us.

He said, "If there's any problems out there on that court and we feel that you guys are responsible for it, or if there's any problems coming off the floor after the game, we'd just as soon lock you up as the fans."

I was in the process of telling him he could take a hike along with his sergeant when John spoke up. He didn't feel real comfortable about where this was going. "Wait a minute, Earl, let's cool it. If they haul us off to jail, you're gonna get a suite and I'll be down in the dungeon never to be heard from again. Let's just forget the whole thing." I could see his point and complied.

Spencer Haywood brought immediate success to the Denver Rockets after his controversial leap after his sophomore year directly into the pros. He had been a star at the 1968 Olympics and really raised eyebrows when the ABA took him in violation of the code that pros didn't touch players until their class had graduated. They packed 7,000 into Denver Auditorium, and it was a rowdy crowd at that. Then Haywood went to Seattle and things dropped off while the crowds became more surly. My old friend Alex Hannum was there to lead the jeers.

The *Denver Post* chronicled another round of our get-togethers after a game in November 1971. I hit Alex with a technical with four minutes left in the first period and another one fifty-four seconds later. En route to the locker room Alex summed up his feelings to a reporter: "I did tell Strom then that 'you never were a blankety-blank good official, you aren't a blankety-blank good official now, and you never will be a blankety-blank good official,' and I left." I hit him with a third T on the way out. Alex then told reporters, "I've had a great deal of abuse from Strom and he has a short fuse. It's a long-running problem from our days in the other league. I should know enough to keep my mouth shut."

That evening's confrontation had been preceded by another hassle in Denver a year earlier. The Rockets were playing the Texas Chaparrals, and this guy who was usually in the front row started on me pretty good. I always felt it was the responsibility of management to keep those who get loud and vulgar under control—not leaving it up to the officials. But as so often happens with clubs when they're dealing with their fans, especially with season-ticket holders, they just ignored the problem.

This guy was calling me a motherfucker this and a motherfucker that. He was calling me a rotten bastard and finally I walked over and said, "You know, you have a pretty filthy mouth."

"Maybe you should try shutting it," he hollered back.

I told him I'd love to and suggested we meet in the lobby after the game. With that he jumped up and said, "I'll rip your motherfuckin' head off right now." And he charged toward me. He came onto the court. I hit him my two best shots and he didn't seem even to flinch. About that time I was thinking of getting the hell out of there when the police came over and took the guy away. They wanted to know if I wanted him thrown out and I said, "No, I think he's embarrassed enough. Leave him be." We didn't have any more trouble the rest of the game.

I filed a report about the incident with the league office because I knew there was always a chance a report would come in from the club or this character. Sure enough, the reports came rolling in from the Rockets and their radio announcer, who took a great dislike toward me. The stories were distorted and said that I had gone off the court after the guy. I know I didn't because I learned a long time ago, never leave the court. Keep things out in the open.

Maybe three or four weeks later I got a call from Jack Dolph, the commissioner. He wanted me in his office and said he was going to have to take disciplinary action against me. Dolph wasn't in office very long, but I think he was one of the best commissioners in all of pro sports. He was generally fair and honest. I know the Denver management was putting a lot of pressure on him to do something. He told me he was going to fine me $250. I thought that was unjust. He somehow convinced me that maybe I had been wrong, and of course my wife had already told me I was stupid to have hit the guy, that I should have just walked away. I honestly didn't accept the fact that anyone could call me names like that or take a swing at me and not have me at least try to retaliate. He said if it happened again I might lose my job. That was a sobering thought, but how many times do you think about something like that when some idiot's trying to nail you?

If it seems as though I was up to my old Red Ass ways reminiscent of my first years in the NBA, I guess I was. I was being challenged again to prove myself to a new group of players. I had lost some of the stature from the NBA with that miserable first year in the ABA. The players in the ABA didn't know me, so I was being tested. Even though I had been through all this before, and at a time when I was younger, I still found myself angered by the attitudes of these people who just wouldn't let a guy go out there and do the job of refereeing a game. One night I was working a game in Dallas and Cincy Powell got on me for calling a foul. "Strom, you just don't like blacks," he said. That did it. I tossed him. After the game he said he was going to file a report with the league charging me with being a racist. Fortunately, I didn't have to answer that accusation. When someone makes as outrageous a statement as that, you wonder how you can protect yourself.

I got a summons and was charged with violating a city obscenity law by a woman in Salt Lake City who accused me of making an obscene gesture at her during a game. Memphis was at Salt Lake and this woman was raising all sorts of hell. She was a season-ticket holder and used to come with her husband and her teenage daughter. She would bring a megaphone and run up and down the end line yelling at the officials. During a time-out, Jimmy Clark and I were standing at the foul line nearest her end of the court, and she was standing up, yelling and waving her arms. Her daughter was doing the same thing. I just leaned over to Clark and said, "Forget her. Just leave her alone." She thought she was a lip reader and thought I said, "Fuck you." I wiped some sweat off my forehead with my middle finger, emulating the way Mendy used to do it. She claimed I gave her the ol' up-yours sign with my finger and arm.

She ran down to the police officer standing by the court and said she wanted me arrested. She was going to press charges for my obscenities toward her. He didn't do anything then. When I was walking off the court after the game, she and her husband were standing there, and she was screaming for the police to arrest me. When she couldn't get a rise out of the cops, she turned to her husband and said, "Are you going to allow him to use that kind of language and treat me like that?" The guy was pretty small and seemed like a nice guy. How he ever hooked up with a nut like her, I don't know. He looked at his wife and said, "This is ridiculous. Let's get out of here."

She went to the police station that night and swore out a charge. It was a city statute. They were to serve me with a summons the next time I came to town. After the game I had called Norm Drucker, Jack Dolph, and Thurlo McCready in the league office. The latter two weren't real happy with me anyway because they were aware I was going back to the NBA as soon as I could. Vince Boryla, general manager and part owner of the Stars, filed a report that I had treated this woman wrong. So they called me into the ABA office and had me give my testimony to our lawyers. They said I would have to get my own lawyer and fight the thing on my own and that if I lost the case, I would be fired. If I beat the rap, they would let me finish out the season. They obviously were happy to unload me.

I went to my lawyer in Pottstown, and he said I had better get an attorney in Salt Lake City. I did, and he turned out to be one of the nicest guys I ever met. It took a month and a half, but he eventually got the statute declared unconstitutional and the charges were dropped. I went back into Salt Lake City shortly after the case had gone to court. The Stars were playing Dallas, who usually didn't draw flies. I was in my hotel room shaving with the five-o'clock news on TV when I heard the announcer say, "Tonight marks the first time back at the Salt Palace for referee Earl Strom since he was sued by a woman for obscenity."

I couldn't believe they were making such a big deal out of it, and what was really disturbing was that anyone knew which officials were working the game. Assignments are supposed to be kept secret. When I got to the arena, the place was packed. Zelmo Beaty, the center of the Stars, came over to me and said, "You ought to get a cut of the gate tonight. Dallas hasn't seen this many people all year." I thought they were going to raise the roof off when I was introduced, but the game went along without any problems with the crowd. The woman and her daughter acted like little angels throughout the game.

As I neared the end of my third season in the ABA, this being the 1971–72 season, the hoped-for merger seemed no closer than it had when I jumped across. Articles started popping up suggesting that the four of us might jump back to the NBA when our contracts expired. Norm was doing fine, working fewer games and doing more scouting as supervisor. Vanak and Gushue weren't particularly uncomfortable. But make no mistake about it, I was ready to return to that lover I had forsaken, the NBA.

I started to plot my return. Milwaukee general manager Wayne Embry and Chicago GM Pat Williams were encouraging me to come back. It was April 1972. It had been one month shy of three years since Russell had led the Celtics to that championship over Los Angeles. Wilt had limped off the floor. Russell had retired in glory. Then New York had beaten Los Angeles for the title in 1970. Madison Square Garden was sold out every night. Lew Alcindor had taken over the league, teamed with the old master, Oscar Robertson, at Milwaukee, and the Bucks beat Baltimore four straight to win the title in 1971. Now Gail Goodrich and Jerry West were scoring over 50 points a game between them, and Wilt was pulling nearly 20 boards a night as the Lakers had set a league mark of 33 straight wins that winter and were finally about to win a championship. I really wanted to get back to the big show.

I called Kennedy's office. He wasn't in. His secretary said, "Yes, Mr. Kennedy would like to speak to you." We set up an appointment, but she called back and said Mr. Kennedy couldn't keep that appointment. We set another one. On the appointed day I went to the NBA office. The ABA playoffs were under way and I was still working. In fact, I was guaranteed a minimum of twelve games at $500 each by my contract. I knew the ABA would know of my meeting with Kennedy, but I didn't care who saw me or who said what.

I knew having the support of the general managers and the players, as Pat Williams and Wayne Embry had indicated I had, wouldn't mean much unless Kennedy was in favor of my return. The owners have the last say, of course, even over the commissioner. But my efforts to return had to be keyed through Kennedy. When I met with him, he greeted me with open arms. He embraced me. He said, "Of course the ABA will know about our meeting. We're in the middle of merger talks and we aren't keeping anything from each other."

"I know that. I walked in the front door and everybody knows why I'm here. So, fine, let's go from where we are," I told him.

He told me how hurt he had been when I jumped to the ABA and how I had been so special to him. He told me that the hurt was over and done with.

I said, "I'm sorry for what happened. But it's done with in my mind. I'm glad you say it is in yours, too. So, you're telling me we're all set for next season?"

"Well, I just want you to understand that I don't do the hiring and firing of officials," he said. I didn't think that was true to a hundred percent; I think he approved or disapproved and obviously carried a lot of weight. "John Nucatola does the hiring and firing."

"What really matters to me is that when I go to talk to John, I'm going to be able to say to him that you are okaying my coming back. Is that right?"

"Absolutely." And we shook hands on it.

I had the feeling a weight had been lifted from my back. I went in to see John and he was tickled to death to see me and kept saying how great it was going to be for the staff and how great it was that Walter and I had buried our differences and how much Walter wanted me back. There was no collective bargaining for officials; it was still a matter of individual negotiations. John and I sat down and discussed all the salary scales and benefits and where I would fit into the pension plan. It was all spelled out. I would be getting a $25,000 salary. I got up to leave and he said he didn't think we should sign a contract then because I was still working in the ABA playoffs. "Let's wait until they're over. There's so much emotion between the leagues and we don't want to add fuel to the fire." It seemed reasonable to me.

"I do have a job here for next season. That's good enough for me. We're all set then, right?"

"Absolutely."

I guess I was worried something would go wrong. I said, "Well, good. I shook hands on it with Walter and I'm shaking hands on it with you. It's been a long grind, and you can't believe how much I want to just get back and settle into the routine here." He told me to come in and sign a contract as soon as the playoffs were over.

"I'll be here the next day," I assured him.

I stopped off to see Mendy after leaving the NBA office. I told him how everything looked good. He said, "Handshakes aren't contracts. Be careful now." I assured him I wouldn't do anything to screw it up this time.

I went back and worked my twelfth playoff game in the ABA. After the game I was treated rather coldly by Jack Dolph and Thurlo McCready. Vanak and I had worked the game, and I heard Thurlo say to John, "When you come back to the hotel, I want you to come see me. I want to talk about a new contract for you." They knew Vanak and Gushue weren't especially anxious to get back to the NBA, and Norm was too old to want to give up his supervisor's job and have to pound the court full-time again. The ABA knew I was going back, so they really gave me the cold shoulder. I understood.

After my twelfth playoff game, I went home. I didn't get a call to work any more games. I called Norm. I asked him what was going on. He said, "You know the reason. They know you're going back and they told me not to assign you any more playoff games."

"Well, fine. Now that that's out in the open and the picture is clear, I'm going to call the NBA office and sign my contract for next year."

"Sounds like your best course of action," he said. "No hard feelings."

I called John Nucatola. "I'm not getting any more playoff assignments, so as far as I'm concerned, I'm through with the ABA and my contract with them. I'm done. I'm ready to come over and sign."

"Well, maybe you should hold up for a few days, Earl."

"What do you mean? You told me to come over as soon as I was free."

"We want to work out a few more things."

"Okay. How long should I wait?"

"Why don't you wait until the playoffs are over in the NBA."

Two weeks later the NBA playoffs were over and I didn't hear from John. I called him. "I'm ready to come up and sign that contract."

"Well, maybe you ought to wait a little longer. Walter thinks it would be a good idea to go over your situation with the owners at the league meetings. Just so everyone is aware of what's going on."

That made sense. But still, I was getting antsy. I waited until the meetings were over. No call came from John. I called him. "John, I want to know where I stand for next year. Let's get it done now."

"Earl, there are some complications setting in."

"Like what?"

"Well, you know, about your coming back and all."

"Are you telling me I have something to worry about as to whether I'll get back next year?"

"Oh, no, no. We just have to handle it right."

"Okay, when do you want me to check back?"

"Call me in a week."

I was starting to get a little peeved and more than a little nervous. I called Red Auerbach. He had been at the league meetings. I wanted to know what was going on. He said my situation had been discussed. He said there was no problem with the owners. If it was left to a vote of the owners, there would be no effort to stop my returning to the NBA.

A week passed and I called John again. He wasn't in. To hell with this, I thought. I called Kennedy.

"Walter, I'm a little bit concerned. John wanted me to phone him after our playoffs and then after your playoffs, and now I'm getting a runaround about signing that contract."

He very coldly said, "Look, Earl, I have nothing to do with it. I don't handle the hiring and firing of officials. I told you that. You have a problem with John Nucatola. You have to work it out with him."

"He tells me you're telling him to hold it up."

"He said that?"

"He sure did."

"Well, I'm telling you different."

So, I called John back. I couldn't get through to him for a couple of days. He finally called back and said, "Earl, we're not picking up your option for next year."

"Option? What the hell are you talking about? Option?"

"Well, we're not going to bring you back."

I blew. I started screaming at him. "If you're going to be that dishonest, then the next person you hear from will be my attorney. We had an agreement. We shook on it. You assured me we had a deal. And now you tell me I'm out. Walter says it's your decision. You're telling me it's Walter's. Well, I'm through with this bullshit."

I went to Richie Phillips, an attorney in Philadelphia who had represented some players. He tried to talk to the NBA, but they wouldn't hear of my coming back.

In early December 1972, eight months after I had come to my "handshake agreement" with Kennedy and Nucatola, I filed a $275,000 claim against the NBA. What I really wanted was my job back. I had burned my bridges with the ABA. The NBA wouldn't take me back. For the first time in sixteen years, I wasn't refereeing professional basketball.

The NBA had seventeen veteran referees for the 1972–73 season. Mendy had in nineteen years and Richie Powers had fourteen. Salaries ranged from $10,000 to $25,000. I had been at the top of the ladder making $14,000 when I had left three years earlier. The jump had helped a lot of people. I felt damn mad about being left out now. I got a lot madder when I found out what was behind it.

I started to pick up some news when all this broke out. Kennedy had been ready to bring me back, but had gotten a letter from Ed Rush and some of the refs that it would be a bad thing for staff morale and a bad influence on the younger guys. Kennedy apparently ignored that letter. So the officials got Richie Powers to use his weight and write another letter. Richie was very important to the NBA then, and he told Kennedy it wouldn't be good to put me back on the staff. When I heard about it, I didn't want to believe it. I called him.

"Richie, did you write this letter?"

"Earl, I did, but I'm really sorry. I let the other guys con me into it. I'm really sorry how this has affected your family."

"You're damn right it has affected my family. You're lucky you're not where I can get my hands on you right now. Where the hell do you get off depriving me of a chance to make a living and support my family?"

"You're right. I agree. I shouldn't have done it. Is there anything I can do to help?"

"It's a little late for that. I've filed a suit against the NBA. If we have to go to court with this thing, you're going to be called in for testimony. You're a direct party to this boycott."

I started calling some of the general managers: Pat Williams, Wayne Embry, Jerry Colangelo with the Phoenix Suns. I asked them why they didn't come to my defense if they had been so anxious to have me back. They said the word was to keep out of it. I couldn't blame them for not pushing it. I went back to Norm and asked if there wasn't some way to get back into the ABA. He said there was too much hard feelings. I couldn't blame them for feeling that way, either. I wrote half a dozen clubs in the ABA and NBA with which I felt I had a pretty good rapport. These were clubs that had said over the years, "When you get through refereeing, we'd like to have your knowledge of the game in our organization." Nobody seemed to have room for me then.

I took a job working for a travel agency. I wasn't going to make enough at that, so I opened a tavern, Yogi Strom's Country Tavern. Open eleven A.M. to two A.M. It was located four miles south of Pottstown. "Get a kick out of life. Come join Yogi for a Moscow Mule!" Sports celebrities dropped by to say hi. I fit in behind the bar with my sideburns and mod attire, sunglasses and white shoes. I was the picture of some happy-time kinda guy. But I was dying inside.

I had long since dropped my affiliation with the collegiate referees federations. I tried to get into the Atlantic Coast Conference or Big Ten, but the doors were locked by politics. I guess they figured it wasn't fair to the guys who had been loyal to have me come back and take away someone else's assignments. There wasn't much left. I worked in the Hill High School Invitational Tournament. Ironically, that was where I had launched my career as a referee.

The Eastern Pro League commissioner called several times, and finally I went up to work a game in Scranton. They never did like me much up there from years earlier. I'm not belittling the Eastern League, but it hurt my ego when people would call out things like, "No wonder the NBA and ABA got rid of ya, you can't even handle this. Where you headed next, the YMCA?" This particular game turned into a riot near the end, a riot in the stands, that is.

The cops came rushing over to us after the horn sounded and told us to get the hell out of there. The Scranton owner was going crazy. He started yelling for the crowd to follow him so they could storm the Allentown players in their locker room. A cop knocked him out with a knock on the head with his nightstick. His wife was holding him in the middle of the floor, screaming, "Police brutality!" As I was heading down the back stairs, a woman with a cast on her foot and on crutches tried to trip me. When I got past her, she yelled, "Hey, Earl." I turned around and she spit in my face.

It still beat not working, so I took a few more weekend assignments in the only league that would have me. Some people probably thought it was degrading, but I just wanted to keep in practice. I might really have fallen apart if I hadn't already gone through so much when I'd jumped to the ABA. But Yvonne became very bitter, which was uncharacteristic of her to say the least. She said, "I feel like this rival, basketball, that has had my man all these years wasn't even treating him right. I hate her, she doesn't even respect him."

Yvonne sat down and wrote this really expressive letter to Kennedy. She talked about what it had meant to the family when I went to the ABA and was able to make so much more that I could quit my job at GE. She talked about how players jumped back and forth and that all seemed okay, and about how much it hurt to watch me when I had told the family I couldn't get back into the NBA. After making each point, she'd pose the question: "What do I tell my children, Mr. Kennedy?" She talked about the lack of quality officials and about integrity and how all these people said they wanted me back and how we had had a handshake agreement. "We teach that you should not be afraid to trust people. But what do I tell my children, Mr. Kennedy?" It was a real work of art. And it came from a deep anger and hurt that she was feeling. She figured it was imprudent to send it and never did, but I would have liked to have seen Kennedy's reaction.

Meanwhile, the NBA seemed as if it had never been better. Tiny Nate Archibald averaged over 35 points a game to take the scoring title away from Kareem Abdul-Jabbar, who had changed his name from Lew Alcindor a year earlier. New York and Boston played a great Eastern Conference finals that featured some of the best team-oriented basketball in the history of the league. The Knicks went on to win the NBA championship, and since all New York was so pumped, it was as though the league had never been more popular. I watched it on TV.

One day during the summer of 1973, I was working at the tavern when I got a phone call from Richie Phillips. He felt we had a pretty good suit and that Kennedy and Nucatola would have a pretty tough time defending their position when he got through with them on the stand. He said the NBA would take me back if I dropped the suit.

I figured, what the hell, none of us starved to death. I'm just going to go back and forget it all happened. I went up to the NBA office to sign a contract—a year late. Simon Gourdine, the deputy commissioner, and Nucatola were there. John couldn't look me in the face. He said, "I'm sorry all this happened. I'm glad to have you back and I want to forget all about this whole mess. Let's be friends."

I said, "Fine, that's the best way to do it. By the way, where's Walter? Isn't he going to be in on this signing?"

John said, "It's not necessary that he be here."

We signed the contract and we signed a waiver of the lawsuit and that was that. You can see why I don't have much favor among a lot of the referees. I came back against their will. I'm convinced Walter said, "Keep him in his place. He's not going to have the stature he had before."

chapter 8

WELCOME BACK
AND SCREW YOU

Despite everything, I was delighted to get back into the
NBA. There were changes everywhere; it wasn't the same
league I had left four years earlier. Kennedy had proclaimed
pro basketball would be the sport of the seventies. That
proved to be premature by a decade, but the intent was
obvious. There was a new emphasis on turning out a product
that was slicker, more organized, and more controlled than
when I had left it. It was as if someone had said, "Clamp
down on the rogues, clean up the arenas, cut out the rough
stuff, and put the spotlight on the superstars. And by the way,
one thing we don't need is a bunch of referees raising hell."

To show how anxious they were to deemphasize the presence of the referees, Mendy encouraged the league to do
away with the traditional "zebra" shirt and adopt a plain
gray one. It was a nice neutral color, as if we were supposed
to blend into the background. There were to be no interviews with refs without league approval. There were to be
no hassles with fans, coaches, or players. There was to be no
screaming and carrying on. If there was a problem, file a
report. When the four of us jumped, the league took advan-

167

tage of the fact that most of the guys who were left were
younger and more pliable, and it stamped them into the
NBA's new mold.

The titles the Knicks won in 1970 and 1973 provided a lot
of exposure for the league, thanks to the influence of the
New York media. The Knicks' hustling style of play with
Willis Reed, Dave DeBusschere, Bradley, Monroe, and
Frazier featured the ultimate in teamwork. Those teams
were the last gasp of a dying era. For the remainder of the
decade, pro basketball as a product just didn't fulfill
Kennedy's promise. Things just got too loose. Three new
teams, Buffalo, Cleveland, and Portland, came into the
league in 1970–71 as the NBA reorganized into four divi-
sions. In 1972, San Diego moved to Houston. The next year
Cincinnati became Kansas City–Omaha. For the 1973–74
season Baltimore was headed to Washington, D.C., to
become the Capital Bullets. Barely half of what was now a
seventeen-team league was playing in the old joints that I
had known when I left four years earlier.

It wasn't just the environment that changed; something
happened to the quality of play as well. With the expansion
and the ABA, there were three times as many players, and
that, coupled with the inflated salaries resulting from the
bidding war between the two leagues, meant there was a
different type of player on the court. Even marginal players
were in demand. Malcontents and head cases and dozens of
guys who never would have made it before were everywhere. I remember when talented rookies would have to sit
and wait their turn. Now guys with limited skills were making $50,000, $75,000, $100,000 a year. And they were get-
ting it guaranteed in the form of no-cut contracts. Instead of
waiting their turn, rookies, as John Brisker once put it, worried that "if you spend too much time on the bench, your
talent gets up and walks away from you."

The campus scenes were full of all kinds of free-spirited
expression. The players coming into pro basketball were a
product of this and the whole social fabric seemed to change.
When one rookie a year makes a team, he's going to go along

with the old veterans. When two, four, or maybe six players only a year or two out of college can form a nucleus on a squad of twelve, you have a pretty wide-open situation. It was a cultural collision between the new kids, many marginal in skills and tremendously well compensated, and the older players, who had grown up and played under a different system. As John Havlicek once said, "We used to bust our tails to make the playoffs and hopefully win the title so we wouldn't have to go out and get a summer job."

More owners with backgrounds outside of basketball were entering the NBA. They had made it selling cars or insurance or oil or fried chicken or whatever. They had big bucks and lacked only one thing: enough publicity to please them. These weren't like the old guard who had owned dingy arenas and ground out a living with their various sports teams and other promotional events; these were management men with a telephone book full of lawyers and accountants and publicity specialists. They weren't necessarily any more sophisticated than Red Auerbach, but where Red would scream and threaten and stomp his foot, these guys would serve you with a summons.

The arenas were becoming larger and more attractive in pursuit of the upper-middle-class fan and the families. Big, wide-open bowls with colorful seats, bright lighting, and fancy new scoreboards replaced the old places that were dark and stained from all the beer and spit. The emphasis on winning became ever more intense so as to bring in the necessary crowds to pay the big salaries. Trades increased, franchises bounced around, and coaches were readily fired. You could sum it up by saying that these kids didn't think the world owed them a living, they felt it owed them the world. The older players used to feel they were lucky to knock out a living playing ball; they weren't getting rich, but they were making a decent buck doing something they enjoyed instead of having to do some other job for the same money. Now the kids were getting so much money so fast there was no way it wouldn't turn most of their heads around.

You could see it in a lot of the things that went on. The

younger players had a different attitude toward the game. There wasn't that old desire, the old love of basketball. The motivation was for the buck, and for a lot of them, even that motivation was ruined when they got long-term, no-cut contracts right out of college.

The drug scene came off the college campuses and into the NBA. Guys with more money than they'd ever dreamed of, stardom they couldn't cope with, and plenty of time out on the road made for a pretty deadly combination. There were rumors about who was messed up, and then guys started getting caught and suspended. John Drew, Micheal Ray Richardson, David Thompson, some pretty damn good players went down.

Every year at camp we would get a talk from the league's security chief about the drug situation, how they tested people and so on. One year they told us, we want you people to be alert. If you see something that seems suspicious about a player's performance or behavior, let us know and we'll take it from there. I felt uncomfortable with that. First of all, I'm not aware of drugs and how they affect people. I don't even know what marijuana smells like. I don't know if a guy's eyes are dilated because he's on drugs or some medication for a cold or what. I didn't know what to look for. That makes me pretty naive, I guess, but it's the truth. I just made the decision within myself that I wasn't going to go around guessing if some guy was messed up and turn him in. The league promised there would be absolute confidentiality, but there are always ways things leak out, and I sure as hell wasn't about to turn some guy in and then have him turn around and sue me when it's proven he wasn't doing anything wrong. Besides, how was I to get any kind of reading on a guy while seeing him maybe once a month when his coach couldn't see it right in front of him every day?

I've seen games so shabbily played that you'd have thought everyone was on something, but it was probably just guys being tired, injured, sick, and not having their head in the game. Could have been someone on something, but I couldn't tell from the play. I was on a trip to Israel and Italy with Micheal Ray Richardson right before he went down again. I couldn't tell anything from his behavior on or off the court. Same way with John Drew, John Lucas, David Thompson. The only thing I knew about David was that he started to get a little nasty with the referees. A little while later it came out that he had a problem with drugs. If I were coaching that team, you'd think I would know, but not as a referee. I'm not in the drug rehab business, I'm not in the security business. I'm a referee. These guys could be stone sober and act like goofballs. I wanted no part of that role, and eventually they stopped telling us to be looking for guys to pitch in.

Even through the worst days of drug rumors, I never heard anything about games being fixed or points shaved. The league has always been alert to any sign of influence from gamblers. That definitely includes keeping an eye on attempts to influence the refs; after all, the players are much better paid than we are, and we can probably do more to determine a final outcome. The age-old accusation that the referee is on the take gets renewed in at least a few minds every time a call is made. It's something an official hears from the first game he ever works, at the biddy league level. "How much they payin' ya, Strom?" If I were a fixer, I'd sure go after the officials. Thank god we have officials with a lot of integrity. Some of them may be jerks, but they're honest. Pro basketball has been very fortunate to avoid any such scandal, despite periodic problems in the colleges. There was a big deal made out of Earl Monroe's flip of the ball into the opponent's basket as the horn sounded, preventing the Knicks from covering the spread. It turned out to be an innocent thing, but they put in a rule that if a player tosses up a shot at the other team's basket at the end of the game, it doesn't count. In New York you always hear the gamblers bitching about calls and fussing over the final score, even when the winner is obvious. I'm sure there are guys who'd love to wire a game, but the NBA has kept them out since day one. Throughout my career, I was never approached in any suspicious way.

When I returned to the NBA, the referees were making double what they'd been getting before we jumped. They had pension, health, and insurance plans. Travel was first class and expenses were paid in monthly allocations. There were twenty officials working regularly in the NBA, including five blacks. Barriers and quotas were falling. Bill Russell had been lured out of retirement in 1973 to coach the Seattle SuperSonics. Ball clubs were carrying as many as ten blacks on twelve-man rosters and drawing well at the gate. Some people blamed the high ratio of blacks for the lack of fan support in the late seventies, but I never did buy that. If that's the case, how do you explain the amazing success that these same black-dominated teams have had at the gate a decade later?

During the twelve years I was in the NBA, I had worn number 10 on my referee's shirt. When I came back, Darrell Garretson had it. I took number 12. That September the officials training camp was held in Milwaukee, and I found the reunion with my old colleagues, and all the new ones, to be free of the animosities that had led to my being black-balled. Who would have believed these were the same guys who a year earlier had been saying I would pose a serious morale problem if I was returned to the staff? Hard to believe for almost everyone—everyone except me. Thanks for the year off, fellas.

Generally, the players, coaches, fans, and officials received me well. There were a lot of new faces. I hadn't worked with Kareem Abdul-Jabbar. He came in the year I went to the ABA, so he had four years in the league by the time I worked a game with him in it. In that game I made a call that upset him, and he started walking away with the ball. I said, "Give me the ball, Lew." He kept walking. "Give me the ball, Lew. I want the ball, Lew." He turned around and glared at me. "The name's Kareem." I said, "Well, excuse me, I've been away. Now give me the damn ball, Kareem." He smiled and we got along pretty well over the years.

Bob McAdoo had just come into the league the previous year and was now winning the first of three straight scoring titles. It was funny to have no rapport with a lot of the younger players. Jim McMillian had come into the league the year after I left. My first game back was an exhibition game between the Celtics and Buffalo. McMillian had just been traded to Buffalo, and after the game he told the Braves' trainer, "Hey, that older ref, number twelve, he's pretty good for a rookie. Wonder where they found him."

The best one was this guy who came up to me in Phoenix and asked, "Hey, didn't you used to be Earl Strom?"

One of my first regular-season assignments took me into Boston. I took a cab to the old Madison Hotel, which was adjacent to the Garden. This place wasn't classy, but it was convenient. They could shoot a 1930s movie in the lobby and not change a thing. When I went up to the registration desk, I noticed the clerk seemed nervous. I didn't think too much about it and headed for the elevator with the bellboy. I really shouldn't call him a "bellboy" since he was old enough to have seen Paul Revere's ride.

As soon as the elevator doors closed, I thought I smelled smoke. As we passed the fourth floor, I knew damned well I smelled smoke because there was a blue haze in the elevator. The elevator stopped on the eighth floor, the door opened, and this little old chambermaid stood there shouting, "There's a fire up here!" She tried to get on the elevator, but the bellboy pushed her back out. "This car is going up. Wait'll I come back down," he told her. This clown closed the door and started up. I grabbed him and tried to get to the button. He looked at me through the haze and said, "Don't you worry. The fire is on eight and your room is on eleven." I finally wrestled the controls from him and got us headed down. When we hit the lobby, the Boston Fire Department was barging through the door with hoses and axes. Fortunately, they got it out in a hurry. I was letting the bellboy and desk clerk know what I thought of them for checking me into a burning hotel when the chambermaid came storming in and unloaded on us for not picking her up on the way down.

I knew I was back in the swing of things the night I had

to unload not only Chicago coach Dick Motta, but also the mascot, Bennie the Bull. It was the third game of the playoffs between Milwaukee and Chicago, being played in Chicago Stadium. I was working with Don Murphy. In the third quarter Murphy called a charging foul on Chet Walker when he rammed into Abdul-Jabbar. It would have been Kareem's fifth foul if it had gone the other way. Motta blew his stack. He ran to midcourt screaming at Murphy. I hit him with a T. There was a time-out then, and Walker was harping at Murphy. I noticed Motta walking toward them, taking off his sports coat. When I stepped in between Motta and Murphy, Motta rolled up his coat and threw it at Murphy. Only it hit me, instead. I called another technical and tossed him. He was still trying to get at Murphy. He yelled, "Give my goddamn jacket to Murphy, he took everything else from us!" I finally got him off the court, and here comes the Bulls' mascot, some jerk dressed in a costume to look like a red bull. He was charging at Murphy and making some obscene gestures at both of us. I promptly had him tossed from the premises.

Boston defeated Milwaukee for the championship, and with the Celtics back on top, at least something felt familiar about the NBA.

During the summer following my first year back in the NBA, I underwent surgery on my right knee and spent six weeks in a hip-to-toe cast, but I was ready to go when the exhibition season got under way. The 1974–75 season featured the addition of New Orleans, swelling the league to eighteen teams, and the arrival of Bill Walton at Portland. He was collegiate player of the year for three straight years at UCLA, but soon was the center of controversy for his unorthodox comments off the court and for missing more than half the season with injuries. Golden State stunned Washington with a 4–0 sweep in the finals. Earlier in that season I got back in Kennedy's doghouse for a little problem I had up in Seattle.

It started when I turned to walk toward the scorer's table to pick up my jacket at the end of the game. I felt somebody grab me from behind. I pushed back, and as I swung around, I saw that it was this woman who had been screaming at me along the end line during the game. Had I known it was a woman, I wouldn't have pushed her like that, but I already had, and all of a sudden here came Seattle guard Fred Brown from my blind side. He pushed me into the crowd and started yelling at me, "What are you doin' hittin' a woman?" I had my arms pinned behind me by another fan, and I told him I was going to kick him in the balls if he didn't let go. Hugh Evans, my partner, and Bill Russell, who was coaching the Sonics, came over and got me free from this fan. I took out after Brown. Russell jumped in between us and I kept shouting at Brown, "I want that SOB! I want to kick his ass!" Brown was just out of my reach in a swarm of fans and players. I kept yelling and Russell kept telling me I was being ridiculous. "Go to your locker room. It's all over," he kept telling me. I was just about under control when a fan hit me in the face with a cup full of beer. Then I really went bananas. Hugh and the police finally got me to the room.

We got in there, shut the door, and I looked down at my arms. They were red and scratched from scuffling with the fans. I looked in the mirror with the beer running down my face. I looked over at poor Hugh, who was beside himself, and I started to laugh. I told him, "You think this is bad, you shoulda been in Syracuse in the old days."

Russell sent word that they would file a report to the league explaining what had happened and how it wasn't totally my fault. When I got back to my hotel, I called John Nucatola. He told me to file a full report by Western Union as was customary in any game where something beyond the ordinary occurred. Nucatola told me everything would be all right, and I flew off to Phoenix the next day. When I got there, I had a message to call him.

When Nucatola was in a relaxed mood his voice was very cordial, but when he was trying to be professional, he became cold and calculating. He said, "You have to report to the league office on Monday." This was Saturday and I had a TV game in Chicago the next day. I said, "I told you what happened. You've heard from Russell and Hugh and me. What more do I need to say?" He said Kennedy wanted a hearing and that I was to meet with Walter and him and Jack Joyce, director of security, on Monday.

It seemed as if every paper in the country were carrying a story and pictures of the incident in Seattle. I was quoted as saying, "I wanted to get my hands on that bleepin' Fred Brown" and how bush I thought the crowd was for tossing beer on me. The pictures showed me lunging at Brown with Hugh and Russell holding me back. I looked extremely mad and upset.

I finished my Sunday game and got into New York Monday morning. It was supposed to be a day off for me. It was also Washington's birthday, and when I got to the office there was a note on the door saying the office wouldn't be open that day. I rang the bell and John came out. He took me in his office and told me he was the only one there. He proceeded to tell me the commissioner was going to suspend me for the remainder of the season and fine me heavily. He told me he had pleaded with Kennedy about how much they needed me in the stretch drive and for the playoffs, so they were reducing the suspension to six games.

I said, "If that's the case, I'm going to my attorney to sue everybody involved because all I did was try to defend myself." He immediately pulled out a picture and said, "Walter put this picture on my desk and said, 'I told you we should never have rehired this guy. All he does is create problems.' " It was a picture of Russell and me screaming at each other. I told John I hadn't been screaming at Russell, I was just telling him how Brown had pushed me from behind. Kennedy didn't care about details, though. This was just one of his ways to get back at me.

I went home. Nucatola called me a day later and told me Kennedy had decided not to suspend me, but he was going to fine me $600. I contacted Mike DiTomasso, an attorney and former official, and had him meet with Kennedy in hopes of clearing the fine. Kennedy wouldn't budge. Mendy was in his final year as an NBA official; he was head of the

National Association of Basketball Referees, our union, and he said they would appeal the fine. If that didn't work, Mendy said the guys would collect the sum from the membership.

A couple of problems got in the way of that plan. It didn't get resolved before Mendy retired, and the NABR came up with a case of "Earl who?" when I asked for the money. Kennedy retired as commissioner and was replaced by Lawrence O'Brien. I quit the NABR and asked O'Brien for a hearing. He said he wouldn't reverse any matters that had been determined by Kennedy. A year later, O'Brien relented and reimbursed me the $600.

After all that, I was left with a bitter taste for my fellow referees. It was plain we didn't have any use for each other. Richie Powers made some statement that I had blown one by O'Brien and that I had a knack for getting into trouble. Can you imagine Powers saying anyone has a knack for getting into trouble? He could find trouble saying good morning.

In the finals of the 1975–76 championship series, Boston took the title over Phoenix. They had a triple overtime game at Boston Garden. In this wild finish Richie was attacked by a fan. He swung back. Richie and the media acted as if this were a real big deal. Sid Borgia was right on when he said, "I don't know why everyone made such a big fuss over it. We had one of those every night when I refereed. I think what disturbed Richie the most was that he punched the guy and didn't hurt him."

The next season became the Year of the Merger. After nine years, the ABA could claim victory to the extent that four teams—Denver, San Antonio, Indiana, and the New York Nets—were allowed to come into the NBA. The price, in part, included $3.2 million per franchise, plus indemnities to the New York Knicks for territorial infringement, compensation to ABA teams that were left out, no sharing in TV revenue for three seasons, and other considerations. It was a pretty steep entry fee, but at least four had made it to the big show. Now all the stars were in one 22-team league.

Julius Erving went from the Nets, after leading them to the last ABA title, to join George McGinnis on the Philadelphia 76ers.

I had Houston at San Antonio one night. In those years right after the Spurs came in the league from the ABA, they had some wild and crazy fans, especially the Baseline Bums. Down 1 with just seconds left, Houston stole the ball and Mike Newlin fired from the corner and missed. Moses Malone went for the rebound and was hammered as the horn sounded. I blew the whistle and the San Antonio fans were on the verge of a riot. Bottles, programs, coins, came flying out of the stands. This tantrum went on for five minutes. After repeated tries to get the court cleaned up, I handed the ball to Moses. "Here, put these two fucking things in and let's get out of here." He winked and did.

Moses was always hard to understand because he mumbled so much. One night I called him for stepping on the baseline. He turned around said, "Mumble, mumble . . . line."

I said, "What?"

"Mumble, mumble . . . line." He looked mad.

I said, "Jesus Christ, I'm standing right here and I saw you step on the line. What's your beef?"

"Mumble, mumble . . . line."

I couldn't figure it out. Then one of the players said, "Earl, can't you understand him?"

"As a matter of fact, no."

"He said, 'That's a helluva place to draw the line.' "

During that 1976–77 season the NABR began making demands. As had always been the practice in the NBA, each official negotiated his contract individually. The union wanted to be recognized as the collective bargaining agent for the officials. It was an interesting twist of fate that the guy representing the NABR was none other than Richie Phillips, the same guy who had represented me when I sued the NBA to get back into the league four years earlier. I had been a little upset at the amount of money he charged me for handling my case. He represented a number of NBA players, and I guess he was used to dealing with people making $100,000 a year. I never used him again as my attorney. Everyone maintained he was a good initial-contact man, able to get the most out of the first deal. Mike DiTomasso had been representing the officials before they started talking seriously about going on strike. He was a nice guy, but a strike wasn't in his nature. When he resigned, Phillips had called me and asked if I would help him get the job. I told him there wasn't anything I could do because, first of all, most the guys didn't exactly look at me as their best friend, and secondly, I wasn't even in the association. I told him to contact Ed Rush and Darell Garretson. He did and they installed him as their attorney.

They wanted him to go to work on me to get me back into the association. Powers was in the association, but said he was dropping out if they went on strike. One thing you have to say about Powers, he stands for his convictions. Whether you like him or not, you have to admit he has the balls to do what he thinks is morally right—which is more than I can say about a lot of people, including more of my colleagues than I would like to admit.

The strike talk had come out of a meeting during the all-star break. I had heard from Phillips when he became the NABR's attorney. He had practically given them his word that he would get me into the fold. They wanted to make it a hundred percent, and they were probably convinced they could get Powers to go on strike when the time came. They figured I carried enough weight with the league that it was important that I be in the group. Phillips said he would deliver me. He called me. "Why don't you join the group?"

"I don't want to belong. They did nothing for me and left me to fight my own battles. When I needed them, they let me down. I don't like the way they operate. I don't want any part of it."

"Well, you're going to have to become a member eventually."

"Then let's just wait until I have no choice."

He had to go back to them and say he couldn't land me,

but he promised to keep working on it. Later in the season I was to work a game in Detroit with Hugh Evans. I was getting ready to leave for the arena when Phillips called and said, "Even though you're not a member of the group, we want you to come to our meeting in Chicago during the all-star break. We're talking of going on strike, and we expect that you would be on strike with us. So this concerns you."

I told him, "Look, Richie, don't you tell anybody I'm willing to do anything. You're not speaking for me. I'm not going to that meeting and I'm not planning on going on strike. I'd have to know the timing and the reasons."

"Well, you can't know unless you come to the meeting.

"Call me and tell me. I'm not going to that meeting."

Powers was supposed to work the all-star game in Milwaukee, but he got sick two days before and Nucatola told me to take his place. While at the airport in Chicago I ran into Phillips. Bum luck. He got on the same plane for Milwaukee. He walked by me and made some sarcastic remark. From that moment on I have had no use for the guy.

It came down to the last Sunday of the regular season and I was supposed to be working in Detroit with Ed Middleton. When I got to Cobo Arena, Ed wasn't there. One of the guys called me and said the officials were going on strike. When Middleton showed up, he was supposed to call Phillips. He came in, went out and called Phillips, and was told to go home. He came back into the locker room, grabbed his bag, and said, "You going to go with me?"

"No. I'm not striking. Our contracts are through the regular season and you guys are violating the contract."

"Okay, Earl, I guess I have to understand your position. I hope you understand mine."

"I do. Be careful nothing happens to you." I worked with a guy out of Buffalo and he did a fairly good job. The NBA had some backup guys standing by around the league in anticipation of the strike, and they handled the games around the various cities. Of the twenty-six regular referees, only Powers and I didn't strike. Richie claimed he was under a multiyear contract and had no right to refuse to honor that contract. I claimed that I couldn't care less what the NABR did since I had told them all to go to hell when they wouldn't back me to get back into the league and when I had the hassle in Seattle.

The officials were seeking the right to collective bargaining, an arbitration clause, life insurance paid up to sixty-five years of age, severance pay, increases in salary and expenses, and an increase in playoff pay. The arbitration clause was a bid for more control of their careers—since an owner or organization could still muster the power to get a referee fired if it was so determined. While I agreed with all their goals, I didn't think they had any business walking out on a valid contract. They left me and Richie Powers to referee the playoff games with a bunch of guys who had no pro basketball experience. It was a tough line to walk for these guys. If they took this shot to show what they could do working the NBA, they would be called scabs by the regular refs and certainly be harassed if they were ever hired full-time. If they didn't work, the NBA would probably forget them for any future consideration. It was a pretty tough baptism.

A game I had in Denver was typical of the turmoil caused by the inexperienced officials. Portland had lost this particular game and a guy came up to me as I was leaving the court. I didn't know it at the time, but it turned out to be Jack Scott, a political activist who was traveling with Bill Walton. He jammed a microphone in my face and said, "I want to talk to you. I have a lot of questions to ask you."

I said, "I'm going to the locker room," and sort of pushed him aside.

He was really being aggressive. "I have a right to ask you any questions I want."

I asked him if he was a member of the media and kept moving toward the locker room.

"Yes, I am, and I want to ask you some very important questions about the way you worked this game."

He just kept it up. I noticed there were more cops around than usual. I wondered why they didn't get this guy away from me. I told him to get the hell out of my face or I'd lay him out. He kept getting more belligerent. He said, "I want to know if you're picking on Walton because he called you a scab."

When he said that, I grabbed him and banged him up against the wall. Just then Walton came running down the corridor yelling, "Earl, Earl, I'll take care of him."

"Is he a friend of yours?"

"Yeah."

"Well, get him out of here or I'll take care of him myself."

Now Jack Joyce and the police moved in. "Come on, Earl, we've got to get you to your room," this cop said as he started to push me down the hall. As soon as they got me in the room, Joyce said, "We had a phone call threatening your life at halftime. Somebody called the switchboard and said to tell you that you weren't getting out of the building alive."

"Nice of you to get around to telling me," I told him. Actually, I was glad they hadn't told me. It would have scared the hell out of me. I was scared now. I didn't know if it was an irate fan who was losing fifty cents on the game or some guy who just didn't like me or if it was just some union goon. I had no idea. It even crossed my mind that it could even be one of the referees on strike playing a bitter joke on me. I hated to believe that. The police checked the corridors and the parking lot around McNichols Arena. They backed a squad car up to the door and ushered me into it. When we got to the hotel, I got out. The cop leaned over from behind the wheel and said, "Okay, buddy, looks like you're safe. See ya."

I said, "Whatta ya mean you'll see me? You're not leaving me here alone are you? What if the guy's in the lobby or my room?" So the cop came in and checked out my room. No one around. I felt pretty safe by that evening, but I bolted my door and put the chairs up against it and left the lights on all night.

I flew to Houston the next day with Jack Joyce. I had a playoff game and we discussed the possibilities. We decided it was probably just some prank and that I should go ahead and work. That was the first death threat I ever had—at least that I knew about. It was obviously pretty scary. I don't think anyone who has ever had a death threat could laugh it off. I remember Kareem received a death threat over the Hanafi terrorist tragedy in Washington, D.C. The Lakers came into Milwaukee and had all kinds of extra guards around the arena. I was working the game and Jerry West was coaching the Lakers. I asked Jerry, "You don't mind if whenever I have to hand Kareem the ball, I just kind of toss it to him from the sidelines, do you?" He said, "You'll notice we haven't invited him into the huddles."

Of course, it was just our attempt to laugh away our fears. It's really something to have hanging on your mind—a death threat. There are plenty of sick people out there and you just never know. People don't always look at players or especially officials as living, breathing, feeling human beings. People tend to say, "Why are you afraid? It's probably just some crank call." Look, people shoot presidents. What's to stop them from shooting some jerky referee? Who's gonna remember a referee? Hell, they'd probably give the guy five years with four years off for good behavior.

Fortunately, there were no more death threats during the strike, but the bad feelings grew between my so-called colleagues and me. The media poked queries at Powers and me everywhere we went, including a Boston-Philly game we worked together. *Philadelphia Bulletin* writer Mark Heisler asked me about Jake O'Donnell's statement that he would work with Powers or Strom but wouldn't socialize with either. "That's kind of him. As far as socializing off the court, I can't ever remember socializing with Jake O'Donnell. . . . I think Richie and I got along well tonight and there's no love lost between me and Richie." I did feel awkward about not backing the efforts of some of the guys, but I just couldn't buy into the mentality of the group overall, and certainly not Phillips. I received harassing phone calls, hate mail, and my kids were harassed in Pottstown. Fans fired off their salvos from the stands.

There was this little guy in Detroit who used to run up and

down behind the Pistons' bench and really get on the officials with filthy, obnoxious language. One night a few years earlier he was really getting out of hand, and I called him over to me during a time-out. I said, "You really get on me and I don't mind that. But I do take offense to your language. Not only are there women and children sitting around you, but you have to remember I'm a minister in my real job and it offends me to hear blasphemy."

He looked at me suspiciously. "Really? Are you really a minister?"

"Yes, I am."

"Well, I'm sorry, sir. I won't talk like that anymore. You don't mind if I get on you a little though, do you?"

"Naw, just so you don't use that filthy language."

From that night on, he always called me Preacher. Like, "You blew that one, Preacher."

One night during the playoffs he started in on me. He kept yelling, "You're a rotten scab, Preacher. They ought to run you out of town. We don't need vermin like you in this town, Preacher."

Finally, Bob Lanier turned on the guy during a time-out and said, "Why don't you sit down, you fool. We need him a helluva lot more than we need you."

After fifteen days and nearly two rounds of playoff games, the NABR gained recognition as the bargaining agent for officials with the NBA. Playoff pay went up by $150 per game to $750, $850, and $950 for the three final rounds of the playoffs. The rest of the matters would be discussed when the season was over. The striking officials believed Powers and I had stayed on the job to bid for the supervisor's job, which was being vacated by Nucatola. During the strike O'Donnell, Drucker, and Garretson were each reportedly offered the supervisor's job if they would leave the ranks of the strikers. Drucker was named to that post, but there was a lot of bitterness toward Powers and me when we started meeting up with these guys to work the rest of the playoffs.

The first game I had with guys from the union after the strike was in Portland. Manny Sokol and I were working it with Jim Capers as the alternate. I never had much use for Sokol, and he had about the same regard for me, so our relationship was the same for all intents and purposes. He's such a jittery guy he'd make coffee nervous. I don't think he liked working with me under any circumstances, let alone just coming back from something as heated as the strike. He knew there was nothing he could do on the court to try to show me up or embarrass me. Being the nervous type, he just rambled on about how the strike had cost him and all that crap. Larry Brown, who was coaching Denver, and Carl Scheer, who had become general manager of the Nuggets, were patting Manny on the back before the game. "Gee, it's great to have ya back. We sure need you guys." When we were introduced, we received a standing ovation. Manny looked at me and said, "How about that? They really wanted us back, didn't they?"

"Wait'll you make your first call against them, Manny, and see how they feel about it," I told him. It took about a minute before they were at his throat. "Who needs you back, ya chump." I just laughed. We're going down to the wire of the first half, and Manny made a couple of calls against Denver that were, well, a little shaky. Larry Brown went crazy. He followed us to our dressing room at the half, and he was screaming and calling Manny every homer, gutless-bastard name in the book. And Carl Scheer was right behind him, yelling and screaming. We got to the room and Manny said, "We're starting the second half with a technical foul."

"Fine. They've got it coming," I told him, pleased that he called them on their efforts to intimidate him.

Manny started pacing around the room, mumbling and cursing. "Who do they think they are? They can't talk to me that way." He went on and on. "I'm going to start the second half with a technical and I don't care what you say."

"Hey, I didn't say anything. It's okay by me. You're a referee same as I am. Hit him with it if you think he's got it coming. But shut up about it, will you?"

"Hey, you can't talk to me like that." He was surprised and upset.

"Fine. Drop it."

We didn't say much after that and headed out to start the second half. Scheer started in on Manny again, then turned to me and said, "I thought you were going to straighten him out."

I said, "Now wait a minute, Carl. You bitched about the subs and now you bitch when the vets come back. I don't want to hear about your sob stories. Nothing changes with you guys."

Manny started the second half with a technical on Denver.

Portland went on to win that series and then to take Philadelphia's cast of stars, 4–2, in the finals. Walton emerged as the spectacular center people had expected him to be three seasons earlier. I think for that one season, and half of the next before he got hurt, Walton was on a par with any of the all-time great centers. He was a better shooter than either Russell or Chamberlain; he was a better passer than either of them or Kareem. He could block shots as well as either of them and better than Kareem. Had he been able to play to that level over an extended period, he would have been the greatest center of all time. But part of the test is doing it year after year, and injuries just never allowed him that chance. He elevated the play of everyone around him so dramatically. Look what he did for Maurice Lucas, who was certainly a good but not a great player. Walton made him look like a great forward. Look what he did for those guards—Lionel Hollins, Dave Twardzik, Herm Gilliam, and Bobby Gross. That was a team of journeymen made into champions by Walton and Jack Ramsay's system. They were so active.

People have speculated that if Walton had stayed healthy, there would have been a rivalry with Kareem that could have been like Russell and Wilt. As two great talents, they certainly would have made for a great matchup over a period of time. But I don't think any rivalry in sports ever quite had the focus of Russell and Wilt. Part of it is the focus a basketball fan gets on head-to-head competition between players. Outside of boxing, there isn't anything in sport as visible and personal. Plus, Russell and Chamberlain were so dominant when the whole of pro basketball was concentrated on so few teams. They were such prominent personalities in an era when the centers were the main force on teams.

I didn't try to get into joking sessions with Kareem. He would sometimes try to kid with me, but I was always cautious of him because he was very moody, and I didn't trust where he was coming from all the time. But we had mutual respect for each other's work and we went about our business. I took the game ball into the locker room after his last game and gave it to him. He gave me a big hug. I guess any hug from Kareem would be big, wouldn't it?

When Walton first came into the league, he loved to nod or shake his head depending on what he thought of the call. I told him I didn't need to know his opinion, and I sure as hell didn't appreciate his telling the crowd what he thought of each call. He cut it out with me and we had a solid rapport from then on. It's funny how none of the great centers ever gave me much grief. In fact, that holds true for virtually all the greats. Elvin Hayes, Oscar Robertson, and Rick Barry were the three notable exceptions; they were always bitching.

Barry would give the choke sign behind your back and rag on and on. Long after he retired, he told a reporter, "Earl would allow me to be an asshole, but only to a point. But then, you have to remember Earl has mellowed over the years, too." We were like water and oil. Sometimes you'd just have your fill of a guy like that. In the playoffs the year after Golden State had won the world championship, the Warriors were playing Phoenix. Ricky Sobers was a tough kid for Phoenix. Joe Gushue and I were working the game. Barry and Sobers got into it, and Sobers was really cleaning his clock. None of the Golden State guys went to help Rick. Joe started to move in to break it up. I held him back and told him out of the side of my mouth, "You stay the hell out of there, I've been waiting for this for a long time." Poor Rick really got the crap kicked out of him. Then he went into a shell; he was so mad at his teammates he hardly took another shot the rest of the game. Phoenix went on to knock them out of the playoffs.

Barry was always so intense, and he'd probably make a pretty good coach now, but he's got to go on my all-time Ref Rider team along with Hayes, Oscar, Kevin Porter, and Norm Van Lier. Of course, when it comes to harassing referees, players are at a disadvantage to coaches. The latter don't have to get distracted by playing the game.

I put the coaches who are particularly prone to bait refs into two categories, Butchers and Bitchers. The Butchers were from the old school; they attacked your character, your ancestry, your courage. They accused you of being on the take. They could be downright vulgar and ugly. Basically, they tried to cut off your manhood. The Bitchers are more subtle, more typical of what you have today. They pick away at you, trying to con you with a little humor, challenging your judgment, your knowledge, trying to get you to give up your manhood without any bloodshed. The Butcher honors go to Auerbach, Seymour, Hannum, Loughery, and Al Cervi on a close call over Bobby Leonard and Al Bianchi.

Most of the contemporary coaches worry more about coaching their players than coaching the referees. But Bitchers distinguish themselves by spending time-outs yelling at officials and constantly nagging throughout the game. As I said, any coach can get into it in a given game, but the guys who made it more of a habit to bitch include Don Nelson, Hubie Brown, Doug Moe, Dick Motta, and Butch van Breda Kolff.

Kevin Loughery was just consumed with harassing referees. He's a throwback to the old days; in fact, he might have been as nasty toward officials as any coach in the history of the league. I guess what made him worse than Auerbach was that he had worse teams. He had the misfortune of coaching the second half of the season with the 1972–73 Philly team that went 9-73, the worst record of all time. He bounced around with the Nets, Hawks, and Bullets without a whole lot of success, at least not when I was there. He did win two ABA titles after I had jumped back, but it didn't help his disposition or won-lost record when the Nets sold Dr. J to the 76ers the day before they were to make their NBA debut. I wouldn't be surprised if he wasn't the all-time leader in technical fouls. He was just a maniac as a coach, ranting and raving. He drove Richie Powers so crazy one night that Richie called three technical fouls on him. After the second one he kicked a chair and tossed a glass of water onto the court. Still, two technicals and ejection was the limit, so they had to cancel out what turned out to be a double-overtime game and go back and replay it from the middle of the third quarter when Loughery got the third T. Richie got suspended for five games for that one.

Al Cervi was a pretty nasty guy, really from the old school since he played before the league was even officially started. He was the first coach Syracuse had, and he rode his players so hard that when they won the title in 1954–55, they didn't even cut him in for a playoff share.

Bobby Leonard was a real maniac as coach of the Indiana Pacers in both the ABA and NBA. He once threw a rack of balls at Ed Rush. Another time he went after a player on the opposing team—I can't remember who it was—and Len Elmore was holding Bobby. The other guy yelled at Elmore, "Let 'em go. Let me have him." Bobby hissed back over his shoulder at Len, "Don't you dare let me go." He was a real wild man. He loved to get things stirred up, kick a ball into the stands, toss his coat. He was hell for most officials, but I got along with him pretty well. When I was working in the ABA, we went out for a pop one night after the Pacers had played at Pittsburgh. We had more than a couple and he looked over at me and said, "You know the reason you have problems getting along with people is because you're too arrogant." I said, "Yeah, you're right. As a matter of fact, we're a lot alike."

Al Bianchi was always on the refs even as an assistant at Phoenix—like the time he threw a clipboard at Hugh Evans. The fans gave him a clipboard shaped like a boomerang for Christmas. But Bianchi had a real heart, and a sharp perspective on life. When Bianchi was coaching the Virginia Squires, we were on an exhibition tour, and the bus was travelling down a road early one morning and the players were all bitching about how tough life was. Bianchi told the driver to stop the bus and ordered everyone off. There were a bunch of guys digging a ditch, and Bianchi said, "Guys, would you really rather be doing this than going down the road to play basketball?" They all trooped back onto the bus and nobody said a word the rest of the way to the airport.

There was a time when I didn't think Red Auerbach was the genius everyone made him out to be. I thought a lot of his act was contrived; he'd get all riled up and maybe get a T or even get tossed and his team would respond with a great burst. Maybe it wouldn't have worked with another set of players, but he had a system and he made it work. When you look at his record and all the maneuvers he made over the years, I really do have to put the guy at the top of the stack. You don't see many guys working that emotional stuff nowadays. To a degree Chuck Daly and Den Nelson do it, but I don't think players get as involved with their coaches as they used to. It's more technical and less emotional. In the earlier era, you had tough, hard players who turned right around and became tough, hard coaches. Cervi, Seymour, Kundla, Hannum, Mikan, Tommy Marshall, Bobby Wanzer, van Breda Kolff, all fit that mold. And Red, although he didn't play as a pro, was a molder of the tough, hard environment in which the league was founded. Red kept his distance; he worked at protecting his hard-ass image with officials. He wanted you to believe he hated them all. He was just a blood-and-guts kind of guy who was born to stick that mug of his out there and defy anybody to stand in his way. And if you did, you'd better have been willing to go to war, because he'd declare it.

As a player, Tom Heinsohn was a protégé of Red's. He was a pain in the ass on the court, and when he was on the bench, he sounded like an echo. Red would say, "Aw, come on, Earl, you're missin' a good game," and you'd hear this echo from Heinsohn, "Aw, come on, Earl, you're missin' a good game." I called them Edgar Bergen and Charlie McCarthy. Heinsohn was very fiery as a coach, but he was usually pretty fair. I remember one night the Celtics got hammered real bad up at Hartford and we were walking off the floor. He said, "Now I don't want your ego to get ahead of you and worry about what I'm gonna say. But Earl, my man, I have to tell you, tonight was not one of your better efforts."

I looked up at him and I said, "Do I get equal time?"

"But of course."

"Well, Thomas, my boy, I've seen some bad coaching in my day, but your performance tonight tops the list." He blew and started hollering, "I knew your ego wouldn't stand for any constructive criticism."

Bill Sharman was another ex-Celtic who entered the coaching ranks, although he wasn't the madman at courtside that Red was. He introduced the superorganized approach to coaching in the NBA, having his practices planned out to the minute. He felt that all aspects of the game, especially shooting, could be drilled into you until it became an instinctive response. While coaching the Lakers, he decided to start having the guys shoot around on the day of the game to loosen up and hone their shooting. When Wilt didn't show up, Sharman sent Rod Hundley, who was working as a broadcaster then, up to his room. "Hey, Wilt, they're having a shootaround."

"What's this shootaround stuff?"

"Coach thinks it'll help you loosen up, get ready for tonight's game."

"Well, you tell him I go to that building once today, eleven A.M. or seven-thirty P.M."

Obviously, Wilt wasn't too eager to embrace the new era of coaching that Sharman was pioneering. When I look where it's gone, I have to wonder myself. I can't understand why they need all these assistant coaches. They say this guy is a great defensive coach, and that guy is great at teaching centers. I think they're making it more complicated than it needs to be. It seems as if the coaches spend half the time-outs huddled among themselves. What's really amazing to me is the way they have these assistants keeping a chart on

what kind of calls are being made by which official. They get
a time-out in a crucial situation and look over to determine
which official is under the basket. Is he likely to call a charge
or a block? It must be a sign of the times, making everything
more complicated, but if they want to put that much emphasis on it, why not just go hire an ex-official as an assistant?
Their knowledge of the rules and the personalities of the
officials could be a factor. There certainly is such a thing as
working a referee. You just have to know whom you can get
to and under what circumstances. There are some referees
who will definitely knuckle under. I'd bet a referee as an
assistant coach could win you five games a year. But I'm
afraid if I were in a job like that, I'd be a Butcher. After all
the study I've had under the masters, I'd go for the man-
hoods every time.

Actually, Charlie Eckman ruined it for any other NBA
referee who might ever want to try coaching. Charlie went
out as coach as I was coming into the league thirty-two years
ago, and nobody has been inspired to hire a referee as a
coach since. After working as an NBA referee, he coached
the Fort Wayne Pistons with pretty good success in the fifties
and had a really good thing going. He almost won the title
two years running, and everyone was starting to think he
was some kind of a genius. But then he started popping his
mouth off, which he had a propensity to do. He said, "Hell,
anybody can coach in this league. Look at me. I'm no coach.
All you gotta do is be a cheerleader, keep everybody happy."
He started making all these goofy trades and finally talked
Fred Zollner into moving the club to Detroit, where they
struggled, and Charlie got canned before the year was out.

He was one of the great con artists in the history of the
game. He had so much talent on that Fort Wayne team—
Larry Foust, Mel Hutchins, Bob Houbregs, George Yardley—he could hardly lose. One night they had a game against
the Lakers in Fort Wayne. They were down by 1 with just
a few seconds to go. The Pistons had the ball under their own
basket and they took a time-out. Charlie said, "This is what
we're going to do, fellas. You three guys line up across the

free throw line. Larry, you come around the screen, and Mel will hit you with the pass. Just pop it in and you'll be a hero." But while he's talking, Foust says, "Coach, I've got to go to the can." Charlie said, "Oh, come on, you can wait a couple seconds. Just give me a couple seconds and we're out of here." Foust said, "Coach, I can't wait," and he took off on the run. He had diarrhea.

The fans all thought Charlie and Foust had gotten into a beef. Charlie turned to Houbregs and said, "You come in and get in the middle of that line, and George, you take the ball out, and Mel, *you* come around the screen and take the shot. *You* be the hero." Charlie told the three guys who were to form the screen that under no circumstances were any of them to take the shot. "You don't touch that ball," he told Houbregs, who in turn took offense at the lack of confidence in him. After all, he was nicknamed Hooks because he had been an all-American with a great hook shot. Well, they lined up across the free throw line, all three of them. The pass came in and Houbregs reached up and grabbed the ball. He took one dribble and let fly with his hook. The ball was in the air as the horn sounded. It went in. Everybody was swarming around congratulating Charlie for his great strategy of taking Foust out and using Houbregs for the winning shot. At least he had the humility to admit later that the time he looked most like a coaching genius was when his star had to run to the can.

If I'd seen where things were headed for me with my fellow refs in the late seventies and early eighties, I might have preferred to take my chances as a coach. After the strike talks were completed at the end of the 1976–77 season, Powers and I were forced to join the union. We had helped the NBA through the tough times, but officiating, like anything else in the business world, is a matter of what can you do for me today. The NBA had said they would never let the union dictate that we had to join, but they were willing to give that up in exchange for something they wanted more. I could accept this as a fact of life.

The following September we went into the referees camp

for the 1977–78 season. The headquarters were at the Shera-
ton Hotel in Manhattan, and I went over on the train with
Joey Crawford. He was going to be a rookie that year, having
worked during the strike. As soon as we walked into the
lobby, a lot of the guys were standing around and they just
turned and walked away. I told Joey, "You'll get the cold
shoulder, maybe not even for the whole week. Just take it
easy. They won't let up on me, but they understand the
position you're in. Just let them have their way for a few
days."

Norm Drucker was the new supervisor. I went into his
room and was talking to him. Other guys would walk in and
would ordinarily have stayed and talked, but as soon as they
saw me, they'd say hello to Norm and leave. Nobody else
would acknowledge me until I ran into Vanak and Gushue.
They didn't like what I had done, but since we went back a
ways together, they weren't about to shut me out. My roommate was Dick Bavetta. He had written me a nice note
during the strike saying that he understood my position and
to assure me we were still friends. He was never that popular
with the guys because they considered him some sort of a
politician type, and now that he was rooming with me he was
really low on their list. They thought he was carrying tales
back to me. Powers and I had been forced to join the union
at a $2,000 initiation fee and $1,000-a-year dues, but they
didn't want us to know what they were up to. They kept
saying, "Strom and Powers know exactly what we are doing.
There's a leak here." So much for the brotherhood.

Things were pretty uncomfortable for Bavetta, and since
he lived right there in New York, he decided to go home and
commute. He hadn't been filling me up with a lot of info, but
at least that way the other guys got off his back. I had come
to camp knowing this was going to happen. Powers was
taken aback by the cold shoulder. Richie and I were sitting
in a bar one evening, and he was getting half a glow on. He
was beside himself about how the guys were treating him. I
said, "What do you expect? We took money out of their
pockets during the playoffs."

"You feel that way, Earl, because you were never liked by the guys. But they used to like me."

"You're wrong. They hate your guts. They just never told you to your face."

Richie was pompous. He had a reputation for getting other officials in hot water. Hell, he had something to do with my being boycotted. They were jealous of him, too, because he was then pretty much the fair-haired boy after coming back from the ABA. I've known him since we came in together in 1957, and the first day he walked on the court he was pompous.

One year he worked a couple of playoff games and Podoloff called him to give him another assignment. Richie said he was going to start working in baseball, and Podoloff was so upset he fired him on the spot and ripped the phone out of the wall. Literally. Podoloff was so upset that he ranted and raved after he pulled the phone out of the wall and promised that Richie would never get back in the NBA. But he was too good an official to keep out forever.

The biggest bitcher and moaner about me was Jake O'-Donnell. He didn't like me. I don't have much faith in him as a person, and with him on the executive board of the union I wondered where the ship was headed. It was so funny, nobody would talk to me when there was a group around, but as the week went on, guys would come up on their own and say things like, "How about that O'Donnell. Ed Rush had to baby-sit him during the strike to keep him from going back before it was settled." They were a bunch of followers without much in the way of leadership.

Four new officials were added to the staff. They couldn't do much to Bernie Fryer, who worked during the strike, because as a former player he was important to the league. They wanted to get former players started in refereeing, and they weren't going to let anything happen to the first one. Joey Crawford was also on solid footing because he was so obviously a capable referee. The other two guys were Milt Cooper and Mel Whitworth. Neither of these guys were ready to come into the league when they did. They should have had more experience outside the NBA, but because they worked during the strike, they were given their chance. These two guys were not strong enough to fend for themselves, so every time they got into trouble in a game the other guys would just let them hang. Crawford was good enough to survive and Fryer had to survive; Whitworth and Cooper went under and were fired at the end of the season.

How can a veteran hang a guy? I'll give you an example. Powers did a classic on Joey Crawford during Joey's first or second year. Richie was out of control by then. Milwaukee was at Los Angeles, and Joey was handling a throw-in, Jamaal Wilkes of the Lakers was trying to get the ball in, and John Gianelli was jumping up and down in front of him. Joey was counting off the seconds against Wilkes, who finally called a time-out. Richie, who was positioned forty feet away, came over and said that Gianelli was encroaching on the sidelines and not giving Wilkes enough room. They came back out and the same thing happened, so Wilkes tossed the ball to Joey and said, "Give me room!" Joey tossed the ball back to him and kept counting. Richie blew the whistle, came over, took the ball, and said, "I'll handle this."

Joey was furious. "What the fuck do you think you're doing?"

Richie said, "You just go over there, I told you I'd handle this." Richie told Gianelli to get back and either he didn't or he said something to him. Whatever, Richie hit him with a T. Milwaukee protested the game because if Richie hadn't done that, they would have had a five-second violation and gotten the ball down only two points at the time. It was a horseshit thing for Richie to do to take Joey off the play and embarrass him like that. I don't know that Joey had any business cussing Richie like that, but I can understand the sentiment.

Richie knew no bounds when it came to doing a trip on people. Like the night Richie went up to Hubie Brown and Kevin Loughery before a Knicks-Nets game and said that he wasn't going to call any illegal defenses. "Go ahead, use your zones. It won't make any difference." I'm sure Hubie and

Kevin thought he was screwing with their minds, which they probably deserved for all the grief they had given referees over the years. Richie just felt it was a joke to pretend that teams weren't using it, and he wanted to make a mockery out of the rule, but it about blew away Drucker, who was supervisor then. Powers got fined big time and damn near fired.

Hanging a guy. It sounds pretty brutal, and as I mentioned, it can be lethal to the inexperienced official if the veteran has it in for him. All referees get accused of doing that at times. I have been. I like to let a younger official handle things so that they learn, but if I see it's getting out of hand, I step in and get the guy out of trouble if I can. A lot of it's done on the side. A coach might come up to a referee who is more established and start knocking the lesser official, saying, "Your partner sure made a terrible call," and the guy says, "Yeah, there's nothing I can do about him, he's pretty weak." That's hanging a guy. Or if there's a tough call that's in a spot where either official would have equal coverage on it, the veteran might back off and let the less-accepted guy take it and catch all the heat. Instead of coming up and saying, "Good call," and helping sell it, the other referee might just hang back in silence or even worse, come in and say, "You've got what?" or roll his eyes as if to say, "Can you believe this guy?" When I was breaking in, some refs would jump in on a call that was equal distance between us and yell something like "I've got it, I've got it" to take charge of the call and not leave the rookie to have to sell it. I do that now.

In the old days you could see a veteran official rush up and shake his head and overrule the younger official's call. It's like saying, "You ain't got a clue, pal." Now they have a rule in the book that stops that. Years ago the senior official would have priority on a call where the two officials disagreed, but now if there's a difference of opinion on, say, an out-of-bounds play, you have a jump ball. This is a case where hanging a guy means *not* overruling him. The ball goes out of bounds and you maybe saw that someone had a little flick on it. The other referee didn't and he's calling it the opposite way. Instead of helping him, you leave him to hang in the eyes of everyone else. Much better to step in if you had an angle the other guy didn't as long as you're not using body language that says he's hopeless.

At the start of that 1977–78 season, the league experimented with three-man officiating crews. The third man could only call things like three-second violations, out-of-bounds plays, and goaltending, and so you couldn't tell if the guy could referee or not. I had a game in Seattle and Jerry Loeber couldn't make it due to fog. Bruce Alexander came up from Tacoma and did a good job. I took him down to Portland the next night, and he did a good job there, too. I had worked with him during the strike and was convinced he was a promising official. After a Detroit game, Bob Lanier and the Pistons' coach, Herb Brown, both came over and were singing the praises of Alexander. They said he belonged in the league. I told them if they felt that way they should let the league know. But the next day it's forgotten and the next year they're back bitchin' about the inadequate officials.

That summer Alexander worked in the Los Angeles Summer League. Garretson ran the officials there and Alexander had a beef with him. Garretson got him labeled as a wise guy, a big mouth, and that stood in his way in getting into the league. It was about this time that Garretson was starting to get some pull, although he thought he had more than he did. Two guys who declined to work during the strike, Phil Bova of Cleveland and Joe Forte of Washington, received letters from Garretson telling them how much he respected what they were doing and how he was going to do everything in his power to see that they were hired. He also sent letters to all the guys who worked and promised he'd keep them out of the league. The league hired four of the guys who worked during the strike and didn't hire either guy Garretson said he'd get in.

If anyone would have had any pull on who got hired, it ought to have been me, considering my friendship with

Norm, but I couldn't get Alexander in, I couldn't get Bova in, I couldn't get a kid named Paul Campbell of Boston in. These guys could referee, but I couldn't get them in. The only pull I had was in 1978 when Manny Sokol had his heart attack; they had fired Jess Kersey the previous year and I felt that was unjust, so I started a move with Simon Gourdine, deputy commissioner, and Norm to get Jess back. He was just sick about having been fired and he deserved to be in the league. I called Si and Norm and told them it was worth the league's swallowing a little pride, admitting the guy deserved to be in the league, and getting him back. A couple days later Jess called and said he was coming back to work.

It's a shame when someone as promising as Alexander has to battle the way he did to get in. He quit his job with the county government and threw his whole life into getting into the NBA. He took himself out of a family business and gave up a good college schedule as a referee. Once he worked in the pros during the strike, the colleges figured he was tainted and wouldn't let him back in. It took him several years of really being hung out to dry before he finally got in the league.

As far as I can tell, the three-man system has two advantages: it provides the locker room attendant an extra buck in the tip tray, and it provides a way to bring along some younger talent, which the league desperately needs to develop. I don't think we need three referees, and I don't think the colleges need three referees. If you have people who are in good condition, able to run and get on top of the play, then you have enough whistle-blowing with two people. I don't think so much goes on that a third man is going to pick up much that two people can't pick up if they so choose. A lot of things aren't called, but they're let go by choice and ought to be.

The owners didn't think the third official was worth it and dropped it after the one season, only to revive it ten years later. They gave the third official more involvement this time around, and the league seems much more committed to it now. They made a big deal about how the third man would cut down on some of the fighting that was going on. Let me tell you, if they think there was a lot of fighting in the eighties, they should've seen Syracuse. Ten refs wouldn't have been enough.

Of course, some guys are never going to change their view of the officials. Early in the season of three-man officials, seventies version, Auerbach was sitting in the stands at Madison Square Garden. He yelled out, "Jesus Christ, Earl, you get three referees out there and you're still missin' half the calls." I yelled back, "That's okay, Red. Next year we're going to bring in four of 'em. One just to keep an eye on guys like you." He didn't laugh.

chapter 9

NEW AGE/OLD
WARRIOR

As the seventies became the eighties, pro basketball finally lived up to its promises, becoming the fast-paced, exciting "sport of the decade" it said it would be ten years earlier. The wide-open play and open-court skills made the game faster and flashier, and the crowds kept growing everywhere in the league. Instead of hearing about teams being on the verge of folding, you heard about attendance records being set by expansion franchises. And if you ask me, the success off the court was definitely caused by the changes on the court.

For so many years, everyone looked for a great center who would guarantee success. Everyone wanted a "franchise" kind of big man. Kareem validated that idea when he came in. Milwaukee was 27–55 in 1968–69, won a coin flip over Phoenix, and outbid the ABA for Kareem. In his first year he led them to a 56-26 record, and the year after that he teamed up with Oscar Robertson to go 66-16 and win it all. Twenty years later people still seemed to think the answer lay in a great center, but the eighties sure showed how great forwards and guards could dominate a game. Julius Erving,

Magic, Larry Bird, Charles Barkley, and Michael Jordan are the most obvious examples. These guys all have good size, but it's their mobility and all-around talents that are so dramatic; these guys can rip rebounds, shoot with finesse, hammer inside, block shots, steal the ball, make great passes. It's just an indication of the mobility there is in the game now. And instead of a couple of big horses battling for the rebounds, you can have ten sets of hands up over the rim. It has certainly made for a faster, more active game, and therefore one that's a helluva lot harder to call than it was twenty years ago.

The eighties provided a steady recovery from the damage done by the rivalry between the ABA and NBA. With a trend inspired by Bird and Magic, the work ethic returned—when superstars come out to bust their butts on both ends of the court every night, the quality of play goes up for everyone. Salaries continued to climb toward an average of a million dollars a man by the end of the decade, but at least guys looked as if they cared to be there. It's as if the players caught on that the public doesn't mind spending a good buck for sports entertainment, but you give 'em a show, baby, or you ruin a good thing.

And you'd better believe the superstars are the heart of the show. Does that mean that superstars get away with things, get favored treatment? To some slight extent, maybe. When you watch someone make a move, it's tough to eliminate completely all your built-in expectations, and I suppose that gives the edge to the superior talent. If a rookie shuffles his feet, he's apt to get called on it; if it's become part of a man's game, a patented style, he can probably get some leeway. A Dr. J or Jordan taking off from the free-throw line and slamming the ball might have taken an extra hop before going airborne, but he's done enough spectacular things to cause people to give him the benefit of the doubt.

On the whole, though, I say the question's all wrong. Superstars don't hold an edge because referees look the other way. It's the referee's job to make sure the game's played right, and if we do our job well, that's going to *allow* the superstars to do their thing. They benefit most by what we do call, not by what we don't. It's imperative that the referee make sure the super talent isn't taken right out of the game by desperate defense.

I was conducting an instructional clinic at the 76ers preseason camp in the late seventies when we were trying to crack down on heavy-duty hand-checking. Henry Bibby, a stocky guard, piped up, "Earl, how am I going to check a guy like George Gervin if I can't use my hands? He's taller than me. He'll overpower me if I can't defend myself with my hands." I reminded him that, first, he didn't have hands on guys in college, and secondly, it's not up to the referee to neutralize the talent of one player so somebody else can keep up. And the year before, I had a game in San Antonio where Billy Paultz came up to me at the half and said, "I've got four fouls and Kareem's got twenty-five points. Earl, if you don't let me play him my way and stop calling all these fouls, he's going to score a hundred on me." I didn't have much sympathy. "What am I supposed to do, Billy? Maybe I should tell him, 'Kareem, you're not supposed to be seven foot two and that good. This guy can't keep up, so I'm going to let him bludgeon you to death.'"

A couple of years ago, Atlanta was playing Chicago and an Atlanta player undercut Jordan as he went in for one of his flying dunks on a fast break. I called a flagrant foul. Some guy yelled out from the Atlanta bench, "Ah, you're just protecting the superstars."

"Damn right I am," I told him. "You eliminate these guys from the game and we're all out of work."

Dominique Wilkins looked at his teammate and said, "Amen."

It really isn't so much a matter of protecting the privileged few as it is ensuring that the guys with the great skills, the guys with all the flair and finesse and touch, can play their game without being pounded right out of commission by some of these muscular assassins. Don't get me wrong, it's a tough, physical game and there are some guys who are big and strong enough to bruise the ordinary man on the street just by bumping into him. But a grinding, rugby-match approach isn't tolerable in the new era. This is the era of flash and flair, and it's paying big dividends.

Where two-thirds of the league's teams were losing money at the beginning of the eighties, virtually all of them were profitable as the decade concluded. Of course, having four teams come into the league at $32 million a pop doesn't hurt. And to think that the four ABA teams came in for one-tenth that amount a dozen years earlier. The growth through the eighties was driven by the emergence of a handful of truly spectacular players, more competitive teams, and the prominent decade-long rivalry between Boston and L.A. For ten straight years, beginning in 1980, one or the other was in the finals, and they faced each other three times. They certainly weren't the only teams with talent during that time; Houston made the finals twice and Philadelphia three times, winning it in 1982–83. But the Celtics and the Lakers provided a catalyst for media and fan interest. They were personified as the glamorous Lakers and the lunch-bucket Celtics. Magic Johnson and Larry Bird. Jack Nicholson and that big jerk under the basket in Boston Garden.

Average attendance has more than doubled since I came into the league, while the league expanded more than threefold. TV coverage, particularly the expansion into cable, has really opened up fan interest. NBC's 600-million-dollar deal to cover the NBA for the next four years is an incredible step forward, and I lay a lot of the credit in the lap of David Stern, who, as commissioner, has shown more leadership and vision than any of his predecessors. Actually, that's probably unfair to Maurice Podoloff, whose leadership got the whole thing started and kept it afloat for its first decade and a half. But what Walter Kennedy kept going and Larry O'Brien tried to enhance, Stern has caused to blossom. He's proven to be a marketing genius; every aspect of the NBA has been treated as a product to be packaged and developed.

It's showtime all the way. Given what trouble the league was in a decade ago, I can't fault the results. A lot of it isn't really my style, though; I still kind of miss the old Minneapolis uniforms, with those huge "MPLS" letters on the front, but maybe that's why I'm not in charge of marketing the era of slickness in the NBA. I mean, Charlotte came out with designer uniforms; really, developed by a world-famous fashion designer, and this got Larry Brown thinking about putting a little more class in San Antonio's uniforms. Me, I'm more in line with Doug Moe; someone asked Moe, whose Denver Nuggets have pretty colorful uniforms already, what he thought about the new look in NBA dress, and he responded, "I really don't give a shit what they wear."

That probably goes for coaches as well as players. Coaches have become more businesslike, Pat Riley probably setting the trend in motion with his *GQ* clothes and slicked-back hair. John MacLeod, Bernie Bickerstaff, Larry Brown, Lenny Wilkens, most of the modern era coaches, seemed to be real conscious of being neat, controlled, and stylish. The league went from the rumpled suits of the fifties and sixties to the seventies when guys wore wild sports coats to the spiffy eighties. Doug Moe never quite got to the eighties. He's a rumpled wild-sports-coat kind of guy, inside and out. Doug's never been afraid to speak his mind; it was not out of character for him to say, during Kareem's final season, "The guy's been a jerk his whole career. I don't see why we're gettin' so sentimental with all this farewell-tour crap now that we're finally getting rid of him."

Starting in the late seventies, the NBA made moves to bring the pro game into the new age. They put in the three-point shot to open things up for the Dr. J's and David Thompsons and the Michael Jordans to come. They turned the All-Star game into a weekend show with slam-dunk contests, three-point contests, and old-timers' games to go with the main event. They've set up international games such as the annual McDonald's tournament in Europe. The crowds in some places are enormous. The playoffs have taken on prime-time prominence. I support—in fact, I enjoy—what all of this has created in the NBA.

But at the same time that all of these personalities were getting bigger and bigger, the league was doing everything it could to make those of us who have to take charge out on the court seem smaller and smaller. The NBA says it wants the spotlight to be just on the players, but it sure seems to me that the spotlight's big enough and bright enough to include some referees, too. It takes a big ego to run the game right, but the NBA has been trying for the last ten years or so to take anyone who stands out and push them right back down.

I may accidentally have given them the impetus for some of this a number of years ago when I was writing a weekly column for a couple of papers near Pottstown. It was kind of fun and it gave the local readers a little of my perspective on life in the NBA. I would write about things such as the terrible loss it was to basketball when Billy Cunningham finally had his career ended by injuries: "Billy was making one of his patented moves to the basket. Suddenly he crashed to the floor, without player contact, and with an agonizing yell of torturous pain that brought to an end his season of playing, and perhaps his career. His shriek of pain was audible among the 18,000 roaring, horrified fans."

I would write about the emergence of an Abdul-Jabbar vs. Bob McAdoo rivalry that never quite became Russell vs. Chamberlain. I would write about getting kicked in the solar plexus after tossing up a jump ball between Charlie Johnson and Paul Silas, and with the last gasp of air going out of my lungs, blowing a time-out. After lying there motionless for a couple minutes, I actually drew a cheer from the crowd when the trainers got me up again. Or I would write about Mendy: "It was during a time-out in a game at Boston and everything was in an uproar. Mendy and I stood at center court, the abuse surrounding us like a shroud. Mendy nonchalantly gazed into the stands filled with irate spectators, and as eggs, tomatoes, and other refuse were hurled at our feet, a slight smile began to form on his lips. Remembering that we were of the same ethnic background, he turned to me and said, 'You might think there were fifteen thousand

Arabs occupying those seats and they all know what we are.'"

Sometimes my opinions would come out about things that I felt weren't right in the NBA. Like the firing, forced resignation, whatever you want to call it, that the Milwaukee Bucks imposed on Larry Costello in 1977 as he was eighteen games into his ninth season as coach. "The new owners, obviously, were blinded by the present dismal record and did not consider what Costy did for the organization since its beginning."

They didn't give me a beef about what I wrote until a piece that ran in the *Reading Eagle* came out in the spring of 1979. As it happens, the story involved another firing of Larry Costello, this time by the Chicago Bulls:

The Bulls are in deep trouble. Not only has attendance dipped to the lowest average in Bull history, but those few thousand who do come out to Chicago Stadium spend the evening booing their own team. When the season began, the Bulls management decided to hire Larry Costello to coach the club—mistake No. 1.

Larry, being from the so-called old school, wasn't going to stand by and watch players making an average of $145,000 a year not put out to the best of their ability. Of course, Larry's opinion of playing ability may differ from that of Bulls management. Some moves were made early in the season by Jonathan Kovler, the team president, that were suspect, and made one wonder about the president's knowledge of the game. Many of these moves were reportedly not even discussed with Costello. Anyway, when the team began losing, Costello made the cardinal sin of working his players extra hard in off-day practices. Can you imagine that—asking a player who is making a couple hundred thousand to work a little harder in practice!

Well, as it always happens in the NBA, Costello was fired, and his assistant coach, Scotty Robertson, replaced him—mistake No. 2. Scotty was picked as interim coach until former player Jerry Sloan decides he can work for Kovler. You see, Sloan would probably have taken the job before Costello got it if he thought he could have full rein over the team's playing roster. Kovler was not about to consent to this sort of nonsense. After all, how could Sloan, a

13-year NBA veteran, think he could know more about playing talent than Kovler?

You get the idea. So did Kovler, who actually held the title of "managing partner." Just how he came across this particular copy of the *Reading Eagle,* I'm not sure, but once he saw it, he went to the NBA office demanding my head on a platter.

While this was hanging, I had a little incident with our old friend Kevin Loughery. He was coaching the Nets in a playoff game. I was working with Joe Gushue and Jess Kersey. Loughery had been carrying on throughout the game, and near the end he came onto the court and went after Jess. I got into it and screamed at him to get off the court. He wouldn't back down so I tossed him. Then the trainer got on me and I tossed him. That got a lot of coverage in the papers. The next night Joe and I had a game in Atlanta. Hubie Brown was coaching the Hawks and he came up to us before the game and was saying, "Gee, that's too bad things like that happen. I'm sorry to see you and Kevin get into it like that." And Joe said, "Don't worry about it, Hubie, tonight it might be you." And sure enough, before the first half was over, I ended up having to unload Hubie.

After the Hubie incident I went to Phoenix and got into a pushing match with a fan coming off the floor and got into a shouting match with a security official working for the league. Joe Gilmartin wrote in a column in the *Phoenix Gazette* about how the crowd chanted in the game's final minutes, "We beat Strom! We beat Strom!" He told about how fans had hurled debris at us and came after us leaving the court. " 'At first,' said a member of what is surely one of the league's best security forces, 'we were holding the fans back. Then we had to hold Earl back.' " Gilmartin wrote about how I was known as a "roader," saying, "It implies that Earl will not be intimidated by even the largest and most hostile crowds. Now, if only Earl will stop trying to intimidate large and hostile crowds." He also wrote: " 'One of the rules of the league,' said mild-mannered center Alvan Adams of the

Suns, who was tagged with a technical by Strom, 'is that you don't rile Jabbar. Or Strom.' "

All this stuff kept building up in reports to the league office, and Richie Phillips must have been loving every bit of it. So they suspended me for the rest of the playoffs. That cost me about $12,000. I was directed to fly to Chicago and apologize to Kovler. Once I had convinced Rod Thorn, then the Bulls' general manager, that I wouldn't harbor any animosity when working future Bulls games, the league dropped their threat to fire me. I dropped the column.

Norm Drucker, who was supervisor of officials at the time, issued a statement: "I think Earl understands now that public criticism of the league is unacceptable. Things are tough enough for a referee without teams complaining that an official is prejudiced against them. Earl and I were NBA referees twenty years ago when things were different. You could tell off a coach or take a punch at a fan who insulted you. But we don't allow any of that because we don't want the riots and lawsuits we'd surely have as a consequence. Taking abuse is part of the job and officials just have to put up with it. Earl knows what the rules are and I don't think there will be any more problems."

Yeah, Norm was right. Kovler had every right to object to the article, which I used poor judgment in writing. I think the league overreacted by their banning me from the playoffs and almost firing me, but I got the message.

I decided I would adopt what I called my "walkaway image." Instead of going nose to nose with a player or a coach, I was determined to use the mechanics specified by the league. I would merely call a technical and walk away. If they followed me and continued to beef, I would call a second technical and expel them from the game. As for the spectators, I would merely look at them and smile. I realized after many altercations with fans over the years that I always came out the loser one way or another. With the increase in arena security, it was best to leave them with the chore of keeping peace; I would simply concentrate on the game.

As I sat on the sidelines during the 1978–79 playoffs, Seat-

tle captured its first NBA title. Lenny Wilkens was coaching
the Sonics then and he said, "If there's one official who can't
be intimidated or influenced by players, coaches, and fans,
it's Earl Strom. The thing I respect him for, aside from being
a very good official, is that you can get hot with him one night
and have a few words, yet the next time you get him working
your team he's ready to start fresh. No grudges or antago-
nism from him. It was more like that in the old days than it
is now around the league. And I'll tell you something else:
When the Earl Stroms are kept from working the biggest
games, the league suffers."

I was grateful for the nice words, but I was starting to get
very wary of drawing attention; it seemed every time there
was the slightest bit of publicity, things would come back to
haunt me. Chuck Newman, a sports reporter for the *Philadelphia Inquirer,* wanted to do a story on the life of a referee. He got permission from the league office to spend
three or four days on the road with me. After a game in
Chicago we went back to the hotel. The visiting team was
staying somewhere else, so I figured it would be safe to go
down to the lounge without running into any players or
coaches. John Killelea, who was then assistant coach to Don
Nelson at Milwaukee, was in there, in the city to do some
scouting. He saw us sitting at the bar and came over. We got
to talking and he started getting wound up about referees;
I just told him, "Look, John, if you've got a problem with the
refereeing, take it to the league office." We kicked around
life in the NBA a bit, had a few laughs, and that was that.
When Newman wrote his article, he put in there that we had
run into an assistant coach from another team in the lounge,
who was scouting. He said the guy bought me a drink, but
he didn't mention anything about our talking about referees.
He also mentioned how I would go into the pressrooms for
a cup of coffee or sit up in the stands before games and chat
with folks I knew. It seemed harmless enough, but Darell
Garretson and Richie Phillips got a hold of it and went to Joe
Axelson, Vice President of Operations, saying they wanted
me fined. They set up a meeting at the league office. I walked

in and there was Phillips at the table with O'Brien, Russ Granik, Chief Legal Counsel, Axelson, and Garretson. I felt as if I'd been set up by Axelson, who had approved the article only to turn around and use it against me. They fined me $2,000 and suspended me for part of the playoffs.

A couple of years after that they tried to get me booted from the playoffs, and instead I ended up getting paid for games I wasn't even working. Garretson and Mike Mathis had worked a playoff game between Milwaukee and Philadelphia. When I went into Philly for the next game, I supposedly told someone in the media or on one of the teams that I couldn't believe they hadn't made a fuss over a lousy call I supposedly felt Garretson or Mathis had made in the previous game. It was all rumors and hearsay and it was all crap. Phillips went to the league office and threatened to take the referees out on strike if they didn't suspend me for the rest of the playoffs. Here I was a member of the union and my own union rep is trying to get me bounced. Scotty Sterling, had succeeded Axelson as vice president of operations, and he said, no way. Immediately after, there was a game at San Antonio and the league sent me out there to stand by at my hotel in case the refs refused to work. I didn't even go to the arena. If they had gone out, I was then to work the game with Garretson, who was now the supervisor of officials and was expected to work as management. Now that would have been ironic, wouldn't it—here was Garretson, clearly at odds with me, and yet he would have been the only regular NBA official working the game with me if they had carried through on their strike threat.

It was all secretive. No one was supposed to know I was going down there. I had to fly from Philly to New York, meet Scotty and Matt Winick, then Director of Game Operations, before flying to San Antonio, with a connection through Dallas. While we were in Dallas changing planes, I bumped into Bill Russell, who was doing color commentary for CBS. Everybody was coming down on me for how I talked to the media, players, and coaches, yet here popped up Russell, who started talking to me and joking around. Scotty said afterward, "I didn't know Russell was that friendly with any-body." I told him, "See what I mean? I don't initiate these conversations. What am I supposed to do, tell 'em to get out of my face?" It gave him a better understanding of what was going on.

I spent the game at the hotel in San Antonio, then I had to go to Philly the next day, leave my gear in the car, and sit in the stands in case they walked out there. After two games, the league realized the guys weren't going to walk out and cost themselves their playoff money, and meanwhile, I was sitting in the stands eating hot dogs and getting paid as if I were working. They finally figured it out and dropped the issue.

The animosity toward me was so strong with some of the refs that they'd rent a car at their own expense to avoid having to ride to the arenas with me. I'd actually go through entire games where there wouldn't be one word of nonbusi-ness discussion between us from the time we hit the locker room until we headed out into the night. I'd just sit in the locker room listening to my Walkman and reading a book, do the job, and move on down the road. Great fun.

Sometimes I felt like some old frontier marshal trying to see that justice was done when all around me were attorneys and administrators playing games with petty and preten-tious rules. On and off the court, what I called common sense, they called taking the law into my own hands. That was the charge that a Detroit reporter instigated in the mid-dle of the 1981–82 season. In the second quarter of a game between the Pistons and the 76ers, Detroit's John Long went up for a jump shot and thought he had gotten fouled. The shot missed, Philly got the rebound, and the teams took off downcourt, except for Long, who trailed behind complain-ing to me.

He kept motioning to me with a hacking motion on his arm. I told him, "You keep trying to show me up this way and I'll give you a foul, except it's not going to be the kind you're looking for. I'll give you a technical." After a time-out a little later, as they broke the huddles, Long came up to me and said, "Earl, I wasn't trying to show you up. I was just telling you I was fouled." I told him, "You don't have to do it in that manner. If you thought you were fouled and think I missed it, you can just tell me and let it go at that." That was the extent of the dialogue between us.

The newspaper article accused me of saying, "I missed it, I'll make it up to you."

Later in the game Isiah Thomas was on the line, and the article said I turned to Long and told him, "Well, I didn't get you on the line, but I put Isiah on the line to make up for the one I owed you."

Jack Joyce called to question me about these allegations. I told him he knew me well enough to know I don't make up calls, and I thought the whole thing didn't even deserve a response. I asked him, "Who's going to investigate this?" He said Joe Axelson, who was then chief of operations. I asked to talk to him and explain this away, but he said Axelson was not available. I never got a call asking for my side of it. The "investigation" was still going on. I felt they were getting awfully preoccupied with this, but if they wanted to waste their time on it, that was their business.

Two nights later, I had a game in Utah between the Jazz and Detroit. During the warm-ups John Long came over to me and told me he had never made those statements and that the writer was just a sensationalist. He told me he had said the same thing to Jack Joyce. I called Jack after the game and told him what Long had said. He said that coincided with his reports, but by now this had hit the papers all across the country.

About a week later, I called Jack and asked him what the hell I was supposed to say to reporters who kept asking me about this. He said the NBA had issued a statement saying there was no evidence to substantiate that such a statement had been made. The NBA's release also said the films showed the foul on Isiah Thomas had been valid. He said they had to protect the integrity of the league in investigating any such charges. I told him the whole thing was ludicrous.

You didn't have to be a paranoid to start putting together

the idea that there were people looking for ways to get me. It seemed especially ironic that Richie Phillips had represented me when I fought to get back into the league and then seemed fully intent on running me back out. It was about this time that the first-half ratings came out. The rating system for the NBA referees is based on the following percentages: 25 percent coaches, 25 percent director of operations, 20 percent supervisor of officials, 15 percent observer scouts, 15 percent general managers. I was rated fifth overall because the league officials in concert with the observer scouts put me down so low. Only top ranking by the coaches and G.M.s kept me from dropping deeper.

This harassment continued. In a 1986 playoff game with Atlanta at Boston, I had thrown Danny Ainge out for kicking Scott Hastings. Near the end of the third period, I looked up and saw Atlanta coach Mike Fratello in a fight with a fan in the aisle behind the scorer's table. I saw the fan throw a drink in his face. I went over to the scorer's table where Dick Bavetta was the standby, and I asked him what was going on. He said he didn't know, except that Fratello was headed for the dressing room and got into it with this fan. Fratello came back and said he had to talk to me. I told him it'd have to wait until after the game. Atlanta lost and we were in our locker room. Neither Billy Oakes, who had worked with me, nor Bavetta knew what had happened. I came out of the shower and was getting dressed when Fratello came in. He said he needed to tell us what happened. I told him he probably shouldn't be in the room, but I needed to know what had happened so I could turn in a report. He told us how he had been headed back to the locker room and this fan had shoved him and he'd shoved back, and then the guy had hit him with the drink.

We have a league rule that if a player or a coach goes into the stands to fight with a fan, he is to be expelled from the game immediately, but since I hadn't known what had happened, I didn't see how I could take any action during the game. I sent the telex report to the league office and went home. I got a call from Rod Thorn, who had become Director of Operations. He was upset with me. The year before Don Carter, the owner of the Dallas Mavericks, had come into the locker room accusing me of having a vendetta against Dick Motta, who was coaching the Mavs. I had gotten fined for letting him into the room (to harangue me!), and now Rod was getting all worked up about Fratello's being in the room. I tried to explain that I needed to find out about the incident so I could file my report. He said it wasn't my jurisdiction, that's why we have security. He just ranted and raved and finally hung up on me. He called back an hour later and told me I was off the game I was supposed to work at Philly that Sunday. He said, "You won't work another playoff game until I call you." I tried to explain again, but he said, "Ah, you think you can do anything you want and explain it away. I'm tired of your bullshit."

I was still going to get paid for the minimum number of playoff games, but I was pissed to be treated like this. But there wasn't much I could do, so Yvonne and I went down to North Carolina for a few days to visit friends. On the way home I checked my answering machine and there was a call from Thorn. I called him from a pay phone in a restaurant. He started in again about how if this ever happened again my ass was going to be fired, and I finally had enough and started yelling back at him. People were looking around and Yvonne was all upset. I ended up getting fined and working just a couple more games.

If it was just a matter of keeping a lower profile and staying out of trouble, I could handle it. It wouldn't make me happy to work with guys I can't get along with, but it wouldn't be the first time, either. The real problem is that the way they want refs to act and to call the game hurts the game and keeps a ref from developing good judgment. At the heart of my confrontations with the league is a basic disagreement over how the game works.

As I've said, I believe in common sense, whatever the rule book may say about a particular action. If you've been allowing Robert Parish to put his hand in the middle of Kareem's back all night, you don't suddenly start "calling it close" at the end and nail the guy. If the game's a rout and there's almost no time left when Michael Jordan seemingly takes off from midcourt and stuffs one in out of the rafters, you don't call the extra step he took. The crowd loved it, it didn't affect the outcome, why take it away from him?

People are always crying about shuffling feet, guys taking little stutter steps. James Worthy probably has the quickest first step of any forward in the game. It sure looks as if he's got to be doing something illegal to blow by people the way he does. But if you can do it quicker than the human eye can register it, I guess you're entitled to it. The rules about traveling and fouls haven't changed since Naismith invented the game. It's the same game, but it's played with so much more speed and ability now that you have to use judgment in determining what really gives one guy an advantage over another. And that's really what the rules are all about— keeping the conditions the same for both sides. The challenge is for the officials to keep up with the talent.

In a playoff game against the Lakers in 1988, Isiah Thomas came up with a move from the top of the key that Ed Rush figured had to be traveling, and he called it on him a couple times. Isiah told him to check out the films. Sure enough, it was a legal move.

But Garretson as supervisor of officials and the rest of the league office don't want to hear about common sense or what the rules are supposed to be about. They want refs who are just going to follow The System, Garretson's beloved guidelines for where you're supposed to be and how you're supposed to stand, and never mind developing the judgment and command that will let you react to anything that might come up. Everything is planned, diagrammed, and ruled to death.

No extraneous conversation. Or to be exact, "Refrain from talking to players, coaches or trainers during the game, unless it is absolutely necessary. At no time should officials speak to fans seated about the court. During timeouts stay away from the scorer's table. Do not face the benches or spectators, face each other, but stay at least one-quarter of the court from each other and do not talk to each other unless necessary." In other words, be a zombie. Never mind that part of getting people's respect is being able to show them that you're a human being. Never mind that a little extra word here and there might head off a big blowup later in the game. And never mind the fact that, whether the league likes it or not, we *are* people out there. People are exactly what Garretson doesn't want getting in the way of his precious System.

You can't believe what kind of robots they want us to be out on the court. Here's an example from the *Official's Manual,* covering one man (of three) in one simple situation:

Half-court Coverage, Lead Position—With the ball above the free throw line extended: "Lead" official will maintain a position which is in line with the ball, while refereeing "off the ball." He will anticipate the next pass by refereeing out of the top of his eyes, not by watching the ball all over the court. "Lead" official will go no farther than "half the distance" between the free throw lane line and the left or the right sideline. Keep your body turned slightly, so as not to "square-up" to the baseline. Do Not Allow Your Shoulders To Become Perpendicular To The Baseline.

Got that? I've been doing this my whole life and I'm not sure I can follow it.

You just can't reduce refereeing to that kind of regimentation and keep a feel for the game. Given the wide differences in philosophies between my approach to the game and that defined by the system, it's not hard to understand why we bumped heads. Granted, there were times when I probably acted unprofessionally, like shouting back at a fan or kidding around with someone at courtside during a time-out. Like maybe telling the folks sitting next to a heckler, "Jeez, that's the last time I'm going to get him tickets." Mendy used to like to holler over his shoulder to hecklers as he was running down the court, "Ah, you're just pissed off because my team's winning." I admit I haven't always been right in line. But really, what's wrong putting a little spirit into the evening?

In the old days, you often had to go into the stands after
unruly fans or deal with them as you were getting to and
from the court. It was all a part of keeping control of your
turf, and if you don't see the court as your turf, you'll never
be able to run the game. I can remember one time when
Mendy and Norm were working a playoff game in the old
Cincinnati Gardens and I was the alternate. We were going
through the walkway, the crowd was pressed in pretty good,
and we had a couple of little ushers who were supposed to
be parting the way. As we were going through, some guy was
crowding in toward us. Mendy said, "Let that guy keep coming." This guy was calling us dirty, rotten bastards and carrying on. As we got to the dressing-room door right under the
stands, Mendy said, "Grab 'em!" and Normie and I grabbed
this guy and threw him in the room, and we each took a
couple shots at the guy. He was like a pinball, bouncing off
the walls. We opened the door and tossed him back out into
the crowd. He's all disheveled. The ushers were standing
there with their mouths open. He was in and out of there so
fast I don't think anybody knew exactly what had hit the guy.
He sure didn't. In those days, you did things like that; it was
just the way it was. It was almost an accepted thing. They'd
slap the guy on the wrist and maybe slap the official on the
wrist for taking the guy on. But now if you went at it with
some guy on the court, you'd get your ass sued by the fan and
fined by the league. What they want us to do is just ask the
security to remove the guy. Well, I did that with a fan in
Seattle a couple years ago and still caught shit from the
league about it.

That was such an innocent thing, I didn't even know what
Rod Thorn was talking about at first when he called me the
next morning: "Something happen in the game last night in
Seattle?"

"No, not really."

"Nothing unusual happened, huh?"

"No, Rod. It was an easy game. Wasn't very well played,
but it was an easy game." To tell you the truth I had forgotten about the fan.

"Didn't something happen between you and some guy in the stands?"

I said, "Oh, you're talking about that guy I threw out."

"Did you know he was a fan?" Thorn asked me.

"No, not until after the game. I thought he was a member of the media. And that's something I want to talk to you about. How can you condone that team selling tickets to fans so they are actually sitting at an official table? That's supposed to be for statisticians, press, timekeepers, the scorer, and what have you. Do you think if that guy had been sitting in the stands and giving me the choke sign, pinching his nose, screaming and yelling, that I would have gone into the stands and thrown him out? I'm not in the habit of throwing fans, am I? I simply thought he was a member of the stat crew."

This incident came as the first in a series of unusual events during a week in January of 1988. A couple of nights later I had a game between Golden State and Los Angeles. I was working with Bennett Salvatore, who hurt his leg, so I worked the last four or five minutes of the game alone. After the game Magic Johnson told the media, "Earl's the best in the business. If it had to be one ref, I'm glad it was him." Warriors coach George Karl said, "We absolutely need three officials. It's impossible for two to work this game. So you can imagine how it is with one." Guess which team won.

A couple of nights later, Indiana was playing in San Antonio. Just seconds before the end of the first half, the Spurs got off a couple shots, missed, and Mike Mitchell picked up the ball and shot and I heard the horn. My hands were down at my sides. Normally, in a situation like that I raise my hand with two fingers extended, signifying that if it goes in, it will count. Or if I know it's been released too late, I'll blow the whistle and wave it off so there's no doubt in anyone's mind. Well, I didn't do either, but when the ball went in the basket, I scored it. Indiana coach Jack Ramsay came walking toward me as we're going off the court. He wasn't screaming, he just said, "Earl, that was so blatantly late, I can't believe you missed that."

I said, "Ah, it had to be closer than that."

He said, "Earl, it wasn't close at all."

I went into the dressing room. I was working with Tommy Nunez, and I asked him if he got a good look at the shot. He said he had. I asked him what he thought. He said, "Earl, it was so late." I said, well, then I have to go out and change it to start the second half. He said, "I would." I took the goal away from San Antonio at the start of the second half.

They don't like it much when you change a call, but I had it hammered into me from the moment I came into the league that the most important thing is to *get the play right*. I was working with Mendy the first time I ever saw Baylor play. I was standing under the basket when Elgin beat his man and another defensive guy jumped in front of him. Elgin went up in the air. I figured he was going to wipe the guy out, but as I blow my whistle for an offensive foul, he slips around the guy and dunks the ball. There wasn't any contact and I'm standing there with my fist in the air. Mendy came over and said, "Hey, rook, if you feel you made a mistake, change it."

Why should someone be punished because I kicked the shit out of a play? Instead of trying to sell a bad call, step back, admit your mistake, and get it right. Still, if you have to change too many, you probably shouldn't be in the league.

There's nothing in the book that specifically said that I could wipe out Mitchell's basket or that I couldn't, so I used what is called in Section III of the rules "Elastic Power," which says the officials shall have power to make decisions on any point not specifically covered in the rules. The league didn't buy it and fined me $150. (Ed Rush did the same thing a year after my game in San Antonio. When I found out he had only been fined $100, I had Dick Markowitz, attorney for the union, notify the league that I was due a $50 refund. Instead they notified Rush that he had to pay another $50.)

A week or so after the San Antonio incident, I got a call from Garretson. He said, "You had a great year last year. The last couple weeks you've been on a roll. You tossed a fan in Seattle, changed a call in Phoenix, changed the score in San

Antonio. One of your colleagues called me and you know what he said? He said, 'Earl Strom is about ready to do something terrible.' "

Don't tempt me, I thought.

Ah, the "Whispering Society" strikes again. In every workplace you have people playing politics, taking shots at each other to gain an edge with the powers that be. Because our working group is never in the same place, most of our communication takes place on the phone. Guys spend half their lives on the phone talking to people in their cliques. Just who is in or out of each of those cliques seems to vary daily. Sometimes I hear from a guy so often I figure he wants to get engaged; then I'm suddenly off-limits and I don't know he's alive. When these guys aren't singing to each other, they're wooing Garretson. He puts up a good front of condemning it, saying he doesn't want to hear all the bitching and backbiting. He calls it the Whispering Society. He complains that guys are calling him night and day. The guys have a saying: "I'm cuttin' off the backside, stayin' out of the paint, and callin' Darell once a day." I told him he could save the league $20,000 a year and himself a lot of grief if he just told the guys he doesn't want to hear from anybody who doesn't have specific referee matters to discuss. But the truth of the matter is that it's his power base.

Garretson has put together a program that is both amazing and unnerving. It's like a police state, it's everywhere. It feels as though he's working twenty-four hours a day, trying to control what every guy is doing every minute. His system has broken officials' responsibilities in working the game into such an exacting regimen, it's like he's forgotten those are living, breathing people out there on the court.

What concerns me most about the system is how it takes away the thinking process. Officials who are following its code to the letter are being taught that structure is everything. If your full concentration is on where you're standing, how you have your shoulders aligned, how many steps you are away from the other officials, you're not thinking about the flow of action. Certainly, a sense of order is necessary.

But the system is trying to protect the referees from being vulnerable to human error. You can't fear that vulnerability as an official. You have to have enough confidence in yourself that you just wade right in there with your knowledge and instincts and put 'em on the line. The players and coaches sense how you're coming at the game. If you have control of the whole show, they'll respect you. If you approach the game like some mad engineer dissecting it into all these little parts, they'll question you and they'll keep testing you. Your lack of confidence will carry through, and the game will never really hit its full potential.

By the way his system approaches the game and by the way he treats the officials, it's evident to me that Garretson doesn't have much confidence in these guys. Everything is aimed at standardization. It's as if he wants every official to be interchangeable with every other official—same mechanics, same interpretations, same zombielike stare. A lot of the young guys say they like it, that it really helps them to develop. But develop as what? They're learning how to make calls, but they're not being given enough room to learn how to take command. They know there's always someone watching over their shoulder, and that's no way to learn how to take responsibility in anything.

The league is set up to get a video of virtually every game via satellite. Garretson goes over these and does a voice-over and sends them to the guys. They watch them in their hotel rooms before a game, then they come back and watch more after the game. When they get home, they might have eight hours of video to go over.

I think the video helps to a degree as a teaching tool, but I think it works better when the observer scouts from the league office teach guys right at the arena. If I were running the show, I would try to get qualified officials to work as scouts and have them come into the room at halftime and point out things the guy needs to do and then give him feedback after the game. They just use a checklist now and usually only cover things that are more technical in nature. I say, teach them when it's fresh, don't send them a critique sheet two weeks later when they've had half a dozen or more games in between. Years ago you'd go out and have a couple drinks and talk about other things. You'd develop a rapport as a crew that would help your communication out on the court. Now it's expected that the officials will get together and talk about the game, that the senior official will discuss what took place and all. This is what you did, this is what you should do, and this is what you have to do to keep out of the crapper. That stuff just distances you; it's better when you've got some interaction as people instead of just as refs.

There are more security people now. Any atypical situation, any fight, you have to send in a telex report to the league office. And you have to call Matt Winick, director of game operations, that night and tell him what happened and that a telex is coming in. Then you have to tell the ball club to send in a video and an official play-by-play sheet. Then you have to call Matt in the morning to be sure he got everything. Then you talk to Horace Balmer, who is the security chief. All this stuff is compiled and taken in to the commissioner to have him act on anything that is appropriate. You call an 800 number and dictate the report. You have to dictate the exact language—he called him a motherfucker and he said fuck you—and sometimes they giggle. I might have half a dozen a year that have to be treated that way.

If you change a call, you're expected to send in a telex. Years ago, if you had a fight or had to toss a guy, you just sent in a technical foul sheet and it was over. You didn't have to call the office and go through all this stuff. But, I guess it's just a more sophisticated way of doing business.

The supervisor of officials pretty well holds the cards to play any way he wants when it comes to the tabulation of numbers for ratings. Jake O'Donnell is one guy who's totally hung up on the ratings. He doesn't accept the fact that politics has more to do with it than anything else. I told him, "Considering some of the clowns Garretson's giving high marks to, it's a little difficult for me to take these ratings seriously. I was rated number one when the league had good referees." I've routinely been rated the top official by the

coaches and GMs and been marked down by the league. It
bothered me at times, but as long as I was among the top
eight, I was still eligible for the top salary and playoff assignments. Officials are paid for each round of playoffs they're
assigned, regardless of how many games they work. If you're
among the top eight and therefore eligible to work all the
way through the playoffs, you pick up about $35,000 above
your base salary. Even Garretson never put me down so low
that I was in jeopardy of falling out of the top eight.

It's pretty hard for me to respect a system that plays political games with the ratings and as a result, insults the quality
of play by having lesser officials working important playoff
games. If they want to rate me below Tommy Nunez, which
they did one year, then I guess the priorities are pretty clear
to see. Nunez has been around a long time, but he's not
regarded around the league as being in the top group. I've
learned to tolerate him over the years; most officials think of
him as one of the most adept political animals in the frater-
nity. We all used to sit at these union meetings where guys
would be coming down on Garretson because he was working during the '83 strike, which shows their ignorance when
you think about it. I mean, Garretson is management, and
when the league says you work, you work or you lose your
management position. They'd say, "Yeah, but he was union
president." Yeah, he was, he was, but he isn't anymore.
"Well, we ought to break his legs." Tommy would get up in
the face of everybody and stand up for Garretson. I have to
say, I admired him for that. He was loyal to the man. Standing up for someone in front of a hostile group is more than
just ass-kissing.

A lot of the problems were cleaned up for me when Richie
Phillips got out of the picture. I still referee the same way I
always have, and I still do the same things on the floor, but
nobody is pitching me in anymore. Several of the officials
told me Richie would say, "You gotta get this son of a bitch.
Anything he does, we want to know about it. Don't take any
shit from Strom." That was the climate in the early eighties
when I got into an incident with Bavetta in the dressing

room up in Boston. I had always worked closely with Dick, even helped get him into the league. He used to phone me all the time and ask me advice. I regarded him as a decent official and was really surprised when he blew up at me while we were in the locker room at halftime. In the first half I had to throw Bill Fitch, the Celtics coach, for carrying on. As we got into the room, Dick, who is a very nervous individual, put his jacket on and kept pacing back and forth and rubbing his hands. Finally he said, "How about Fitch?" and he got all cranked up about it.

"Forget about Fitch," I told him. "He's gone. What happened happened and he'll be turned in."

He said, "Is there anything out there you want to talk about?"

"If you're asking for advice, yes." I told him about a three-second call I thought he kicked.

He looked at me, hesitated, and said, "Okay, okay, anything else?"

"You can't reset the twenty-four-second clock when there's no change of possession." I said it in a normal tone of voice. He had reset it on a loose ball situation, where the defensive team touched, but never controlled, the ball as it went out of bounds.

He stopped pacing and all of a sudden he looked up and yelled at me, "Well, fuck you! Fuck you! Who the hell are you?"

I looked at him. "What?"

"Fuck you! Who the hell are you to tell me what to do? You didn't give me any help on the thing."

"You asked me for advice and I'm giving it to you."

"Well, fuck you! I don't want your advice."

I stood up and put my hands on his chest. "Hold it!" He had this towel around his neck, and there was no way I could possibly get to his neck.

He pulled away and said, "Don't put your hands on me."

I sat down. He said, "You always were a prick, you're still a prick!"

"Hold it a minute!" I stood up again and took hold of his

jacket and sort of shook him. I realized this was ridiculous and let go. I walked into the bathroom and when I was in there, I said, "You know what really bothers me, Dick, is that you always called me and asked for advice and now when I give it to you, you pull this crap. What is it with you?"

He said, "Don't you talk to me! I don't want to talk to you!"

That was all that happened in the locker room. There were no punches thrown. When they gave us the three-minute notification, I went back out on the floor. Dick stayed in the room. When he came out, I saw him stop and talk to the Boston trainer and point over to me. Later on, when he related his side of the story to others, he had me grabbing him around the throat, strangling him. He had me punching him, knocking him to the floor, almost knocking him out, and he had to recover so he could go back out and do the second half. I don't recall anything like that happening. But hey, when it's over, it's over. Players have clubhouse brawls, but they don't go whining off to everybody in the world that they had a beef.

I tried to talk to him at the hotel after the game, but couldn't get in touch with him. If Bavetta had gone right to Norm Drucker, who was the supervisor then, that thing would have been handled in-house. Normie would have slapped me on the wrist, it wouldn't have hit the papers. But instead, Bavetta called Phillips, who then called Garretson, which was the worst thing that could have happened. Apparently they thought, "Hey, here's our chance to get that SOB." So they had Bavetta call Jack Joyce, the security chief. Phillips could have kept it within the association, but he didn't.

I went back to my home the next day and Jack Joyce called and wanted to know what had happened. I told him my side of it and told him Bavetta was lying to say I punched him or tried to choke him. I only admitted to having initiated the touching. The league fined me $2,500. At my hearing, I protested that they were calling it a fight, but they took his word over mine. It was like these certain people stick you with a reputation and you're stuck with it. I had been trying to avoid confrontations, just being the new Walkaway Strom. But if someone wants to put your tail in a wringer and they have control of the politics, you're in for a tough time.

It used to be, we'd come off the court and ask, "We got any complaints, any problems? If not, good, it's over. Let's get a belt and get on down the road to the next one." Now you're only as good as your last videotape. And sometimes you aren't sure where the hell they'll come from. One official is suspected of sending an occasional video to the league office. He supposedly has a dish and tapes a lot of games. Alexander and Madden had a game in Boston in which they had a violation on a free throw shot; nobody said anything from the office, but the word in the Whispering Society was that this guy saw this on his tape and sent it in. (The official denies it.)

Joe Gushue used to love to grab every paper he could, to see what everyone else in the league was doing. He'd say, "Let's see what kind of trouble our friends got into last night." I never looked at that; I figured the supervisor of officials needs to worry about everybody, I just needed to worry about doing my job. Some guys are aware of every stat, every winning streak, every incident that happens. Some guys get sympathy pains, and if their buddy had trouble the game before with a certain coach or player, they aren't above being real quick to nail the guy. I don't say that it happens often, but there are some paybacks that these guys pull.

There are guys who will tell a coach, "That's fine, I'll put that in my memory bank and I'll get ya the next time." I think that's terrible. I would never say that. I might think it, but I would never say it. I've actually heard a referee say, "See this face? Remember it. I'll be back and I'll take care of you." It makes Garretson's job awfully tough when he has officials going on the record with that kind of prejudice. That leads to the player's or coach's calling him at two o'clock in the morning, saying, "Hey, so-and-so says he's going to screw me the next time he works my game. Whattaya gonna do about it?" Garretson's got a tough job, no doubt about it; he's got some weird people working for him.

The guys became much more cordial in the last several years. At camp they all talk to me now and carry on. Heck, even Jake talks to me. What a blessing. Jake has to be the worst guy I've ever known for screwing up the King's English. You listen to him try to express himself sometimes and you think you're listening to a comedian doing it on purpose. When Darell was working during the last strike ('83) and everybody was coming down on him, Jake got up in front of the group one day and said, "I've known Darell a long time, and I know he's been perspiring for that supervisors job for a long time."

I said, "Jeez, Jake, has he really been perspiring all that long?"

Joe Forte came into his first referees' camp straight from Korea, where he had worked the Olympic finals. When he got there, we were in the middle of a meeting. Garretson greeted him as if he were some long-lost brother and was going on about what a big deal it was to have a guy joining our staff right from the Olympics. Of course, most of the guys figured working a game between the two weakest teams in the league was tougher than any Soviet-USA match, but Garretson encouraged Joe to share his stories, and he was going on and he said, "The biggest problem the officials had was communicating with each other." I said, "Joe, did you ever meet Jake O'Donnell?"

When I said it, a chuckle went through the group. Jake, who was sitting in the back, hollered, "He knows who I am. He knows who I am. You don't have to tell him who I am. He knows." As Garretson jumped back in and repeated how we were all honored to be working with a guy who'd worked the Olympic games, Jake hollered, "Fuck them Olympics!" Everybody just sat there in stunned silence.

The guys coming onto the staff now are much better educated than the old guard. Most of them are college educated, which I suppose the league considers beneficial for its image. But they'll have to go a long way to match Jake's abilities on the court. The abuse we took in the old days was considerably more. The rules that the owners, general managers, coaches, and players have to abide by today are considerably more stringent. The old days were wilder, coarser without a doubt.

A lot of this has to do with how the owners and general managers want the league to be run. That style starts with the way the preseason camp is run and the types of things that are emphasized. They want the time put in on the rules. We study them and we have examinations. Years ago we'd just go over the rule book and that was it. We didn't have examinations or go over the casebook and manual like we do now. I think the written examinations are a plus, and I think the greater emphasis on physical conditioning is a plus. We have a tough job and the time we commit to camp is important. The job, in the way they've chosen to teach it, is more sophisticated than it was when I came in.

But I'll tell you something you'll think is crazy: The worst thing they ever did was make refereeing in the pros a full-time job. Why? Because it's gotten to be so high paying that everybody is running scared. The supervisor of officials can take this really good thing away, the salary, the expense allowances, the benefits, the pension program, the playoff monies. Now, it's just too good a deal.

Remember the old saying "Don't give up your day job." I was in the league a long time before I did. Mendy used to say, "If you come in and you do a good job and it's a supplement to your regular income, then if they give you shit, like you won't be around, screw you, you're terrible, we're gonna get you fired, then you can turn to them and say, 'I'm doing the best I can. If it ain't good enough, fuck you, fire me. But if it is good enough, then get off my ass. Because I'll go back and work college ball and you'll be left working with some guy who's a lot worse." That's the security having a regular job gave you. Sure, you can say that's convoluted thinking; after all, I fought for more money and security for my family when I jumped to the ABA. Sure, I'm a better official if I don't have to use up time and energy running back and forth to another job. But there's a price and the league knows that. The price is your balls. The league knows it can attract top talent and keep them under its control.

And nobody can deny that Garretson has control of the group. He is using Ed Rush and Hugh Evans—*president of the union,* mind you—as observer scouts. Their reports have an impact on guys' ratings. I feel Garretson's greatest value to the league, through his power over these guys, is the ability he will have to get them to agree to whatever contract the league serves up. Garretson has set up the whole program to have total control.

He would accept that I was among the top group of officials, but it still was impossible for him to tolerate any deviation from the uniformity he demanded. At our preseason-camp dinner a couple years ago, Garretson was addressing the group. He said, "I don't want this to be taken the wrong way, but I could never teach officials to referee the way Earl Strom does. I'm not sure I could referee the way he does. I can't teach guys to go into huddles and yell back at players and have guys out there admitting mistakes." A couple of the guys in front of me turned around and said, "If it was good enough to get you where you are now, there must be something to it." I thought how I had picked up things that I felt were effective from each guy along the way and then fitted them into my personality. But in Garretson's eyes, that's what was wrong. Personality isn't supposed to be a factor anymore. And the guys working the game now and for the next twenty years won't have the chance to benefit from some of that experience.

The way Garretson marked things and the comments he made on my rating at the end of the 1988–89 season illustrated that he just couldn't accept my working the game my way. To begin with, these ratings are ridiculous. They break the game down into so many different component parts that half the time I can't even figure out what he's talking about. You get rated as Excellent (E), Good (G), Average (A), Poor (P), or Unsatisfactory (U) in over fifty categories. Some make sense—Judgment/Consistency; Game Control; Application/ Knowledge of Rules; Appearance/Physical Condition. But how do you do an evaluation of somebody's signals? How do you put a letter grade on someone's eye contact with other officials? And what's the point of giving grades in subcategories like those under Transition Lead to Trail: Left/Right of Ball; Trails by 3/4 Strides; Remains OOB until Ball INBDed after FG? What's that got to do with developing good refs?

And if all this wasn't proof enough that what they want was robots, the Additional Comments on that evaluation put it all in focus for me:

CONVERSATION: You continue to talk to anyone and everyone in sight. You may be assured that your talking and complete disregard for being warned about it will come to a COMPLETE halt in the future. The statement in the Official's Manual will be followed to the letter.
INADVERTENT WHISTLES: You lead the league in changing your mind on a call using this as a "cop-out."

Oh, what the hell. Rather than go and pop my mouth off and get fired, I figured the time had come for me to retire. The league had become too mechanical, too full of computers and videos and too caught up in the clinical, regimented approach. I knew I could still work a pro basketball game as well as anyone in the business, but they were denying me the chance to work *with feeling*. Without the license to use my judgment and to interact with the people in and around the game, I was being cut off from the real pleasure I got from my job. The NBA loved having Jack Nicholson at courtside, but they didn't want Earl Strom talking to him. Well, I didn't spend the past thirty-plus years in this game to become a piece of furniture. They wanted me to stay, but they didn't want the color and individuality of my personality. It seemed they really didn't want me rolling along reminding them of a crazier, less sophisticated, less financially successful time. Fair enough. I gave notice that the 1989–90 season would be my last. But I never said I'd go quietly.

chapter 10

I'M OUTTA HERE

When Julius Erving announced his retirement effective at the end of the 1986–87 season, he spent that season taking a bow in each city, getting rocking chairs and other more lavish gifts of gratitude for the entertainment he had provided basketball for sixteen seasons, the first five in the ABA. John Havlicek did it several years earlier, and Kareem Abdul-Jabbar followed up a couple years later, spending his final season getting a send-off in every city. The idea is to give the fans around the league a chance to say thanks. Dr. J's last game was a playoff game in Milwaukee. I tossed Bucks coach Don Nelson during the game, and somebody called in a death threat against me. After the game I gave Doc the game ball and kept giving him a kind of hug as we headed off the court. A writer said, "Gee, Earl, you're being pretty palsy with the Doc." I whispered back over my shoulder, "Even a jerk wouldn't risk shooting the Doc after his last game."

Brian McIntyre, head of publicity for the NBA, said the league wouldn't allow a farewell tour for me because all I would end up with would be twenty-seven Seeing Eye dogs.

That's okay, I didn't expect to receive any special treatment. Just letting me do my job without a lot of harassment was a gift in itself. But I did dare to ask to go to Rome for the McDonald's preseason tournament. Instead, they sent me to do a preseason game in Newfoundland.

Fond farewells don't always work out, even for the legends. I had the all-star game in San Francisco the year after Red retired, and they brought him back to coach the Eastern team. Willie Smith was working the game with me. They told us not to let Red get under our skin; the game was televised nationally, and they wanted to let him have his swan song. Early in the second half Red started getting after Willie pretty good and Willie nailed him with a T. Red said something else and Willie tossed him. Bang, bang, just like that, Red was officially retired as a coach. Walter Kennedy was fit to be tied. Mendy was referee in chief and Dolph Schayes was supervisor of officials. Neither could believe it. The newspaper people came up after the game and asked Willie, "Do you think Red knew he had one technical on him already before you hit him with the second and ejected him?" Willie, who came from Pennsylvania Dutch country and had this accent, said, "Of course he knowed it. Of course he knowed it. He wanted to get thrown, so I obliged him. He knowed it." That was the beginning of the end for Willie; he just kind of slipped from there and eventually went out of the league. Nice guy, but his common sense left something to be desired.

It was kind of sad to see Kareem so ineffective his last year. I think Wilt would have been more capable at the same age. Wilt played with power and he used his muscle to force his way inside. Kareem was a finesse player who by the end had lost his legs. He couldn't do the things that had made him great. He should probably have quit a year earlier as far as the image of him on the court goes. He could have gone out a winner, making those last free throws to beat Detroit in the sixth game en route to the 1987–88 title.

Kareem extended his career for at least a couple of years by putting a real emphasis on his fitness. So did I. Over the years I paid better attention to my health, cutting down on the rich foods and coffee, dropping the cigars altogether. The road life can lull you into trouble, either by too much sitting around or by being worn-out from early-morning or late-night flights. I figure I ran about five miles each game, and I made sure I got in a good jog any day I didn't have a game. I finished up my career at 6', 171 pounds, the same as when I came in. There was a time ten years before I retired that I got heavier, and I felt it in my knees and my general stamina. The league is real strict about guys being in shape. We have a mile-and-one-half endurance run each year at camp. Joe Gushue was fond of saying, "You guys got the wrong sport. I never saw a referee toss up the ball and take off on a mile-and-a-half run." Poor Joe could have put in another dozen years in the league if he had taken care of himself.

Traditionally, officials have put a lot of importance into the way they look. Some guys used to wear these stretch tops to hold their gut in, but Garretson banned those. Looks are a part of how you earn respect. Years ago if a referee walked into a dressing room with a hair blower and hair spray, he'd have gotten laughed out of the room. Now it's part of your equipment. Billy Paultz once told Jess Kersey, "Don't fall down, you'll break your hair." My hair is always flying around and I don't worry about it, but a lot of the guys really put a lot of effort into their appearance—polish their shoes, get the lint off their pants. But that part of it isn't new. Willie Smith used to be like that when I first broke in. You could cut your finger on the crease of his pants. That's the way he was with his street clothes, too. He was immaculate. He used to put newspapers down when he changed clothes so he wouldn't get the dust from the floor on them. Mendy personified dignity on the court and was always well dressed off it. He was meticulous. He bought the best suits. Sid Borgia was a great dresser; he used to wear these three-piece suits and a long cashmere topcoat. We all dressed well. It was just a myth that we were making money for our families; it was really just to buy nice clothes.

Everybody likes to be acknowledged for what they've put into something over the long haul, and I have to admit that even though you know you've done a good job, you do take stock of the perspectives others put on your career.

A couple years ago Roy Firestone did a TV feature on me called "A Tribute to Earl Strom" for a Lakers' pregame show. He said:

Quick with a joke, calm, but in complete control, almost impeccable instincts. The one referee road teams can always count on to give them a fair shake. These are all the Strom trademarks. He's the so-called Road Ref, the ultimate arbiter, the law unto himself, the ref who overshadows, even intimidates, his partner. After thirty years, well over two thousand games, and enough frequent-flier miles to start his own travel club, what you're left with is an image. Earl Strom is a throwback, a reminder of the days when the refs had colorful personalities, the days when war-horses like Mendy Rudolph, Norm Drucker, and a younger Earl Strom were called the father, the son, and the holy ghost. We're left with an image of a man who has made the transition gracefully—from a hell-raiser to a grandpa. A man who has gained in grace without compromising the qualities of his work. And that, in the end, is his greatest legacy of all.

On that same show, Danny Ainge said, "There are times when it seems he almost wants to go the other way, to shut the crowd up, or to get them riled up." He must have gotten me confused with Sid Borgia.

Among the responses I got from that show was this note I received in the mail: "Earl: Saw the feature on you by ESPN! Terrific! You are honest at 60 about your age! Hell, I'm a kid compared to you at 57—58 in October! Remember 1955, rookies! I always said if you could work alone in an NBA game you were a star! You could work alone . . . maybe should!!! A compliment, my friend! Don't go too much further! My best, Richie Powers."

In that same season, *USA Today* came out with a poll on the best coaches, players, and referees based on a vote by the coaches and players. Pat Riley was tops among the coaches with 76 of the 219 votes cast, followed by Doug Moe, 42; K.C. Jones, 16; Lenny Wilkens and Mike Schuler, 15. Of the 237 votes cast for players, Michael Jordan had 129, Larry Bird, 56; and Magic Johnson, 28. Of the 193 votes cast for officials, I had 83, Jake O'Donnell, 43; Darell Garretson, 15; Hugh Evans 14; Jess Kersey, 10; Jack Madden, 8.

The *Detroit Free Press* did a piece on the best official in each sport. They queried about five hundred people—players, coaches, general managers, broadcasters, writers, and fans. They listed the best as Bruce Froemming, baseball; Jim Tunney, football; Andy vanHellemond, hockey; and me. They also cited me as the top official in all sports. I think they just felt sorry for me because I had the most gray hair. In the story they told about this game where Morganna, the kissing stripper, walked onto the court toward me: "Before accepting a hug and a smooch, Strom threatrically held her at arm's length and gazed at the body of the celebrated entertainer. Pistons announcer George Blaha said on WWJ radio: 'Earl had to step back and look twice to make sure he made the right call.'" Thanks fellas, that played real well at home.

I was inducted into the Pennsylvania Sports Hall of Fame the same night with NFL supervisor of officials Art McNally and the late (and gerrr-rate) 76ers PA announcer David Zinkoff. Talk about a guy who could liven up the place. I participated in celebrity golf tournaments and other fund-raisers such as the annual Kutcher's benefit games. A couple years ago, Frank Layden did a stand-up comic routine up there. I wonder if he didn't miss his calling as a professional comedian. Norm Drucker and I were sitting in the first row and we were sort of needling him. His first remark was, "It's nice to see a lot of celebrities from around the league here today. Here we have Earl Strom right down front. Earl's a nice guy. Earl, stand up. Let's give Earl a hand. Yeah, Earl's probably the best referee money can buy."

I got a call from the league office one day telling me that the Mavericks were having an auction for the Special Olympics and they wanted to auction off an Earl Strom referee shirt. I thought they were kidding. No, they wanted to do it, and they wanted it autographed. So I sent it off and got a letter from the club a few weeks later saying it had gone for $271. Every time I went back there I fully expected to see it stuffed and hanging from the rafters with pins sticking out of it.

Anytime I ever dared think of myself as a celebrity, all I had to do was remember back about thirty years. You didn't see all these autograph hounds and stuff to the degree it's around the players now, but there was still fan adulation. I was up in Boston in maybe my second or third year in the league, and I was starting to feel my oats. The Celtics were playing the old Philadelphia Warriors. I came out after the game and was talking to some friends in the lobby of Boston Garden. Here were Cousy and Ramsey and the other Celtics being surrounded by fans wanting their autographs, and over there were the Warriors Paul Arizin, Wilt Chamberlain, Tom Gola, Guy Rodgers.

This little redheaded kid came up to me and asked for my autograph. Well, of course I was flattered and I thought, this is pretty neat to be getting a sense of identity with all these stars around here. I signed it and turned back to talk to my friends. A couple minutes later the kid came back and wanted another autograph. I signed it again. Well, he came back four or five times, and finally my curiosity started to get the best of me.

"You know, son, I appreciate your wanting my autograph, but why do you want so many of them?"

He looked me right in the eye and said, "Because if I can get twenty-five of yours, that kid over there will trade me a Bob Cousy."

It was flattering, of course, to have my career given some tributes, but what meant the most was to hear folks say, "He lets you know where you stand, what you can and can't do, so you know how to play. He's fair." I might write my own epitaph as: He was man enough to admit he was wrong, if he had ever had the occasion. Naw, I booted my share.

In my first regular-season game of my last go-round, I had Boston at Chicago. Michael Jordan picked up Robert Parish on a switch. Parish hooked his arm over Jordan's and started stumbling as if Jordan were holding him. As I blew the whistle on Jordan, he yelled out, *"He's* holding me, *he's* holding *me!"* But I had it the other way. Jordan shook his head and said, "After all these years, Earl, I wouldn't think you'd fall for the oldest trick in the book." I said, "I'm afraid you're right. I kicked it."

What do they say, first the eyes go, then the legs?

Not even a month later, I made a call that, to my knowledge, was the first time in my career that I made a mistake that cost someone a chance to win at the end of a game. San Antonio was playing the Clippers in the Sports Arena and was up by 3 with a couple seconds to play. I was in the lead position just past midcourt when the Clippers threw long to Charles Smith. I was concentrating on the light, the clock, and the horn to be sure I could tell if the shot would get off in time. He fired before the horn and hit it. I saw him land inside the three-point line. Shot good, two points or three? Terry Durham was back about midcourt, and Tommy Nunez had been down on the other end. Neither of them offered anything on the call. The easiest thing would have been to let the home team have the benefit of the doubt and go into overtime. But I was sure he had been inside the line when he fired up and I called it a two-point basket. Clippers lose by one.

I said to Durham and Nunez when I got into the room, "It seemed pretty obvious to me that he was inside the line." Neither of them said a word. Later, I was in the bar at the hotel, meeting a friend. He got on me a little about blowing the call when he first sat down. I said, "Was it really that bad?" He said, "Naw, it looked like it was close." I was a little curious, but didn't think too much about it until ESPN came on a little while later and the replay showed it wasn't even close. I said, "Jesus, he was a foot and a half behind the line. I totally kicked the shit out of that call." He had drifted way over the line after his shot, but he was clearly behind it when he fired. I was sick. If I'd known that even after we had gotten back to the locker room, I would have gotten the teams together and gone back out to play an overtime. It would have cost me some money, but at least the call would have been right.

Durham got his butt chewed by Garretson for not being in position to help better on the call. I asked Durham later, "Did you think it was a good shot at the time?" He said, "Yeah, but if I had come up to you and said I thought he was clearly behind the line at the time of the shot, would you have changed your call?"

"Of course I would have. Did you think he was clearly behind the line?"

"Yes, I did."

"Well, isn't that great."

A couple nights later I was talking about it with Kevin Loughery, who was working as a TV commentator, and he said to me, "Those guys aren't going to overrule you. They're all afraid of you." Yvonne told me the same thing. I thought, am I that much of an ogre that my fellow refs won't even offer their opinions?

I knew that wasn't the case. I had a play in the previous spring's final game of Detroit's sweep of L.A. where I was the trail official, Kersey was the slot, and Madden was the lead. A shot was taken by Detroit just before the 24-second clock went off. It fell short. Somebody from Detroit knocked it into the backboard. I blew the whistle and said it was a 24-second violation. Madden and Kersey came up and said it had hit the board in time. I said, "Are you sure? If you are, let's give Detroit the ball back." We did, and Detroit scored. There was a time-out a couple minutes later, and I was over getting a drink by the CBS announcer. He said, "Earl, you were right on that play. It never touched the glass before the horn sounded." I told those guys they had it wrong, after all. They said, "Well, what do you want us to do in a situation like that?" I said, "When it's that questionable, just let me live or die on the shot."

This just illustrates how there's no exact system to protect against mistakes. We can't stop the game every thirty seconds to look at tapes. It's a game played by human beings being judged by human beings. But when I talked to Rod Thorn about my mistake in the Clippers game, we agreed that there just might be a place for instant replay in the pro game. I think it would make sense to use it on shots that are launched at the horn at the end of periods, and on controversial three-point shots where there wasn't an agreement by all three officials. Every game is recorded, even if not televised, so the tapes can be sent to the league. It wouldn't be a problem to have instant replay available to officials. I wouldn't use it for anything else, because you'd have a game stopped every minute for some call. And there are so many things in the pro game that aren't that clear-cut, let alone needing to be called.

In addition to recommending the very select use of instant replay, I have my opinions on some rules and their interpretation that always seem to come up among basketball followers:

1. *Don't raise the basket.* It would just take the basket farther away from the shorter player, forcing him to change the trajectory of his shot. You'd take the dunk away from 5'7" Spud Webb, but the 6'7" guys could stuff at eleven feet just as frequently.
2. *No foul-out.* Instead of losing the guy, just add a technical to any other free throws that are to be shot when he goes past six fouls. I don't think they need to let the fouled team keep possession as well; the extra shot's enough. People think that some guy could just sit in there and hammer on people, but you still have the flagrant-foul rule. If a guy rips someone, toss him. A blown call on a third strike with the bases loaded or a holding call on a touchdown run can be pretty devastating, but at least the star is still in the game to take another shot at winning. It just doesn't make sense that a referee can call a couple, three, ticky-tacky fouls and render a star useless for huge chunks of the game. In fact, when I was aware that a star player had five fouls, I would make real sure his disqualification was a solid foul. Usually he's being extra

careful by then anyway, so you've got a good chance of keeping him around, which is what the fans paid to see.

3. *Widen the court.*   They've widened the foul lane several times. That wouldn't be enough now. All it would do is provide more space for guys to get cheap three-second violation calls. Widen the court itself by three feet on each side and give these bigger guys more room to maneuver. It'll cut down on the body contact and provide better flow to halfcourt offenses.

4. *Put back the force-out rule.*   There is such a thing as a tie. Two guys can hit the same spot at the same time and they both fall out-of-bounds. Let the offense put it back into play with the same time left on the shot clock. Same thing when a nudge causes a guy to step back over the 10-second line; if the nudge isn't really enough to call a foul, let the offense keep the ball and the game goes on.

5. *Take out the 10-second line.*   They don't have it in international rules. With the shot clock, we don't need it. If you press full court, you're keeping them from getting into offensive position; defense would still be rewarded.

6. *Toss the jump balls.*   Years ago they made rules to benefit the game. Now they make rules to protect against refereeing deficiencies. They worried that the toss wasn't always high enough and straight enough, so they left it to one toss at the start of the game and on held-ball situations. In college, they've even resorted to the possession arrow. There has to be at least one guy among the three officials who can toss the ball up right and he ought to be used throughout the game.

7. *Palming and walking.*   When a guy loses control of the ball, it can look pretty bad, but it doesn't necessarily mean he's walking. If it's by the visiting team, the crowd is going to get on the official to call it, but generally things like that should just be allowed to pass. If a guy slides his foot or scoots a couple inches, and he hasn't really gained any advantage against the defender, let it go. Keep the game moving.

8. *On rebounds, let a guy go up and over.*   Inside position

isn't always enough. Don't automatically call over-the-back, even if the outside rebounder comes down and bumps the guy. You can't have guys climbing and thrashing people in there, but there's going to be plenty of contact. I tried to lean on the side of allowing aggressive play, unless someone was being malicious about it.

9. *Continuation.* If the player with the basketball has picked up his dribble when he's fouled, he's entitled to a one-two-count step to the hoop. If he takes another dribble, it's not continuation. If the offensive player fires up his shot, then runs over the defender, he loses the basket. What I think officials need to concentrate on is where the defender plants himself. Is he checking the man or a spot under the basket? If he's just camping out to draw the foul, he's not playing honest defense, he's playing a zone. Run him over and count the hoop.

The block/charge is probably still the toughest call in basketball at all levels. Who got there first? In the pro game, given the incredible leaping abilities and quickness of the players, I think the toughest call is goaltending on the defensive player and basket interference on the offensive end, particularly on a lob pass. On the latter, the rules now say that you can take a lob and tip it in if you're weakside (on the far side of the rim from the guy who took the shot), but not if you're strongside—then you have to decide if it's a pass that the guy has a right to jam through or if it was over the cylinder and he's guiding it in. A very tough call.

Despite Richie Powers's infamous invitation to Kevin and Hubie to go ahead and play any defense they wanted, zones must be discouraged. Guys are clever enough the way they stunt and sag off their men, but you have to force them to play a man unless they're doubling the ball. I called a zone in Philly against Washington in the exhibition season one year. I had three guys—Kupchak, Unseld, and Hayes, I think it was—standing in the lane not checking anybody. I blew the whistle and called a zone.

"Who's it on?" they all sang out.

"All three of you, take your pick."

Unseld said, "Hey, we just lost our men, we were trying to find them."

Motta, who was coaching Washington, came charging up. "Earl, that's impossible. We haven't even had a chance to work on a zone defense yet." That might be my all-time favorite alibi.

Every once in a while I would find myself struck by the contrasts in the pro game since I broke in. From days when a player took his wife on a road trip for their honeymoon and shared the room with his roommate to save a buck, to guys with shoes named after them making more on those deals than whole teams were when I started. From dank, old locker rooms where you showered with the winning team to carpeted suites where you were supposed to hide from interacting with the rest of the world. From a league that was almost within driving distance to coast-to-coast jet lag. From dark, old arenas where doubleheaders might only draw several thousand fans to bright arenas where they're selling out 20,000 seats for losing teams. From schedules that looked like this:

> December 3, 1957
> Phil vs. Syr at NY, 7:00, MSG
> Cinn at NY, 9:00, MSG
> St.L. vs. Minn at Det, 7:00, Olympia
> Bos at Det, 9:00, Olympia

to:

> December 3, 1989
> Utah at Washington
> Chicago at Miami
> Philadelphia at Atlanta
> Minnesota at Cleveland
> Dallas at Houston
> Charlotte at San Antonio

Portland at Denver
New York at Phoenix
Sacramento at L.A. Clippers
Milwaukee at Golden State
Detroit at Seattle

From familiar slurs from the Auerbachs and Hannums to pleasant foreigners such as Drazen Petrovic, a guard for Portland. He came up to me before a game and reminded me he had played for Czechoslovakia in the Madrid tournament against the Celtics in a game I had worked a couple summers earlier. He said, laughing, "Remember me? Remember I tell you I couldn't understand when you say something to me about something I said?"

"I remember."

"You said, if I didn't understand, I better learn or I wouldn't be around for end of game."

From 20¢ whistles and $12 shoes to six-dollar whistles and a union contract with Converse that pays us over $100,000 a year to wear their shoes. From learning from Sid Borgia to officiating alongside his son, Joe.

I always liked it when former players and coaches would come up to me if I met them at an airport, mall, or arena around the country. I always tried to stay in contact with people in the league when they were having a tough time. If a coach got fired, I might call him up and wish him well. The toughest one was when Gus Johnson was dying. I called and his wife said he was pretty weak. He picked up the phone and said, "Earl Strom—shootin' two." I asked him how he was doing. He said, "Earl, I ain't gonna make it. But I've got a lot of fond memories." I broke down. Big help, I was. But I always felt a kindred spirit with the guys, especially the ones from the early years.

A couple of summers before I retired, I gave a speech in Cambridge, Massachusetts, to the National Association of Sports Officials. The promotional pitch they put out read like this: "Without a doubt Earl is among the best-known active

NBA referees. He has achieved a measure of success seldom equaled, but to do it, Earl had to look inside himself to change the way he did things. That learning process makes for fascinating listening and will undoubtedly help you in your officiating. Come hear this remarkable NBA referee."

The first thing I did when I got up in front of the room full of officials was take out a big cigar and start puffing on it. I told them about working a game early in my career, I think it might have been NYU and somebody at the old Madison Square Garden. A woman sitting on the end line was giving me crap the whole game. Right near the end she stood up and yelled, "If you were my husband, I'd feed you poison mushrooms." I said, "Lady, if I was your husband, I'd eat 'em." Everybody laughed but her.

Then I said, "I suppose a lot of you saw the promotion piece for this speech. It cracks me up. They said, I had to look into myself and change. That's a bunch of bullshit. I still referee the same way I always did. They just changed the way they want me to work a game. And for a while, there were a bunch of guys running around trying to pitch me in to the league office every time I took a breath. 'Earl had to look inside himself . . .' Come on."

I did talk about how I had adjusted some of my responses. About how I had tried to adopt a "walkaway image." But I told them I could never allow any doubt about who was in charge on the floor each night. A lot of guys feel they have to be out there twenty years before they can have command of a game. But there's no magic formula. You get respect the day you draw a line and stand by it. If you don't start doing that, when are you going to? You do it, and let it be what you're accepted as. There isn't any magic to putting in the years; it isn't as if you suddenly become a "command" official. You earn your reputation every time you step onto the court, starting day one. And you learn that with some guys, the harder it is for them to intimidate you, the more they'll criticize you.

Phil Jackson, who is now coaching the Chicago Bulls, was a rawboned, rough-and-ready kind of player with the Knicks and the Nets in the sixties and seventies. He was anything but graceful and knew he had to be slam-bang to be effective. He once said of me, "I used to feel a great deal of hostility when I'd encounter officials who wouldn't let me play. From my point of view, Earl Strom was always the worst offender. He officiates with a chip on his shoulder, and when ballplayers try and question him about anything, he freaks out. His attitude is that the control of the game is solely in his hands, and anyone who challenges him is going to suffer in the end."

I wonder how Phil would feel today if I let guys play Michael Jordan the way he wanted me to "let him play" back then.

If being in control earns you the reputation of having the Red Ass, I can live with that. Be consistent. Be fair. If guys don't respect that and don't want you back to work their next game, then they're looking for an edge and to hell with them.

Here are the five things—in inverse order of importance— that I look for in an official:

5. *Professionalism.*   Hustle. Maintain concentration. Don't get distracted by a hassle, a coach nagging at you. Look fit. Be in shape. Make sure your running and other mannerisms look athletic. Look together and sharp in your appearance. Exact mechanics aren't so important; just get the call right. Don't play the politics. Concentrate on becoming a better official and skip the knocking of other guys.

4. *Continuity.*   Keep it moving. Ticky-tacky fouls can throw everyone off-balance. Let a couple of little ones go by and guys will start to get into the flow of the game. Don't squeeze the life out of a game, give it some fresh air. If the game's been determined and the players are just going through the motions, get it over with. If it's a blowout, don't call an illegal defense on the winning team with a minute to go. That's a "pacifier call," trying to show

how diligently you're working the game and how concerned you are about the rights of the vanquished.

3. *Judgment.*   Know the rules. Each rule has been written
for a purpose. Now apply the rule with common sense.
Just because you saw it, doesn't mean you can't let it pass
if it didn't give someone an unfair advantage. Don't call
something in crunch time you've let go all night.

2. *Self.*   Believe in your knowledge and your right to be in
charge. It's my court, my law; you will decide who wins
this game playing by the rules I have set out. Adopt a style
that is appropriate to your personality.

1. *Courage.*   Ultimately, this is what determines the stature
of an official. Have the balls to stand in there and make
the right call, regardless of what kind of heat you're going
to get. Be ready to admit a mistake when it's appropriate
and correct it if at all possible. I say it over and over, be
consistent and fair. Whatever the pressures, give them
only what they have coming, home and away. More than
anything else, that will determine how you'll feel about
the guy you see in the mirror when the game's over.

I guess all of these factors had some role in my last call,
which came in game four of the NBA Finals last summer in
Portland. The call decided the game, put Detroit up 3–1 and,
for all practical purposes, lifted the Pistons to the championship. The Blazers had put the ball in play under the Detroit
basket with 1.3 seconds left, trailing by three points. Portland's Danny Young had the ball. I was in the trail position,
with Mike Mathis and Hugh Evans upcourt. Young let the
shot fly from barely past midcourt. Mike raised his right hand
to signal it would be a three-pointer if it went, and it did. The
horn sounded as the shot was taken. Did it count? I knew
what call I had, but it was Hugh's responsibility to make it.
I whipped my eyes over to him. There was no signal from
Hugh. The Portland fans were going berserk, screaming that
the game should be tied. I rushed up to him and hollered,
"Hugh, what do you have?" He said, "I had 0:00 with the ball

in his hands." I asked Mike and he said the same thing. We didn't have the luxury of referring to the video, even though the national TV audience could see the replay while I was huddling with my partners. Actually, if I had had any doubt about the call, I would have been willing to take a fine and use the video. But I had no doubt it had been launched too late, and I would have overruled Hugh if he had said otherwise. (The video clearly showed that the shot was too late.)

I would have loved to see the game go on forever. If the series had gone to 2–2, it would have increased my chance of working at least one more game. But none of that mattered. I turned to the mob of players and media that was crowding around and yelled, "This game is over!" As we plowed our way off the court, a Portland fan snarled, "Ah, we didn't have a chance of it being good. The Road Ref strikes again." I couldn't help but laugh.

And just like that, my refereeing career was over.

I long feared, absolutely *dreaded* the time when I was not going to be working as a referee. I still have the same drive and desires that I had when I started. I don't mind living out of a suitcase. I don't mind getting on airplanes. I love meeting people. I like being around the ballplayers. I like being in the midst of the sports world, being part of people who are facing up to extreme challenges night after night. Once it got so that I was able to get the rest I needed, it was a very attractive life to me. My wife has been after me for years to get out, to come home and have what she calls a normal life. I know she's right in what she wants, but I don't know if I'm going to like it. I do have to be fair to her, though. My God, she has put up with a lot all these years. And she's understood that I'm just not a nine-to-five kind of guy. I had to have the adventure, the intensity, the being on the spot, under pressure, tested, having a hand in something dynamic, living first class, big crowds, big-name people in my everyday life. I guess it's that hunger to be somebody special that drives anybody to seek the top. I might have been happy being good at some other field if I hadn't known this one, but now it seems like the ideal thing to have done all these years. I know I was good at this, and the people who count know. And I guess it's a matter of pride; it's important to me to let it go before I lose that feeling of being on top of it.

So it's off to the golf course and maybe something in broadcasting or some project that will keep my juices flowing. And when I lean back to think about it all and savor what has been, I'll play out my fantasy game. It'll be a corker. It'll be two teams that have been going at it tooth and nail against each other for years, and it's now the seventh game of the finals, everybody is playing in the last game of their careers, and Red Auerbach and Pat Riley are coaching their last games. We're in Boston Garden and I'm working the game with Mendy Rudolph. Red gets a T for coming out of the coaching box. He gets in my face and screams, "Whaddya make up a stupid rule like that for?" Riley gets a call to play Frank Layden in a show called *Salt Lake City Vice* and leaves at halftime.

It's a great game. Every time Mendy or I tell 'em to knock off the bullshit and concentrate on playing good ball, they do. We're down to the wire in the third overtime. Dr. J breaks loose on a fast break, takes off at the top of the key, hears Connie Hawkins yell, "Doc, ya gotta cock the rock like a tomahawk," and rams the jam home. As PA announcer David Zinkoff's cry "ERRRRRRRRRRR-ving" echoes for a full thirty seconds, Elgin Baylor puts up a spectacular hanging bank shot to tie the game. Michael Jordan comes flying back the other way, winding up for a windmill dunk, but Kareem comes flying out of nowhere to slam the shot off the glass. Magic Johnson picks it up, flips it without looking the length of the court to Oscar Robertson, who roars down the lane and collides with Jerry West. Mendy and I hit our whistles at the same instant. Oscar jumps up shouting that he was fouled. I tell him, "You are absolutely right, Mr. Robertson, and if you'll kindly step to the free throw line you will be granted two shots as compensation." Oscar looks over at Rick Barry, who has been run up into the stands earlier in the game for making fun of guys who miss free throws. Oscar puts on a blindfold and nails them both. With three seconds to go, Larry Bird connects on a three-pointer from midcourt. Red figures it's in the bag and lights up his cigar. I toss him for violating the building's no-smoking code. Wilt gets the ball in low and tries to jam it. Russell blocks it, but I blow my whistle as the horn sounds. His other hand was on Wilt's shorts, pulling him off-balance. Nice try. No time left on the clock, Wilt's on the line with two shots and his team down by 1. He makes the first one to break a string of a dozen straight misses. The crowd's going crazy, tossing everything from beer cups to chairs onto the court. Wilt bounces the ball. He takes aim and fires; It hits the back rim, goes straight up, comes down, rattles, and drops in. As we all run for cover, Red's standing on the press table. He yells, "Hey, Strom, ya blew that one, too. But I'm not gonna get on your ass, because you're finally outta here!" Then he jumps down off the table, reaches in his jacket pocket, and pulls out a long cigar. "Ya know, Strom, did it ever occur to you, you've been in this game seems like a hundred years and you've never been on the winning side?" He sticks the cigar in my mouth and lights it. "Yeah, you never had the pleasure of smoking a victory cigar." I puff a big cloud over both of us and grin at that old mug. "You're wrong, Red. I had one every night."

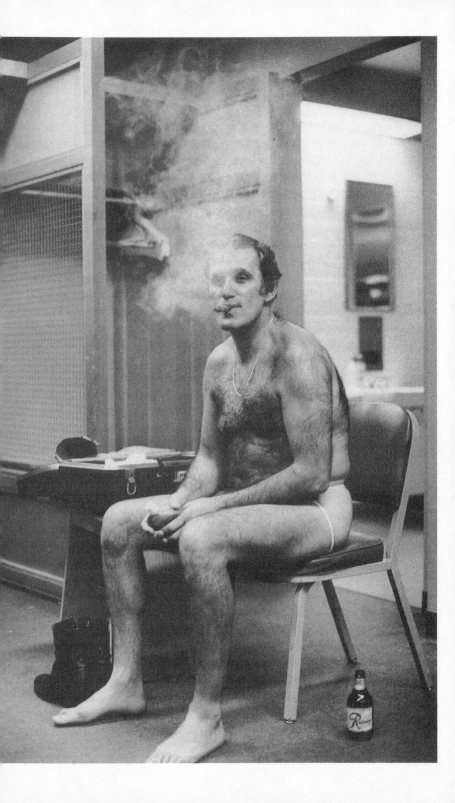